One man

One car

Pictures from 1999 season

One tyre

Formula One tyres by Bridgestone

BRIDGESTONE

ULTIMATE PERFORMANCE

FORMULA 1 YEARBOOK
1999-2000

Pictures
Thierry Gromik / SIPA Press
Daniel Reinhard
Steve Domenjoz
Masakazu Miyata
Jean-Marc Loubat

Conception and texts
Luc Domenjoz

Translated by
Eric Silbermann

Statistics and results and page layout
Sidonie Perrin

Drawings and circuit maps
Pierre Ménard

Contents

PHOTOGRAPHIC CRÉDIT

Thierry Gromik: 5, 10(1), 11(1,3), 13(1, 2, 3), 20-21, 46-47, 50, 51(3), 53(1), 54, 55(1), 57(1), 61(1), 63(1), 72-73, 90(3), 91(1,3), 93(5), 96(1, 2), 98-99, 101, 103(2, 3), 104-105, 106(2), 110, 111(1),, 112-113, 118(1), 119(1), 120(6), 121(3), 122-123, 124, 126-127, 128, 129(2), 130, 132-133, 134(3), 135(4), 136-137, 138(3), 140-141, 142(2), 143(1, 2), 150, 151(2), 154(1, 2, 3), 159(1), 162(1),166(1, 2), 167(1, 2), 170(2, 3), 174(1, 2, 3), 175, 176-177, 182, 184-185, 186(1, 3), 188-189, 190(2, 3, 4), 191(1, 3, 4), 192-193, 198(1), 199(1, 4, 7, 8), 200(1, 5, 6, 7, 8), 202-203, 204(3), 205(1, 3, 4), 206(2), 208, 214(2, 3), 216(2), 217(1, 3).

Daniel Reinhard: 12(3), 13(4), 18, 19, 48(2), 49, 51(2), 52(2), 53(2), 56, 57(2, 3), 88-89, 90(1,2), 92(1, 3), 93(1, 3, 4), 94-95, 97, 100 (1, 2), 102(3), 106(3), 111(2, 3), 114(1, 2), 116-117, 118(3), 119(2, 3), 120(1, 2, 3, 4, 5), 121(1, 2), 129(1), 135(1), 138(1, 2), 146(1, 3, 4), 152-153, 154(4), 156-157, 158(1), 159(2, 3), 160-161, 162(4), 164-165, 167(3), 170(1, 4), 172-173, 178(2, 3), 180-181, 183, 186(2), 190(1), 191(2), 194, 196-197, 198(2), 199(2, 3, 5, 9), 200(2, 3, 9), 204(1, 2), 204(1, 2), 205(2), 207(1), 207, 212(2, 3), 213(1), 214(1, 4), 216(1), 217(2, 4), 219.

Steve Domenjoz: 10(2), 11(2), 12(2), 48(1), 52(1), 55(2), 62(1), 86-87, 92(2), 93(2), 96(3), 100(3), 108-109, 114(3), 118(2), 134(2), 135(2), 142(1), 143(3), 148-149, 151(1), 158(2, 3), 162(2), 166(3),, 174(4), 178(1, 4), 199(6), 200(4), 210-211, 212(1), 213(2, 3, 4).

Masakazu Miyata: 8, 12(1), 51(1), 59(1), 102(1, 2), 103(1), 106(1), 134(1), 138(4), 142(3), 144-145, 146(2), 168-169, Jean-Marc Loubat: 60, 61(2), 62(2), 63(2), 135(3), Lukas Gorys: 91(2).

Foreword

"*Dear reader,*

The great English Prime Minister, Sir Winston Churchill once made a speech where he promised his people nothing but "Blood, sweat and tears." Maybe he should have run a grand prix team, because although there was thankfully no blood, there was plenty of sweat and tears during the 1999 Formula 1 season. I understand I have even been accused or credited, depending on your point of view, with starting a fashion for driver's tears!

At the end of the season there were only tears of joy as I took my second successive World Championship title. I grew to like having the "Number One" on my West McLaren Mercedes car this season so I am pleased to be keeping it for the first year of the next century. It is not just my Number One. It belongs to everyone in the team who contributed so much in a year that was action-packed from start to finish.

If we are winners, then so are you, the readers and spectators, because the last season of the millennium was truly exciting from start to finish and, as it should be, the final outcome was not decided until the end of the very last race. That fact is a reflection of how successful the sport of grand prix racing is these days. With stability in the regulations, the level of competition is getting closer at the top, which is proved by the number of different race winners we saw this year.

With so many changes of fortune during the season, I felt pretty exhausted as we approached the Asian finale and events in Malaysia did nothing to ease my mind, but everyone at McLaren-Mercedes is a fighter and we raised our game for the final showdown.

Having won two championships, my next target is simple: to win three. And you can rest assured that we are already planning how best to do that. It will not be easy and I expect another hard fight, although we are aiming to be better prepared.

After winning in Japan, I said I would not be embarking on any gruelling promotional tours as I had done the previous winter. I felt I did too much and now I want to make sure I am mentally and physically at my peak for the next 17 rounds of the World Championship. Of course, the other reason I do not want to spend the winter doing promotional work and attending press conferences is because that way I will have more time to read "The Formula One Yearbook."

Best wishes,"

Mika Häkkinen

When the stars became mortal again

by Pascal Dro
«Auto Plus»

Did you say the 1999 Formula 1 season was exciting? That would be something of an understatement. From memory, none of the previous 49 years of the championship was anything like this one. Sport, grand gestures, mix-ups, victories and glory. All the ingredients of a great event were brought together as the adventure unfolded.

From the moment the starter's gun went off in March we were in a surreal world. In Melbourne, McLaren unpacked a host of new cars. There had even been talk of bringing the 1998 models to the party as the 1999 MP4/14 had failed to go the distance in endurance testing. Perhaps they should have done, because while the new car pulverised the opposition in qualifying, it was torn to shreds in the race. Of course, they made up for it in Brazil with a win for Mika Hakkinen. But Eddie Irvine clung on to the championship lead. Then in Imola, Ferrari, who were outclassed in qualifying, hammered home the advantage with Michael Schumacher winning at home while the reigning world champion retired. The last time the Scuderia had won the San Marino Grand Prix dated back to 1983 and a victory for Patrick Tambay. So with Ferrari leading the championship from the outset, the tifosi started to believe this was their year. Certainly this red effervescence contributed to the unusual atmosphere of the 1999 championship. 1979 - 1999 is a long time and it was hard for them not to get excited at the thought of such a tasty birthday cake. A twenty year period without a drivers' title was more than such a famous name could bear. The drought had to end.

Eight months later and the dream was over in Suzuka. While Ferrari failed to leave Japan with both titles in their luggage, they did at least win the constructors' trophy for the first time since 1983 again, when Rene Arnoux and Patrick Tambay did it for them.

A framework of intrigue

But more than the result itself, it was the way the year was played out on a framework of intrigue that made this a year like no other. In a series of books like the Sherlock Holmes stories or the Adventures of Tintin, the tenth story is never as

good as the first. Like its creators, the hero gets older and the stories follow a pattern. But in Formula 1, the story of its history is collective and prevents routine from creeping in. Each year there are twenty one frustrated drivers and one champion. Usually, it is the frustrated ones who write the next chapter.

That is exactly the scenario we have just lived through. Ferrari was up against the powerful opposition of the heros of yesterday and tomorrow. That was the first key element of the season. Mika Hakkinen and Ferrari emerged as winners. Eddie Irvine and McLaren were losers. Jordan must wait its turn. Stewart confused matters somewhat. Throw in a few mistakes, mishaps and misdemeanours and some over-exposed emotions and you have the ingredients for a great end to the milliennium.

Overexposed

It would be too easy for Formula 1 to follow the rules of a formulaic novel. This is no Barabara Cartland pot boiler we are talking about. 1999

was definitely one of the best years of the decade, and not just because it was hard fought from start to finish and at all levels. From Monza, that temple of pleasure and tears, the gloves came off and the masks came down. Apart from the legitimate emotions of sportsmen who attain or miss out on their objectives, the faces of the main players of the 1999 championship were usually a pleasure to see.

But it's over and done with, the era of the supermen. The invincible and the untouchable are dead and buried. There are of course still plenty of heros in Formula 1 but they appear to have adopted the politic of the caring, sharing Nineties. The schooled and trained faces of the past appear to have made way for humanity. The most published image of the championship in the run up to Suzuka was that of Mika Hakkinen in tears at the side of the track in Monza, We'll come back to that. There were other newsworthy events like the barge boards of Sepang, Michael's Malaysian sainthood and others and above all some great battles on the track and in

A difficult season for Mika Häkkinen, numerous problems, a few offs, and... times losts in front of gravel trap.

▷ ▽

PASCAL DRO,
35 years old, married to Florence, one daughter, Martha. Holder of a Science diploma. Finalist in a racing school championship. Took part in three Pau Formula Ford Grands Prix. Switched to the Caterham Cup. Twice entered the Le Mans 24 Hours and three appearances in the Daytona 24 Hours. Started as a road test journalist with Auto Hebdo in 1989, before switching to the Automobile Mgazine and then Auto Plus, for whom he covers the Grands Prix

the pit lane.

Simple but brilliant

If the track action was pretty much clean and honourable we must remember that Michael Schumacher was missing from action for half the season, but we cannot lay the cause of this increase in driving standards at his closed door. There was the little matter of David Coulthard's actions in Suzuka. If the truth be told, even the German double world champion showed traces of humanity this year. He was certainly badly shaken by his accident and its implications. When he got behind the wheel for the third time at Mugello, he spun off the track and did not hide his feelings: *"It was a very unpleasant experience. Immediately I had some bad memories flood back into my mind. Not exactly the best thing to happen."* it is clear that Michael Schumacher gave himself a fright and for the first time in his career, he admitted it and spoke it. He might have toned it down, but he was being sincere. In Monza, Mika Hakkinen was comfortably dominating the opposition when he spotted a sign on his pit board which said "Push." Maybe it confused him, but for whatever reason, he

came up to the chicane, as he had done hundreds of times that weekend and selected first instead of second. Game over! Off the track and into retirement. We had never seen Mika react like this. He was furious, throwing first his steering wheel, then his gloves to the ground. He stormed off into the undergrowth, dropped to his knees and blubbed like a baby. It would be hard to imagine Prost, Senna, Piquet or Schumacher doing the same.

Mika's tears

The big blonde burst into tears at Monza, but he was not alone this year, joined at the Nurburgring by Frentzen, Badoer, Fisichella and Ralf Schumacher. And then we had Michael Schumacher admitting he was scared, which is only right and normal and a good thing. Because, at a time when major conglomerates dominate the sport it reminds us that the stars are human being after all. It reminds us they have dreams, experience highs and lows. On the Melbourne podium, Eddie Irvine showed real joy; Johnny Herbert's face betrayed happiness and exhaustion in equal measure as he stepped from the Stewart cockpit in the Nurburgring. This was a guy

like you and me winning a race. It is a moment we want to share with him. Then we had Luca Badoer, reputedly with his job on the line for months. Again at the ring, he retired while lying fourth, with just twelve laps to go. He too burst into tears. A gearbox casing for goodness sake! It doesn't move, it doesn't rotate at great speed, it hardly ever breaks. Formula 1 nearly destroyed its players this year and left them red and raw. On the podium in Sepang, Hakkinen can hardly stand after being scared witless by Michael Schumacher. He was not scared of being beaten; he was scared of being caught out, of being duped.

A legitimate fear

Pain in Italy, fear in Malaysia; Mika Hakkinen is a troubled soul. Errors, there have been a few, both from him and from McLaren. In total, between them, they got it wrong on five separate occasions. At the start of the 1998 season, Keke Rosberg warned his charge, Mika that: "You will have mechanical failures, an engine here, a gearbox there, just like your opponents. In the end, the difference will come down to the number of mistakes. If you make less or none, then you

Heinz-Harald Frentzen was the big surprise of the season. Few people would have predicted third place in the championship for the German at the start of the year.
◁

1999 WORLD CHAMPIONSHIP

Drivers:
1.	Mika Häkkinen	76
2.	Eddie Irvine	74
3.	Heinz-Harald Frentzen	54
4.	David Coulthard	48
5.	Michael Schumacher	44
6.	Ralf Schumacher	35
7.	Rubens Barrichello	21
8.	Johnny Herbert	15
9.	Giancarlo Fisichella	13
10.	Mika Salo	10
11.	Jarno Trulli	7
	Damon Hill	7
13.	Alexander Wurz	3
	Pedro Diniz	3
15.	Olivier Panis	2
	Jean Alesi	2
17.	Pedro de la Rosa	1
	Marc Gené	1

Constructors :
1.	Ferrari	128
2.	McLaren/Mercedes	124
3.	Jordan/Mugen Honda	61
4.	Stewart/Ford	36
5.	Williams/Supertec	35
6.	Benetton/Playlife	16
7.	Prost/Peugeot	9
8.	Sauber/Petronas	5
9.	Arrows	1
	Minardi/Ford	1

(continued)

A bad season for Benetton: a lucky second place in Canada and no points after Austria!

▽

can be champion if the mechanical failures are spread out equally."

In 1998 at the Nurburgring, the Finn was like a limp rag before the start, while Michael Schumacher was busy waving to his fans. But once the race started, it was Mika who took control. It was the defining moment of that year. This year, even though he has already achieved the ambition of a lifetime, the Finn summons up all his strength one more time and once again the two men go at it hammer and tongs to the final flag.

Luckily for him, Ferrari was not exempt from the odd error. Even before Schumacher's Silverstone accident there had been retirements in Australia and Canada. Then, David Coulthard did his bit to make life more complicated for his team mate, because of McLaren's insistence on driver parity within the team, which allowed the Scotsman to win in Belgium.

"Are you thinking what I'm thinking?"

Was it a strategic error? Should a decision have been taken before the start?It's hard to say. Hakkinen almost jumped the start, but stopped, allowing Coulthard to get his nose ahead as they headed for the Source hairpin at Spa- Francorchamps. Mika tried an over-ambitious move, the two men touched and Coulthard disappeared up the road never to be troubled again. Four points were at stake here for Mika, the difference between first and second and at two thirds distance a single question asked of Ron Dennis by Norbert Haug sealed his fate:

"Are you thinking what I'm thinking?"

"Yes."

That was it then. David Coulthard built and deserved the win. Mercedes and McLaren recognised this fact and let him keep the victory, rather than clip his wings. Once again it seemed that the heart was ruling the head this season. Hakkinen did not see it quite like this and was sulking. It was probably not the time to remind him that in a fit of post-title euphoria in 1998,

he had promised to help his team mate take the top honours the following year. He drew the line at letting the Scotsman start from pole.

Coulthard might have done better in six of the first thirteen events, but he only won twice to the Finns four victories. So all in all, Mika deserves his position as natural Number One driver at McLaren. In the final countdown, David's Spa win could have cost Mika dear. But re-writing history when one knows the outcome is a futile exercise.

So, with hindsight, this decision might have cost McLaren-Mercedes the world championship, but in fact it had no effect on the drivers' or even the constructors' titles. It was an honourable decision, yet another human decision which cared not for the concerns of multinationals.

At Sepang, Michael Schumacher proved his accident had done nothing to dent his speed. Indeed, if anything, the enforced rest appeared to have given him an extra gear. He was quicker than anyone including Eddie Irvine and even quicker than Mika Hakkinen, who for his part was fully motivated by the prize that awaited him at the end of the road.

It would be wrong to claim that the 1999 championship was fought out in a mood of friendly rivalry, free of acrimony, but the low blows were few and far between, or at least harder to spot. Until we got to the Kuala Lumpur saga, which is best forgotten and swept under the carpet, which is effectively what happened in the Paris Appeal Court. It was an unworthy incident.

▷

Mika Salo was the deluxe stand-in this season, first with BAR and then with Ferrari. It certainly helped him get a job for next year.

The Stewarts provided another pleasant surprise. No wins for Rubens Barrichello, but he did take pole position at a rain lashed Magny Cours.

▽

Heinz-Harald Frentzen: from zero to hero

Everyone is after him, or will be one day. But for the time being, he belongs to Eddie Jordan. Other drivers might announce their transfer plans or decisions to stay put in press conferences, or get their acolytes to put out a platitudinal press release, but for Heinz-Harald Frentzen, one little sentence was enough. *"Eddie took up his option. I am staying at Jordan."* Would he have wanted to leave anyway? Unless he received a miracle offer from McLaren or Ferrari, it is unlikely. At the moment, Jordan is on

the up and in 2000, it will have a Mugen-Honda engine which should be the equal of what BAR will get from Honda itself. And while contracts do not count for that much in Formula 1, Jordan owns Frentzen and Frentzen owes Jordan, as the Irishman is keen to point out to anyone who will listen.

At the end of 1998, it was easy for Eddie to pick up Frentzen for peanuts and for a long time. Because, from the middle of that season, the German's market value was on the slide. Publicly slated by Patrick

Head, Williams legendary Technical Director, he was saddled with the FW20 which was not exactly setting the racing world alight. More importantly, he was being outclassed by his team-mate Jacques Villeneuve.

Frentzen got more and more despondent, gradually losing his competitive spirit. Rather than moan to the press, he simply refused to talk to them. In Hungary he collapsed after the race and had to go to hospital to be rehydrated. There was talk of a new

Tomorrow is here today

Money has always been a Formula 1 obsession. Nevertheless, even by its own standards of financial fascination, cash has dominated conversation and press cuttings even more than usual this year. Jackie Stewart is reckoned to have sold his team to Ford for around sixty million pounds. A few weeks later it was Ron Dennis' turn. At the British Grand Prix he revealed that DaimlerChrysler had bought 40% of the shares in the TAG McLaren Group. The price? Who knows. But Ron Dennis and Mansour Ojjeh now own 30% each leaving the car company as the major shareholder with 40%. Elsewhere, Eddie Jordan sold 40% of his outfit to the financial organisation Warburg Pincus, who aim to find additional sponsors and turn Jordan into a global brand. A similar situation occurred at Arrows where the now departed Prince Malik Ado Ibrahim brought the Deutsche Bank with him. They bought 75% of Arrows and at the end of the year acquired 50% of the Bernie Ecclestone owned FOA at a cost of 1.3 billion dollars. Then Alain Prost gave up 10% of Prost Grand Prix to the luxury goods giant, Luis Vuitton Moet Hennessy, while still pushing Peugeot to invest in the team. Rumours persist that Patrick Head is planning to sell his 45% stake in Williams to BMW.

As for Rocco Benetton's team, his family still seem disposed to sell out to a major manufacturer and Tom Walkinshaw has recently sold his Ixion motor group to buy back the Arrows team. In short, 1999 was the year of the giants. Industrialists and finance houses are sniffing around the main players in Formula 1. The discipline has a great global standing and, according to Bernie Ecclestone, is set to expand still further. "It could double in size in the next ten years. I have no doubt about it." So, for those who can afford it, Formula 1 represents a great investment on all levels. It is growing year by year, counts an audience of billions and is slowly but surely conquering Asia and heading for the USA. Previous attempts to make it in the States have all failed to capture the imagination of the biggest nation on earth. Formula 1 will have a future there and that starts in 2000 with the race at Indianapolis, the most famous race track in the world.

Ralf Schumacher did not have an easy year at Williams, but he did prove that he has matured and that the mistakes of youth are now behind him. He scored all 35 of his team's points. Alessandro Zanardi drew a blank. Indy to F1 is a tough trip.

career in Cart in the USA. It was then that Jordan entered the equation. Eddie knows a thing or two about nursemaiding a driver's ego. He is certainly better at than Williams. Frentzen signed his last-chance contract and went on to out-pace team-mate Damon Hill, who himself went through a crisis of confidence. In short, Frentzen's star began to shine over the winter and proved his worth right from the opening round in Melbourne with a magnificent second place, when he was the only driver to lap in the same times as the winner. He went on to confirm his form with another visit to the podium in third place in Brazil. In the pouring rain in Magny Cours, he won the French Grand Prix. Two more podium finishes followed in Germany and Belgium and then he won again at Monza. What do you say now Mr. Head? In the Jordan team, they began to dream the impossible dream. With three rounds to go, there was Frentzen on pole position in the Nurburgring. If he could win, he would be second in the championship, four points behind Hakkinen. Sadly, he was forced to retire with an electrical problem. But that could not hide the fact, that the washed up 1998 driver had almost become world champion. At the end of the day, he finished third in the world championship ahead of David Coulthard and the dominant MP4/14. That was something new for the Jordan boys.

They say people in F1 have short memories, as can be seen today with the Olivier Panis business. Frentzen, who married girlfriend Tanja in between Malaysia and Japan, has proved that the sport can learn to love those it had nearly disposed of; a fact which must give the likes of Jacques Villeneuve and Olivier Panis reasons to be cheerful.

Farewell to the last gentleman racer

On Thursday morning before the French Grand Prix at Magny Cours, all the journalists are wandering around the paddock clutching "A message from Damon Hill." This fax which has reached all four corners of the globe, announces that "Never for me the lowered banner never the last endeavour!" Damon Hill's mind is made up. The desire, that little something that pushes one to always go further, to concentrate permanently on driving and improving the car, was no longer there. After long discussions with his wife Georgie, his mother Bette, with his long time friend Pete Boutwood, the decision is taken. At the end of the season, he will hang up his helmet. As straightforward as that after 115 grands prix, 22 wins and 15 second places. "One day the desire and the speed are no longer there. When that day comes, it's time to do something else." Knowing when and how to go is an important part of the story of his life. They say other people's experience counts for nothing. But Damon Hill has that experience. Way back when, his father Graham had gradually slipped to the back of the grid. He had never wanted to give up F1. His death was perhaps not the worst price he paid. Because timid little orphan Damon paid a high price. For him, more than was the case for

his father, Georgie and the kids are his whole life. He is a devoted father. He has bought his calm future with his children. He has paid for it all himself. Now he wants that choice to be respected. After putting out this release, Damon demanded to stay silent on the subject. He says he feels better having taken the decision and he is ready to give his all. But on Sunday afternoon, after yet another retirement after crashing off the track, he told the BBC: "I might have just driven in my last grand prix." After that his position hardened and he refused to talk. Maybe we will never know the truth, but it seems that Eddie Jordan invoked the business of contractual obligations. Who knows? Damon stuck to his guns and "no comment" was all we got for the rest of the year. As for his performance level, he reckoned that he had never driven as well as he did in 1996. "I am slower now, that's all." No other racer or world champion has ever been brave enough to admit to that. He had always given his all and achieved his objectives. Twenty two wins and the 1996 world championship attest to that fact. The man can go with a clear conscience. He should be allowed that. He will not grow old in Cart or any other formula. Because the real greats do not grow old on the race tracks.

Ricardo Zonta, Pedro de la Rosa and Marc Gene represented a "Latin" trio of new-boys this season.

MP4/14 - F399: two different conceptions

by Paolo Filisetti

The Italian project was more conservative than the English one which featured several new ideas, many of them very innovative. In fact, Adrian Newey did not settle for simply fine tuning the MP4/13 but pushed harder in many areas, such as weight distribution, a lower centre of gravity and the use of very sophisticated suspension geometry. Although the differences between the two cars are extensive, there are several similarities. This is not a surprise as computer simulation of design is now so sophisticated that it is possible for all the teams to reach more or less the same conclusions in terms of aerodynamic and mechanical solutions.

A common feature of the two cars is undoubtedly the great length of the front part of the chassis that in both cases means that the cockpit has been pushed rearwards in a more central position. The cockpit sides (see both the overall view drawings) have reduced height, two small winglets to respect the rules that are more evident in the past. The driver seat position has been lowered with a flatter driving position.

Looking deeply at the McLaren, it is surprising how the front of the chassis has been lowered in comparison to last year's MP4/13, with the two vertical winglets higher and longer to conform with the rules. Right below this point, the front suspension has been strongly developed in terms of its geometry. This is clearly visible by the dimensions of the push rod linkage hole that is wider than in the past. In this way the design using torsion bars as last year has been revised so as to allow a better use of the new harder tyres, especially in the corners, and improves attitude over the kerbs. At the rear, the suspension has been completely re-designed, using for the first time, torsion bars instead of springs.

The Ferrari F399, like its English rival has a revised concept for weight distribution, pushing back the driver seat, but adopting less radical solutions, so we can consider it as a major evolution instead of a proper revolution. The suspension is strongly developed both front and rear. The front has a revised geometry that mimics the McLaren, especially in terms of its behaviour on the kerbs. At the rear the big change is due to the fact that now the dampers are placed on the side of the gearbox not above it. All the suspension elements are made in carbon fibre and not just covered with this material. The cooler position is the same as the McLaren, and the hot air outlet blows under the winglets in front of the rear wheels, in an attempt to increase the speed of the airflow in this area. This has allowed it to keep the high exhaust configuration that allows better aerodynamics inside the sidepods, with a very narrow coke bottle shape and furthermore it increases downforce.

Drawings explanation:

McLaren MP4/14
1. The new hot air outlet on the top of the sidepods, to obtain a faster air flow in the area inside the rear wheels, so as to have a greater downforce, and a cleaner flow through the rear wing.
2. The sidepod entry is narrow and vertical. In front of it there is a small air intake, for cooling data logging units, that is similar to solutions used on the Williams designed by Adrian Newey. Big turning vanes in front of the sidepods, are kept over from the 1998 car.
3. The front of the car was even lower than the 1998 car with the two vertical winglets of increased dimensions and further forward.

Ferrari F399
1. The engine air intake area has a very narrow cross section. A small splitter beneath it, to separate the air flow to the engine from the turbulence created by the driver's helmet. The headrest has a round shape and big dimensions, and is clearly detached from the air intake.
2. The sidepods have a front arrow shape and a side section higher than the central section as on the Benetton B194 and B195 designed by Rory Byrne. In this way there is a channel for the air flow that touches the exhausts pipes at the rear.
3. At the rear the sidepods have a very narrow Coke bottle shape, with the engine exhausts that exit on top and the hot air outlet placed under the winglets in front of the wheels.

MP4/14 rear suspension

The rear suspension of the McLaren Mp4/14 may be considered as the state of the art «contractive suspension».
It is very interesting to notice how its design is simple and shows the very slim gearbox case. This is because the torsion bars are not placed inside the gearbox casing but at the sides. The torsion bars are very easy to change, even allowing the mechanics to carry out a last minute change on the starting grid.

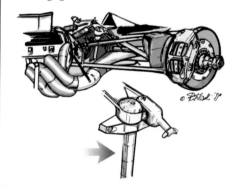

PAOLO FILISETTI,
was born and lives in Milan. An F1 enthusiast since childhood, he turned this interest into a job after University where he studied mechanical engineering, starting working in F1 as technical editor for Italian and foreign magazines in 1996. Today, he is a regular contributor to several publications scattered all over the world.

McLaren MP4/14

Ferrari F399's new steering wheel

The new steering wheel has changed from the previous version mainly in the use of a new wider display pane at its centre, instead of four smaller ones. This new display provides driver different information that the driver selects by pressing two buttons placed on the central area of the steering wheel. The software programme that manages all the data has been changed to give the driver a wider range of solutions.

The number of control switches available has been increased with two more buttons on the top of the steering wheel rim, making a total of 16 switches.

The central part of the steering wheel is removable, leaving the wheel itself in place. This new feature allows the mechanics to change the electronic control system during a race in case of a malfunction, as happened to Schumacher in Australia. In this way the mechanical part of the steering, the two levers for gear shift and clutch remain in place.

It is interesting to note that on the F399 there are no other lights and switches inside the cockpit, except those for the rear light and for the fire extinguisher. This allows the drivers to raise their knees at the level of the steering wheel as the regulations as required for safety reasons. Another change relates to the material used for the hand grip. It is a heat modelling material sensitive to the heat transmitted by the hands that fit perfectly on the steering wheel, providing perfect grip.

Steering wheel drawing explanation:

1-2 Buttons for the brake balance, selecting the programmes of different set up adjusted by the corresponding switch 14

3 Button for the speed limiter in the pits.

4 Neutral button, mandatory in addition to the external one placed on the top of the chassis.

5 Radio switch. When pressed connects the driver to his pitwall crew.

Reverse button for the reverse gear.

7-8 Double switches to select the different information on the main display in place of the old four smaller displays.

9 Drive by wire switch 5 positions

10 Electronic clutch switch (5 positions)

11 Power steering switch (on - off)

12 Mixture set-up switch (8 positions)

13 Electronic differential set up switch (6 positions)

14 Brake balance switch (8 positions)

15 S button, to downchange automatically a pre-set number of gears, in conjunction with the blue button on the bottom right.

16 Hand grip parts in special heat sensitive material, for a perfect fit of the driver's hands on the steering rim.

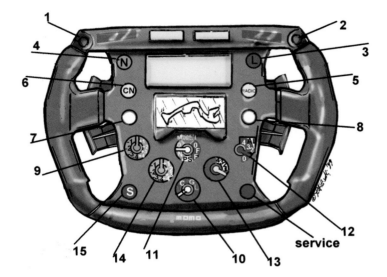

◁
The steering wheel of the MP4/14, very different from the one of the F399.

Ferrari F399

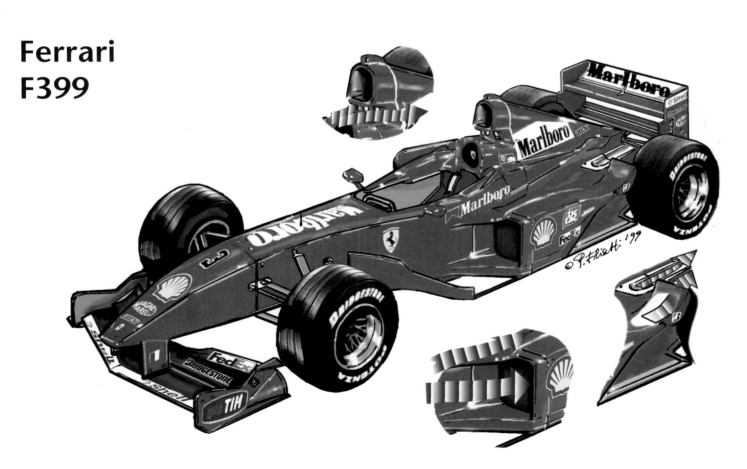

technical

The other interesting cars

Stewart SF3, the white shark

The Stewart SF3 has been one of the revelations of the championship. Powered by an all-new Ford CR-1 engine, built using advanced technology to allow a lightweight construction.

The SF3 is a logical evolution of the less competitive SF2, but it is also a development of the concept found on the 1998 McLaren MP4/13. It is currently the best interpretation of that winning idea which can be summarised as follows: low hull shaped nose; cockpit pushed back in the chassis with a lower and flatter driving position; reduced chassis cross sectional area, using vertical winglets on the top to conform with the regulations. The front suspension is by torsion bar. The aerodynamics are less sensitive to changes in ride height and last but not least, a major weight reduction to allow greater use of ballast which can be moved around to improve weight distribution.

At first sight, the car does not look much longer than its predecessor. It certainly hides its 310 cm. The car seems longer because the sidepods have been moved back by 10 cm and the cockpit by 8 cm. The driver is seater further back than in 1998 and he is in a flatter position which lowers the centre of gravity and improves the weight distribution.

Driver comfort is improved as the lower nose also means the legs are lower in the car.

Moving the weight backwards has improved traction and allowed for a much greater aerodynamic load at the front.

In order to move the weight rearwards, Alan Jenkins' 1998 idea has been retained in terms of positioning the oil tank between the chassis and engine instead of the more conventional place between the gearbox and engine. The main differences in the chassis are the reduced nose height and the rearward displacement of the sidepods.

The efficiency of the car decreased under braking as the rear rose up. It would improve under acceleration which would push the back of the car down.

Improved airflow under the car has been achieved with a V shaped bottom to the chassis (as on the McLaren.) The shorter sidepods have improved the quality of air flow as the front wheels are further away, creating less turbulence. The narrow track caused problems in this area for all the cars in 1998.

The efficiency of the rear diffuser has been improved through a different design which has stabilised the airflow.

Apart from the gearbox, these were the weak parts on the 1998 car, which was hyper-sensitive to aero balance and to changes in ride height.

The efficiency of the car decreased under braking as the rear rose up. It would improve under acceleration which would push the back of the car down.

Rear suspension has retained the '98 multi-link system which compensated for the excessive flexibility of the gearbox. The SF3 gearbox is made of cast magnesium which increased its weight and size. It did bring the benefit of increased stiffness.

The front suspension is entirely new with horizontal torsion bars first seen on the 98 Ferrari and McLaren.

The large ugly top parts of the chassis also disappeared. The surface is now very flat with a flap for pedal access.

Access to the suspension is from the side. The Penske dampers are in a new position, no longer connected with the push rod levers. They are fixed outside the front of the chassis in the place usually reserved for brake fluid reservoirs and pumps. The dampers are connected hydraulically to suspension uprights with an additional third damper.

The steering column is lower than last year and is similar to the McLaren MP4/13. It is situated just above the halfway point of the chassis. Generally there is a much closer attention to detail on the 99 car. The handling and straight line speed are much improved.

The Ford engine is the ultimate in modern engine technology at the moment with a claimed weight of just 95 kg, being very compact and powerful. It is reckoned to put out around 810 ps at 17,250 rpm, only slightly less than the Mercedes. Its weak point has been reliability.

The Stewart SF3 has been one of the pleasant surprises of this championship and it has performed better than its outsider status led one to expect. It is proof of the fact that the smaller teams can challenge and occasionally beat the top two teams, as was proved by its podium finishes and Johnny Herbert's win in the European Grand Prix. Sometimes these sort of performances seem impossible in F1 but Stewart has proved it can be done.

▷

Behind the super powers of Ferrari and McLaren the Jordan team found a way this year to climb to third place in the championships. The car designed by Mike Gascoyne , the 199 is a well developed project, with many clever solutions mainly in terms of weight distribution, the suspension layout and of course also the aerodynamics. The first point is clearly evident in the design of the chassis that sports very low sides. In fact the sides 1) of the cockpit are the lowest in comparison to all the other cars, sporting very big vertical winglets to respect the rules relating to the minimum dimensions of the cockpit side protections. Of interest is the adoption of two small wings 2) profile extensions placed in front of the sidepods beside the splitter under the cockpit. These devices split into two parts the air directed to the sidepod entry, providing greater efficiency from the bottom of the car. In fact in this way the turbulence directed underneath are diverted outwards to produce a clean air flow under the rear diffuser.

1   2

© P.Filisetti '99

50 cm

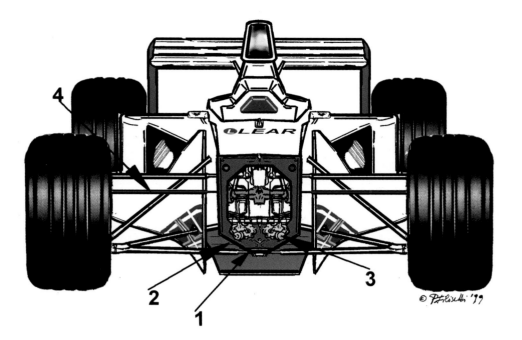

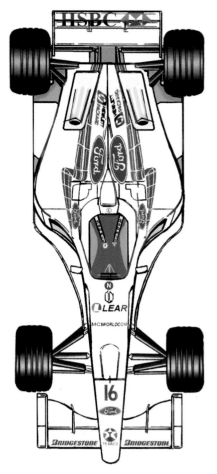

Drawings :

1. The pick-up point for the front wishbone is outside the chassis and is the same as the upper mounts, with titanium plates instead of the more usual uniball joints.

2. The bottom of the chassis as a hull shape with a splitter placed below the cockpit linked to the lower part of the sidepods which include deformable structures.

3. The Penske dampers are a completely new solution. They are connected to the suspension push rods by hydraulic ducts instead of being attached mechanically and are located outside the chassis in the place usually used for brake fluid reservoirs.

4. The position of the steering link is lower than the upper wishbone but not at half the height of the upright as on the McLaren.

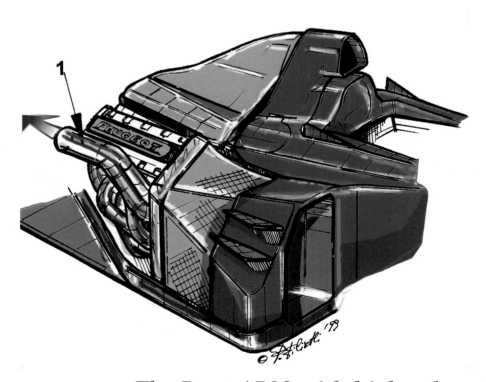

The Prost AP02 with high exhausts

The French team, introduced on the AP02, after the Silverstone test, for the very first time and only in qualifying on Panis' car, the high exhaust configuration following the example of Ferrari and Stewart.
Three teams used this solution and in the case of the Prost car was developed especially for the fast circuits like Spa and Monza, where even a small increase in performance is important.

This configuration has been studied in depth in the wind tunnel and the French engineers reckon it improves the aerodynamic efficiency of the car by about 3-4%.
The air flow in front of the rear wheels in fact speeds up thanks to the hot air coming out of the exhausts, that have a circular section. It is a unique solution, because the pipe is placed horizontally and not diagonally, thus giving a vertical exit.

McLaren/Ferrari: Technical appaisal

by François Granet
«L'Automobile Magazine»

The duel on the track between McLaren and Ferrari is one that is reflected in the shadows of the research and development departments, the wind tunnels and the workshops where a terrifying battle takes place between engineers. At the end of the road, after sixteen grands prix and innumerable test sessions, each team came away with a world championship this year. You could say it was closely fought! Here we look at the battle of the backroom boys, seen through the eyes of a few engineers who watched it take place and three men who were involved in the hand to hand combat; McLaren Technical Director, Adrian Newey, the man behind the Mercedes engine Mario Illien and Ferrari Technical Director Ross Brawn.

McLaren Technical Director Adrian Newey is the designer of the car which took Mika Hakkinen to his second consecutive world championship. He is an aerodynamicist by profession and he played a major role in his team's success this season. "I cannot single out just one element that absolutely gave us an advantage over Ferrari, just as I cannot say which area we have made the progress in since the start of the year," he said with a smile. *"I cannot, because there is not element that stands out. The car moved from one grand prix to another, same as usual, without any real technological revolution."* It is a response that Prost Grand Prix's chief engineer, Vincent Gaillardot agrees with. *"He is quite right to say this. His answer is a perfect synthesis of his design philosophy: a very pure aerodynamic concept, very evolved, fixed during the winter break in order to take his wind tunnel research as far as possible. The evolution takes place over the car as a whole rather than on individual elements."* The end result seems so on the limit that is actually quite fragile, in that the aerodynamic package is so fluid, it is difficult to introduce even the slightest revolutionary element. It would disturb more than improve the package. *"When you look at a McLaren-Mercedes, it is obvious that it is the work of just one man. The engine is conceived as one element of this*

▷ *Ross Brawn*

package. Ferrari does not adhere to the same philosophy. One senses that the F399, which is also very finely honed, is born from the meeting of several different ideas. It mixes different aerodynamic and mechanical concepts," explains Stewart Ford's Technical Director Gary Anderson. *"For Adrian, it is obvious that an F1 car can be summed up in one simple principle: that of a fluid aerodynamic in which one integrates an engine. Everything is based on this idea."* And Adrian Newey always pushes it as far as it will go!

The first performances of the MP4/14 did indeed suffer from this prolonged development: in Australia the car had not been sufficiently developed and it was not reliable. The team had even considered bringing along the 1998 which they had taken the precaution of homologating to the latest safety crash test requirements introduced by FIA.

"Technically, the late arrival of the car and the concerns over unreliability which it had suffered with, were also linked to the fact that we had to fight right to the bitter end of the 1998 season to win the world championship. That final effort prevented us from preparing as well as we would have wished for the 1999 season," admitted Newey.

Unhappy with having a late start to the programme, McLaren seemed to have tried to adopt too many radical technical solutions. *"It is not evident, but we have built a radically different car to the last one. Technically, it is more evolved and in theory, it is more efficient."* Hakkinen did not share that view. *"The MP4/14 was a complicated car, difficult to drive, or at least more so than its predecessors."* Newey admitted that, but had no regrets. *"We had a car with very dif-*

ferent characteristics to the '98 one. But we always knew where we were technically." Nevertheless, because of its complex nature, the MP4/14 was always difficult to set up. It was not just for the fun of it, that Newey played the role of super-race engineer.

This year we felt we had to move forward from where we were in 1998. Without losing sight of the perpetual search for more power

---

The McLaren was certainly the nearest thing to a perfect car as permitted in the regulations, but on the other hand, it was also the most difficult car from which to extract the maximum. It could well be that this difficulty in fine tuning the vehicle is what often prompted Mika Hakkinen to choose the hardest tyre on offer from Bridgestone, which gave a more consistent performance, while Ferrari usually went the other way. *"This could also have been done in order to compensate for the car's natural tendency to understeer,"* explained Anderson. *"While Ferrari were looking for a way to dial out oversteer on the F399."*

"There was no deliberate plan on our part in this area," affirmed Newey. *"It's true we took longer to favour the softer tyres, as was the case with Schumacher. It was only after the Spanish Grand Prix that we noticed how much some teams were getting out of them and so decided to do the same by using them more often."* This preference for harder rubber led the engine men to work more on the driveability of the engine. *"This year we felt we had to move forward from where we were in 1998. Without losing sight of the perpetual search for more power, which all engine builders must do. We wanted to improve driveability as well,"* explained Mario Illien, the father of the Mercedes engines. *"Given our choice of tyres, the way the power is delivered and the torque curve became an essential element so that the drivers could get the most out of the car. The more you use hard tyres, the harder it is to control the car as it has less grip and tends to understeer. For 2000, the driveability and the ease of use will once again be the two key points which we will concentrate on. Weight, size and consumption are other factors which we concentrate on. The*

importance of consumption increases as several races have been won or lost by thousandths of a second spent refuelling in the pits. To succeed in this area the important thing is to increase engine revs and I don't think we are the only ones to have discovered that! Globally, I would say this season has been trouble free from an engine point of view," continued Illien. As with the chassis, so too the engine was com

---

I am very happy about that, as we did not see a single failure in 32 starts; 16 for each car. That was lucky in a way, as we had plenty of failures in other areas

---

pletely new for 1999. *I am very happy about that, as we did not see a single failure in 32 starts; 16 for each car. That was lucky in a way, as we had plenty of failures in other areas: driving errors, collisions between our two drivers, strategic errors, refuelling problems and gearbox failures. We were spared nothing. Nothing apart from worries about the V10! We introduced evolutions at three points during the season: in Canada, at Hockenheim and in Japan for the final race. The Suzuka changes should have arrived for Malaysia, but we did not reckon we were ready and decided to delay the introduction. I have to say that we rarely had the same engine from one race to the next. We almost always had some small modifications which could not be described as "evolutions." As usual, we first tried these changes in qualifying before they were considered safe to race."* Newey is no doubt proud of his work this season and why shouldn't he be. He too confesses to no faults with his car, just some weaknesses in its development, no doubt linked to its complexity. "I think we had a more advanced car than Ferrari at the start of the season, but they were able to catch up by doing a better job of developing the F399 than we did with the MP4/14," claims Newey, adding: "If there had been a few more grands prix I would have liked to further develop the front and rear suspension." That amounts to a confession of sorts as it was the suspension that caused Hakkinen so much bother in San Marino and Monaco. The day after he crashed out of the race at Imola, the Finn had quickly claimed that he did not reckon he was responsible for the accident which cost him what looked like being an easy victory. "Something happened on the car which I do not understand. It happened without warning and there was nothing

I could do about it." It was evident that Mika had a mechanical problem, even if the team was quick to blame the driver. McLaren revealed nothing about its post-race investigation, but it seemed as though something had gone wrong with its sophisticated suspension system.
In Monaco, it was once again a problem of sticking the car to the track which turned the Grand Prix into a nightmare for Mika. This time there was official confirmation that a faulty damper was working erratically. *"I have just driven the hardest race of my life,"* he said at the end of the day. *"I had to fight like never before just to finish third."*
At Ferrari, it is evident that the F399, although not as good out of the box as the McLaren, underwent two distinct evolutions: the first ran from the start of the season to the time of Michael Schumacher's accident at the British Grand Prix and the second began when he got back to work in testing, a fortnight before the Malaysian Grand Prix and ended with the last race of the season.
Ferrari's Technical Director Ross Brawn never wanted to discuss the problem in public. It is clear however, that without the driver for whom he developed the F399 he found himself somewhat at a loss. While Eddie Irvine lacked for nothing in developing a car, he did not have Michael's ability to galvanise the team into doing something about it and

the development of the car seemed to go into a stall. While accepting that the F399 moved on quickly at the start of the season, Brawn disagrees with Newey on one point, in that he believes the F399 was a good car right from the start of the season. *"Our car was fundamentally good. But we suffered from the same problem as McLaren; we were running late by the time we got to Australia. We only really began to develop the car around the time of the Spanish Grand

Prix. To detail the changes we made during the season, we moved on with the floor four times and there were even more modifications to the front and rear wings and side deflectors. We also made several changes to the suspension geometry, the damping system and made notable progress in terms of braking efficiency."* These changes always had the same goal; to find more downforce by reducing drag and improving the dynamic equilibrium of the F399, mainly by playing with downforce, an area where

---

If we had three more grands prix? I don't know what I would have liked to change

---

the car was particularly strong. *"I am also very pleased with what we achieved on the engine side,"* continued Brawn. *"We constantly increased the power of the 048 without compromising its reliability."* Ferrari made improvements to the engine on three occasions. «*Another source of satisfaction was the way we managed to lighten the car. We lost about 7 kg between the start and finish of the season.*»
This is a remarkable achievement when one considers that Brawn and his team came up with a car that was so light that it had to run all year with 50 kg of ballast in the chassis. Those 50 kg could be placed wherever the engineers deemed it would provide the best balance.
"If we had three more grands prix? I don't know what I would have liked to change. You know, I feel we really proved what the F399 could do in Malaysia. But if I can be a perfectionist, I would like to have seen a bit more power! Nothing else. The car was good and the proof of that is that Ferrari won the 1999 Constructors' World Championship. Basically, it is now very difficult to find improvements that have a significant effect on the handling and performance of a car. The regulations have been stable for a long time and we are beginning to get the hang of them."
In fact, Brawn is so happy with his car that he is starting from the same base camp for 2000.
«*Our next car will be an evolution of this one. The main changes will revolve around the centre of gravity, which will be lower. The aerodynamics will be better and the engine will have more power. Basically, I can only find one thing wrong with the F399; it didn't win the drivers' title!*»

▷
Adrian Newey

TECHNICAL SUMMARY

The players

Eleven teams, twenty two drivers, hundreds of mechanics, eleven cars and eight engines which are jewels of engineering.
The Formula 1 cast is vast. Here it is.

McLaren-Mercedes

1. Mika HÄKKINEN

DRIVER PROFILE

- Name : *HÄKKINEN*
- First names : *Mika Pauli*
- Nationality : *Finnish*
- Date of birth : *September 28, 1968*
- Place of birth : *Helsinki (SF)*
- Lives in : *Monte Carlo (Monaco)*
- Marital status : *married to Erja*
- Kids : *-*
- Hobbies : *skiing, swimming, golf, tennis*
- Favourite music : *Dire Straits, Mick Jagger*
- Favourite meal : *finnish food*
- Favourite drinks : *water, milk, coca-cola*
- Height : *179 cm*
- Weight : *69 kg*

STATISTICS | PRIOR TO F1

STATISTICS		PRIOR TO F1
• Nber of Grand Prix :	128	1987 : *Champion F. Ford*
• Victories :	14	1988 : *Opel Lotus*
• Pole-positions :	21	*Euroseries*
• Best laps :	13	1989 : *F. 3 (GB, 7th)*
• Accident/off :	17	1990 : *F. 3 / Champion*
• Not qualified :	2	*West Surrey*
• Laps in the lead :	1024	1991 : *Lotus / Judd. 2*
• Km in the lead :	4903	*points. 15th of*
• Points scored :	294	*championship.*

F1 CAREER

1992 : *Lotus / Ford. 11 points. 8th of championship.*
1993 : *McLaren / Ford. 4 points. 15th of championship.*
1994 : *McLaren / Peugeot. 26 points. 4th of champ.*
1995 : *McLaren / Mercedes. 17 points. 7th of champ.*
1996 : *McLaren / Mercedes. 31 points. 5th of champ.*
1998 : *McLaren / Mercedes. 100 points. World Champion.*
1999 : *McLaren / Mercedes. 76 points. World Champion.*

2. David COULTHARD

DRIVER PROFILE

- Name : *COULTHARD*
- First name : *David*
- Nationality : *British*
- Date of birth : *March 27, 1971*
- Place of birth : *Twynholm (Scotland)*
- Lives in : *Monte Carlo (Monaco)*
- Marital status : *engaged to Heidi*
- Kids : *-*
- Hobbies : *cycling, golf, swimming*
- Favourite music : *Queen, Phil Collins, Texas*
- Favourite meal : *pasta*
- Favourite drink : *tea, water*
- Height : *182 cm*
- Weight : *75 kg*

STATISTICS | PRIOR TO F1

STATISTICS		PRIOR TO F1
• Nber of Grand Prix :	90	1983-88 : *Karting*
• Victories :	6	1989 : *Champion junior*
• Pole-positions :	8	*de F. Ford 1600*
• Best laps :	11	1990 : *F. Opel Lotus*
• Accident/off :	12	1991 : *F. 3 GB (2°)*
• Not qualified :	0	1992 : *F. 3000 (9°)*
• Laps in the lead :	575	1993 : *F. 3000 (3°)*
• Km in the lead :	2834	
• Points scored :	218	

CARRIÈRE EN F1

1994 : *Williams / Renault. 14 points. 8th of champ.*
1995 : *Williams / Renault. 49 points. 3rd of champ.*
1996 : *McLaren / Mercedes. 18 points. 7th of champ.*
1997 : *McLaren / Mercedes. 36 pts. 3rd of champ.*
1998 : *McLaren / Mercedes. 56 pts. 4th of champ.*
1999 : *McLaren / Mercedes. 45 pts. 4th of champ.*

When Mika Hakkinen arrived in Melbourne for the first race of 1999, the world champion surprised everyone with a very un-Mika-like self assurance. Okay, so the car was not very reliable at first, but nevertheless, Hakkinen was totally in control of the game. Apart from at Imola and Monza, the Finn made no driving errors and now has to be seen in the same light as Michael Schumacher, or possibly even superior. Rumours that he was liable to crack under pressure can be dismissed, especially after the final in Japan, where he was in a class of his own in a car that was not particularly dominant that weekend. He now joins Alain Prost, Ayrton Senna and Michael Schumacher, as the only drivers to have won two consecutive titles. Only the great Juan-Manuel Fangio scored three in a row and there is no reason why Hakkinen's name will not be up there with the brilliant Argentinian's come the end of 2000.

The fact that David Coulthard manages to turn up for work at the track with a smile on his face is a tribute to his self-belief and courage. Unlike the situation at Ferrari where Irvine was designated Number Two, Coulthard is supposed to have equal status with Hakkinen at McLaren. Whatever it says on his job card, the fact is that David is not in the same league as Mika. There is nothing to be ashamed of in that, because the Finn is a great driver while the Scot is simply a very good one. Coulthard has nearly always been pipped to the post in qualifying and has come away with two wins from '99 and four second places against his team-mates five wins and two seconds. David is in a difficult position as no other team can offer him the brilliance of the McLaren-Mercedes technical package and having to share it with Hakkinen is the price he has to pay.

△
Erja Hakkinen never missed a race as she travelled the world supporting her husband.

During the driver parade, it was all smile between Mika Hakkinen and David Coulthard, but on the track relations were more strained.
▽

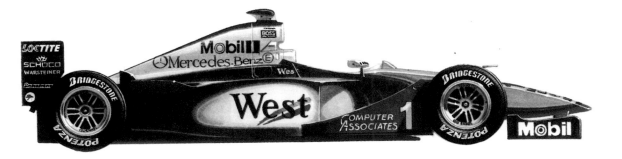

McLAREN-MERCEDES MP4/14 –
MIKA HAKKINEN
BRAZILIAN GRAND PRIX

McLaren-Mercedes MP4/14

Ron Dennis and Norbert Haug: a perfect relation-ship.

SPECIFICATION

- Chassis : McLaren MP 4/14
- Engine : Mercedes-Benz FO 110H V10
- Tyres : Bridgestone
- Wheels : Enkei
- Fuel / oil : Mobil
- Brakes (discs) : Hitco
- Brakes (calipers) : AP Racing
- Transmission : McLaren 6 gears, semi-autom.
- Radiators : McLaren / Calsonic
- Plugs : NGK / GS Battery
- Electronic mgt : TAG Electronic System
- Shock absorbers : Penske
- Suspensions : push rods/torsion bar
- Dry weight : 600 kg, driver included
- Wheelbase : not revealed
- Front track : not revealed
- Rear track : not revealed

TEAM PROFILE

- Address : McLaren International Ltd.
  Unit 22 Woking Business Park
  Albert Drive, Sheerwater
  Woking, Surrey GU21 5JY
  United Kingdom
- Telephone : (44) 1483 711 311
- Fax : (44) 1483 711 312
- Web : www.mclaren.co.uk
- Established in : 1963
- First Grand Prix : Monaco 1966
- General director : Ron Dennis
- Technical director : Adrian Newey
- Team-manager : Jo Ramirez
- Nber of employees : 280
- Sponsors : Reemtsma, Hugo Boss, Tag-Heuer

STATISTICS

- Number of Grand Prix : 492
- Number of victories : 123
- Number of pole-positions : 103
- Number of best laps during the race : 87
- Number of drivers' world titles : 11
- Number of constructors' titles : 8
- Total number of points scored : 2331.5

POSITION IN WORLD CHAMPIONSHIP

1966 : 7th – 3 points	1978 : 7th – 15 points	1990 : 1st – 121 points
1967 : 8th – 1 points	1979 : 7th – 15 points	1991 : 1st – 139 points
1968 : 2nd – 51 points	1980 : 7th – 11 points	1992 : 2nd – 99 points
1969 : 4th – 40 points	1981 : 6th – 28 points	1993 : 2nd – 84 points
1970 : 4th – 35 points	1982 : 2nd – 69 points	1994 : 4th – 42 points
1971 : 6th – 10 points	1983 : 5th – 34 points	1995 : 4th – 30 points
1972 : 3rd – 47 points	1984 : 1st – 143.5 points	1996 : 4th – 49 points
1973 : 3rd – 58 points	1985 : 1st – 90 points	1997 : 4th – 63 points
1974 : 1st – 73 points	1986 : 2nd – 96 points	1998 : 1st – 156 points
1975 : 3rd – 53 points	1987 : 2nd – 76 points	1999 : 2nd – 124 points0
1976 : 2nd – 74 points	1988 : 1st – 199 points	
1977 : 3rd – 60 points	1989 : 1st – 141 points	

The steamroller almost flattens the opposition

There was a period when Ron Dennis seemed to have found the elusive formula to continuous success. In the days of Lauda, Prost and Senna, nothing could stop the McLaren steamroller. But then, with the sudden departure of Honda, when the team was at the height of its powers, winning races and championships seemingly at will, the whole deck of cards collapsed for a while as the team worked its way through a series of unsuitable partners. Eventually, in the shape of Mercedes, it found an engine supplier with the same ruthless, if rather dull attitude to success. 1998 saw a return to form, with the team taking both titles thanks largely to the design skills of Adrian Newey. However, in 1999, the winning machine seemed to run out of puff. At the start of the year, the team had gambled on a brand new car and it paid the price in terms of poor reliability. Then there have been a series of strategic errors and what appeared to be finger trouble, when it came to bolting the cars together. On top of that, both drivers have made mistakes, many of them unforced errors. McLaren did still take the Drivers' title, thanks to a brilliant drive from Hakkinen in the final round, but the Constructors' prize slipped from their grasp; something which will have annoyed Mercedes more than McLaren.

TEST DRIVERS 1999

- Nick HEIDFELD (D)

SUCCESSION OF DRIVERS 1999

- Mika HAKKINEN : all Grands Prix
- David COULTHARD : all Grands Prix

Ferrari

3. Michael SCHUMACHER

DRIVER PROFILE

- Name : *SCHUMACHER*
- First name : *Michael*
- Nationality : *German*
- Date of birth : *January 3, 1969*
- Place of birth : *Hürth-Hermühlheim (GER)*
- Lives in : *Vufflens-le-Château (CH)*
- Marital status : *married to Corinna*
- Kids : *two children (Gina, Mick)*
- Hobbies : *watches, karting,,cinema*
- Favourite music : *Phil Collins, M. Jackson, twist*
- Favourite meal : *Italian cuisine*
- Favourite drink : *apple juice with mineral water*
- Height : *174 cm*
- Weight : *74 kg*

Ferrari President Luca di Montezemolo loves Formula 1 and was a frequent visitor to the pit wall.

STATISTICS

- Nber of Grand Prix : 128
- Victories : 35
- Pole-positions : 23
- Best laps : 39
- Accident/off : 20
- Not qualified : 0
- Laps in the lead : 2013
- Km in the lead : 9193
- Points scored : 570

PRIOR TO F1

- 1984 : German junior karting Champion
- 1987 : European karting Champion
- 1988 : German Champion of F. Ford
- 1990-91 : Sportscar championship with Mercedes

F1 CAREER

- 1992 : *Benetton / Ford. 53 points. 3rd of championship.*
- 1993 : *Benetton / Ford. 52 points. 4th of championship.*
- 1994 : *Benetton / Ford. 92 points.* **World Champion.**
- 1995 : *Benetton/Renault. 102 pts.* **World Champion.**
- 1996 : *Ferrari. 49 points. 3rd of championship.*
- 1997 : *Ferrari. 78 points. Excluded from the championship.*
- 1998 : *Ferrari. 86 points. 2nd of championship.*
- 1999 : *Ferrari. 44 points. 5th of championship.*

4. Eddie IRVINE

DRIVER PROFILE

- Name : *IRVINE*
- First name : *Edmund*
- Nationality : *British*
- Date of birth : *November 10, 1965*
- Place of birth : *Newtownards (IRE)*
- Lives in : *Dublin, Oxford (GB) & Bologna (I)*
- Marital status : *single*
- Kids : *-*
- Hobbies : *fishing, helicopters*
- Favourite music : *rock, Van Morrison*
- Favourite meal : *Chinese*
- Favourite drink : *beer Miller*
- Height : *178 cm*
- Weight : *70 kg*

STATISTICS

- Nber of Grand Prix : 97
- Victories : 4
- Pole-positions : 0
- Best laps : 1
- Accident/off : 25
- Not qualified : 0
- Laps in the lead : 156
- Km in the lead : 838
- Points scored : 173

PRIOR TO F1

- 1983-87 : F. Ford 1600
- 1988 : F. 3 GB
- 1989 : F. 3000
- 1990 : F. 3000 (3rd)
- 1991 : F. 3000 Japon (7th)
- 1992 : F. 3000 Japon (8th)
- 1993 : F. 3000 Japon (2nd)

F1 CAREER

- 1993 : *Jordan / Hart. 0 point.*
- 1994 : *Jordan / Hart. 6 points. 14th of championship.*
- 1995 : *Jordan / Peugeot. 10 points. 12th of championship.*
- 1996 : *Ferrari. 11 points. 10th of championship.*
- 1997 : *Ferrari. 24 points. 7th of championship.*
- 1998 : *Ferrari. 47 points. 4th of championship.*
- 1999 : *Ferrari. 74 points. 2nd of championship.*

Michael Schumacher is incredible. His accident meant he was not in the title hunt, but his comeback proved his amazing qualities and a disconcerting superiority when confronted with the other 21 guys on the grid. Yes, there were mistakes; Canada for example and will we ever find out what really happened at Silverstone. For the rest of the time, the German was classy. Everyone expected he would find it impossible to help his team- mate's title quest, but at Sepang, Michael added honour to his list of qualities by playing with the opposition and handing Irvine the lead not once but twice. In Suzuka, no one really knows if the German could have challenged Hakkinen, but the final result suits him down to the ground, as he helped Ferrari to the Constructors' crown but can still be the first man in what is now almost living memory, to win the Drivers' title for the Scuderia in 2000.

"You never know, one day Michael might quit or break a leg," said a prescient Irvine, a couple of weeks before the British GP. Schumacher's enforced absence was a godsend. Irvine, having already proved capable of winning, with victory in the opening round in Melbourne, went on to win the next two races in Michael's absence. After that, it seemed as though the team had not expected to still be in the fight and Irvine had to fight with a lack of development and the incredible pit lane incompetence of the European GP. Given that Ferrari had never looked further than Schumacher for its inspiration over the past four years, the fact that Eddie arrived in Japan leading the championship is remarkable: it is as much if not more than Schumacher had delivered in the past. Irvine did not win and no one will remember how close he came. Now he goes to Jaguar, where he will be the unofficial Number One. The big cat might take a few years before being capable of offering him as good a shot at the title as did the Prancing Horse.

"The other Mika" as Salo is known, had a busier year than expected after being shown the door at Arrows at the end of 1998. He first got the call when Ricardo Zonta crashed in his home race at Interlagos. Salo was a BAR driver for a few races and then he got the call to replace Schumacher at Ferrari after the British GP. It turned out to be his best ever season in F1. Salo, who added to his racing activities by getting married this year, almost won in Germany, handing the lead to Irvine and then he was on the podium once again in Italy. The understudy was hogging the limelight and it paid off as he now has a nice Sauber contract in his pocket for 2000, which some say was organised by Ferrari as a "thank you" for services rendered.

FERRARI F399 –
EDDIE IRVINE
AUSTRALIAN GRAND PRIX

Ferrari F399

SPECIFICATION

- Chassis : *Ferrari F399*
- Engine : *Ferrari 048 V10*
- Tyres : *Bridgestone*
- Fuel / oil : *Shell*
- Brakes (discs) : *Carbone Industrie*
- Brakes (calipers) : *Brembo*
- Transmission : *Ferrari 7 gears*
- Radiators : *not revealed*
- Plugs : *NGK*
- Electronic mgt : *Magneti Marelli*
- Shock absorbers : *not revealed*
- Wheels : *BBS*
- Suspensions : *push rods (ft/bk)*
- Dry weight : *600 kg, including driver*
- Wheelbase : *3000 mm*
- Total length : *4387 mm*
- Total height : *961 mm*
- Front track : *1490 mm*
- Rear track : *1405 mm*

TEAM PROFILE

- Address : *Ferrari SpR*
  Via Ascari 55
  41053 Maranello (MO)
  Italy
- Telephone : *(39) 536 94 91 11*
- Fax : *(39) 536 94 64 88*
- Web : *www.ferrari.it*
- Established in : *1929*
- First Grand Prix : *Monaco 1950*
- General director : *Luca Di Montezemolo*
- Technical director : *Ross Brawn*
  Paolo Martinelli (engines)
- Concepteur chassis : *Rory Byrne*
- Team-manager : *Jean Todt*
- Chief mechanic : *Nigel Stepney*
- Nber of employees : *400*
- Sponsors : *Marlboro, Fiat, Shell, Asprey*

TEST DRIVER 1999

Luca BADOER (I)

SUCCESSION OF DRIVERS 1999

- M. SCHUMACHER : 10 GP (AUS-BRE-S.M-MON-ESP-CAN-FRA-GB-MAL-JAP)
- Eddie IRVINE : all Grand Prix
- Mika SALO : 6 GP (AUT-ALL-HON-BEL-ITA-EUR)

STATISTICS

- Number of Grand Prix : 618
- Number of victories : 125
- Number of pole-positions : 127
- Number of best laps during the race : 139
- Number of drivers' world titles : 9
- Number of constructors' titles : 9
- Total number of points scored : 2343,5

△ *Technical Director
Ross Brawn was
always calm in the
eye of the storm.*

POSITION IN WORLD CHAMPIONSHIP

1958 : *2nd – 40 points*	1972 : *4th – 33 points*	1986 : *4th – 37 points*
1959 : *2nd – 32 points*	1973 : *6th – 12 points*	1987 : *4th – 53 points*
1960 : *3rd – 24 points*	1974 : *2nd – 65 points*	1988 : *2nd – 65 points*
1961 : **1st – 40 points**	1975 : **1st – 72,5 points**	1989 : *3rd – 59 points*
1962 : *5th – 18 points*	1976 : **1st – 83 points**	1990 : *2nd – 110 points*
1963 : *4th – 26 points*	1977 : **1st – 95 points**	1991 : *3rd – 55,5 points*
1964 : **1st – 45 points**	1978 : *2nd – 58 points*	1992 : *4th – 21 points*
1965 : *4th – 26 points*	1979 : **1st – 113 points**	1993 : *4th – 23 points*
1966 : *2nd – 31 points*	1980 : *10th – 8 points*	1994 : *3rd – 71 points*
1967 : *4th – 20 points*	1981 : *5th – 34 points*	1995 : *3rd – 73 points*
1968 : *4th – 32 points*	1982 : **1st – 74 points**	1996 : *2nd – 70 points*
1969 : *5th – 7 points*	1983 : **1st – 89 points**	1997 : *2nd – 102 points*
1970 : *2nd – 55 points*	1984 : *2nd – 57,5 points*	1998 : *2nd – 133 points*
1971 : *4th – 33 points*	1985 : *2nd – 82 points*	1999 : **1st –128 points**

Getting closer

Twenty years the Scuderia has gone without winning the Drivers' World Championship. So there was some consolation to be had in the fact they at least took top honours in the Constructors' title for the first time in 16 years. Although media attention centres on the Drivers' series, the Constructor's trophy has become ever more important in terms of prestige as more car manufacturers become involved in the sport, but the Italian legend will still not be able to carry the coveted Number One on one of its cars next season. Mind you, even if Irvine had taken top honours, they would not have got it, because the Irishman would have taken it with him to Stewart in 2000. Their season got off to a cracking start and it seemed as though they were going to win by default as McLaren fell by the wayside. It looked as though the reliable but slow tortoise would beat the fragile but fast hare. It was not to be and we will never know exactly what effect Schumacher's seven race absence had on the outcome, although we can hazard a pretty good guess. Ferrari looked stronger than at any time in recent years and if only they can find some early season speed to match the reliability then maybe the first year of the new century will belong to the oldest team in the sport.

Williams-Supertec

5. Alessandro ZANARDI

DRIVER PROFILE

- Name : ZANARDI
- First name : Alessandro
- Nationality : Canadian
- Date of birth : October 23, 1966
- Place of birth : St-Jean-sur-Richelieu, Quebec, CAN
- Lives in : Monte Carlo (Monaco)
- Marital status : married to Danièla
- Kids : 1son (Niccolo)
- Hobbies : model planes, skying
- Favourite music : a bit of everything
- Favourite meal : Grand-mother pasta
- Favourite drink : Coca-cola
- Height : 176 cm
- Weight : 70 kg

STATISTICS / PRIOR TO F1

• Nber of Grand Prix :	41	1981-86 : Karting
• Victories :	0	(Champ.of Italie 85 & 86)
• Pole-positions :	0	1987 : Champ. Europe
• Best laps :	0	of karting
• Accident/off :	2	1988-90 : F.3 Italie
• Not qualified :	0	1990 : Winner of the
• Laps in the lead :	0	Europeen Cup F.3 FIA
• Km in the lead :	0	
• Points scored :	1	

F1 CAREER

1991 : Jordan. (3 GP) 0 point
1992 : Minardi. (1 GP) 0 point
1993 : Lotus / Ford. 1 point. 20e of championship.
1994 : Lotus / Honda. 0 point
1999 : Wlliams / Supertec. 0 point

6. Ralf SCHUMACHER

DRIVER PROFILE

- Name : SCHUMACHER
- First name : Ralf
- Nationality : German
- Date of birth : June 30, 1975
- Place of birth : Hürth (D)
- Lives in : Monte Carlo (Monaco)
- Marital status : single
- Kids : -
- Hobbies : karting, tennis
- Favourite music : soft rock
- Favourite meal : pasta
- Favourite drink : apple juice with mineral water
- Height : 178 cm
- Weight : 73 kg

STATISTICS / PRIOR TO F1

• Nber of Grand Prix :	49	1978-92 : Karting
• Victories :	0	1993 : Jr. Champ. ADAC
• Pole-positions :	0	1994 : Champ. F. 3 (D, 3rd)
• Best laps :	1	1995 : Champ. F. 3 (D,
• Accident/off :	13	2nd), winner world
• Not qualified :	0	final F.3 in Macao
• Laps in the lead :	8	1996 : F. 3000 Champion
• Km in the lead :	36	(Japan)
• Points scored :	62	

F1 CAREER

1997 : Jordan / Peugeot. 13 points. 11th of championship.
1998 : Jordan/Mugen-Honda. 14 points. 10th of championship.
1999 : Williams/Supertec. 35 points. 6th of championship

Zanardi's performance this year was as surprising as his team-mate's, but for all the wrong reasons. The charming and amusing Italian's comeback to Formula 1, after taking two consecutive CART titles was eagerly awaited. There were high hopes that he would upset the F1 hierarchy and set the place alight, just as Jacques Villeneuve did when he made the switch from American racing to Formula 1. But while the Canadian had the advantage of what was then the best car on the grid, Alex had to struggle with the FW20; a car which will never have pride of place in the Williams museum. He never got to grips with the new-style grand prix cars and their narrow wheels, to such an extent that he even tried reverting to steel instead of carbon brakes, despite their 12 kilo weight penalty. He had more than his fair share of mechanical failures in pre-season testing, which kept his learning miles down, but even so, apart from a brief flourish at Monza, he never showed the talent he had promised and a cloud now hangs over his long term F1 future.

There is evidently no logic as to why a driver gets on well with one team and not with another. Frentzen flourished when he left Williams for Jordan and this year the inconsistent, accident prone, and arrogant 1998 Jordan driver, Ralf Schumacher became the consistent, quick and amiable Williams driver. The younger of the two Schumi's came out of his big brother's shadow to put in some stunning drives. He would fight just as hard for eighth spot as he would for a place on the podium. Without a doubt the revelation of the season, it is no surprise that Frank Williams has opened up the bank vault to keep this young talent on his books for the future. Lets hope the BMW engine gets on the pace quickly enough for him to perform in 2000.

Frank Williams never misses a grand prix. With all his experience, he knows his team is going through a difficult phase on its way to a victorious tomorrow.

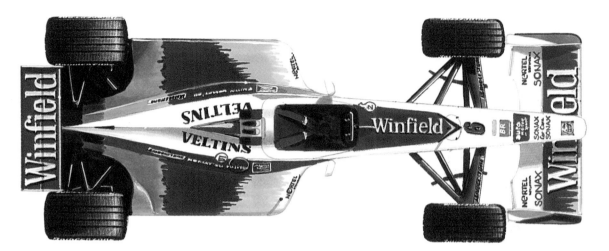

WILLIAMS-SUPERTEC FW21 – RALF SCHUMACHER ITALIAN GRAND PRIX

Williams-Supertec FW21

SPECIFICATION

- Chassis : *Williams FW21*
- Engine : *Supertec V10 FB 01*
- Tyres : *Bridgestone*
- Wheels : *OZ*
- Fuel / oil : *Petrobras/Castrol*
- Brakes (discs) : *Carbone Industrie*
- Brakes (calipers) : *AP Racing*
- Transmission : *Williams 6 gears*
- Radiators : *Secan (water) / IMI (oil)*
- Plugs : *Champion*
- Electronic mgt : *Magneti Marelli*
- Shock absorbers : *Williams / Penske*
- Suspensions : *Williams, torsion and helicoïdal*
- Dry weight : *600 kg, driver included*
- Wheelbase : *3050 mm*
- Front track : *1460 mm*
- Rear track : *1400 mm*
- Total length : *4450 mm*

TEAM PROFILE

- Address : *Williams F1*
  Grove, Wantage
  Oxfordshire OX12 0DQ,
  United Kingdom
- Telephone : *(44) 1235 77 77 00*
- Fax : *(44) 1235 76 47 05*
- Web : *www.williamsF1.co.uk*
- Established in : *1969*
- First Grand Prix : *Argentina 1975*
- General director : *Frank Williams*
- Technical director : *Patrick Head*
- Team-manager : *Dickie Stanford*
- Chief mechanic : *Carl Gaden*
- Nber of employees : *220*
- Sponsor : *Windfiel*

STATISTICS

- Number of Grand Prix : 411
- Number of victories : 103
- Number of pole-positions : 108
- Number of best laps during the race : 110
- Number of drivers' world titles : 7
- Number of constructors' titles : 9
- Total number of points scored : 1982.5

POSITION IN WORLD CHAMPIONSHIP

1975 : 9th – 6 points
1976 : not classified
1977 : not classified
1978 : 9th – 11 points
1979 : 2nd – 75 points
1980 : 1st – 120 points
1981 : 1st – 95 points
1982 : 4th – 58 points
1983 : 4th – 38 points
1984 : 6th – 25.5 points
1985 : 3rd – 71 points
1986 : 1st – 141 points
1987 : 1st – 137 points

1988 : 7th – 20 points
1989 : 2nd – 77 points
1990 : 4th – 57 points
1991 : 2nd – 125 points
1992 : 1st – 164 points
1993 : 1st – 168 points
1994 : 1st – 118 points
1995 : 2nd – 112 points
1996 : 1st – 175 points
1997 : 1st – 123 points
1998 : 3rd – 38 points
1999 : 5th – 35 points

During a race, all the mechanics can do is wait. It is sometimes hard to bear as they watch out for "their" car on the TV screens.
▽

The end of the line

This is the first time since 1990 that the Frank 'n Patrick show has finished as low as fourth in the Constructors' Championship. Why? Well the departure of Adrian Newey a couple of seasons ago certainly did not help and the proof of that can be seen in the corresponding reversal of fortunes between his past (Williams) and present (McLaren) employers. Williams have effectively been treading water this year, with Supertec just about helping to keep its head above water, but a "customer" engine is really beneath the dignity of a team whose natural position has always been somewhere in the Top Three, along with McLaren and Ferrari. Perhaps the balance of power has shifted forever in favour of arrivistes like Jordan and Stewart. Perhaps Frank Williams and his technical supremo Patrick Head belong to a past generation of winners. Unlikely, as these two men are competitive to their fingertips. But we are unlikely to see a great upturn in fortunes in 2000. The new partnership with BMW will deliver the goods, but it will take more than a year together to smooth out the glitches. In the meantime, Williams has paid a big bag of gold to hang on to Ralf Schumacher, one of the stars of 1999. However, the team must be wondering what to do with Alessandro Zanardi, who simply has not delivered the goods. BMW will certainly not be interested in running a one-car team.

TEST DRIVER 1999
- Jorg MULLER

SUCCESSION OF DRIVERS 1999
- Alesandro ZANARDI : all Grands Prix
- Ralf CHUMACHER : all Grands Prix

Jordan-Mugen Honda

7. Damon HILL

DRIVER PROFILE
- Name : *HILL*
- First names : *Damon Mark*
- Nationality : *British*
- Date of birth : *September 17, 1960*
- Place of birth : *London (GB)*
- Lives in : *Dublin (IRL)*
- Marital status : *married to Georgie*
- Kids : *4 kids*
- Hobbies : *golf, music, motorbike, tennis*
- Favourite music : *Elvis Presley, Otis Redding*
- Favourite meal : *traditional english cuisine*
- Favourite drinks : *milk, wine, beer, champagne*
- Height : *182 cm*
- Weight : *70 kg*

STATISTICS
		PRIOR TO F1
• Nber of Grand Prix :	115	1983 : *Motorcycle 500cc*
• Victories :	22	1984 : *F. Ford 1600 (10th)*
• Pole-positions :	21	1985 : *F. Ford 1600 (3rd)*
• Best laps :	19	1986 : *F. 3 GB (9th)*
• Accident/off :	17	1987 : *F. 3 GB (5th)*
• Not qualified :	6	1988 : *F. 3 GB (3rd)*
• Laps in the lead :	1352	1989 : *F. 3000 (11th)*
• Km in the lead :	6248	1990 : *F. 3000 (13th)*
• Points scored :	360	1991 : *F. 3000 (7th)*

F1 CAREER
1992 : *Brabham / Judd. 0 point.*
1993 : *Williams / Renault. 69 points. 3rd of champ.*
1994 : *Williams / Renault. 91 points. 2nd of champ.*
1995 : *Williams / Renault. 69 points. 2nd of champ.*
1996 : *Williams / Renault. 97 pts.* **World Champion.**
1997 : *Arrows / Yamaha. 7 points. 12th of championship.*
1998 : *Jordan/Mugen-Honda. 20 points. 6th of championship.*
1999 : *Jordan/Mugen-Honda. 7 points. 12th of championship.*

8. Heinz-Harald FRENTZEN

DRIVER PROFILE
- Name : *FRENTZEN*
- First name : *Heinz-Harald*
- Nationality : *German*
- Date of birth : *May 18, 1967*
- Place of birth : *Mönchengladbach (D)*
- Lives in : *Monte Carlo (Monaco)*
- Marital status : *married to Tanja*
- Kids : *-*
- Hobbies : *flying model planes, karting*
- Favourite music : *U2, soul, rap*
- Favourite meal : *fish, paella*
- Favourite drink : *apple juice*
- Height : *178 cm*
- Weight : *64,5 kg*

STATISTICS
		PRIOR TO F1
• Nber of Grand Prix :	96	1980-85 : *Karting*
• Victories :	3	1886-87 : *F. Ford 2000*
• Pole-positions :	2	1988 : *Champion F. Opel*
• Best laps :	6	*Lotus*
• Accident/off :	19	1989 : *F. 3 Germany*
• Not qualified :	0	1990-91 : *F. 3000*
• Laps in the lead :	140	1992-93 : *F. 3000 Japon*
• Km in the lead :	698	
• Points scored :	142	

F1 CAREER
1994 : *Sauber / Mercedes. 7 points. 13th of championship.*
1995 : *Sauber / Ford. 15 points. 9th of championship.*
1996 : *Sauber / Ford. 7 points. 12th of championship.*
1997 : *Williams / Renault. 42 pts. 2nd of championship.*
1998 : *Williams / Mécachrome. 17 pts. 7th of championship.*
1999 : *Williams / Supertec. 54 pts. 3rd of championship.*

Damon Hill could have entered the history books as a great people's champion; a hugely popular sporting hero, the first son of a world champion to emulate his father's title winning success and an all-round good book. In the end, the one element of his father's career Damon appeared to copy, was the ability to mess up the end of a great career by hanging on too long. Hill never got on with the "new" F1 cars with their narrow wheelbase and grooved tyres. There is no shame in that, but once he decided to pack it all in, as he did in Canada, he should have stuck to that decision and left Jordan to run a two car team again. Instead, a mixture of misguided sentiment and financial concerns kept him in the cockpit until he parked a perfectly good Jordan in the garage at Suzuka. Hopefully, these more recent memories will fade and we will remember his one world title, his 22 wins, 20 poles and 19 fastest laps. Now that is something to be proud of.

What a difference a year makes. Sacked by Williams, "HH's" career was "rescued" by Jordan at the start of this year. Frentzen never got on at Williams but his talent blossomed in the warm and family environment presided over by Eddie Jordan. We did not have to wait long to see the effects as he pushed Irvine all the way and came home second in the first race of the season. With two wins, which only owed a little to luck, the German was actually in with a chance of taking the Drivers' title as the teams headed for Sepang. It was a remarkable turnaround in a year when he got married to girlfriend Tanja, who is expecting the couple's first child. Next year, with a brand new Mugen-Honda engine and the confidence that comes from knowing you are a front runner, the brothers Schumacher might find they have serious competition in the battle for top honours among the German F1 drivers.

Eddie Jordan claims he is aiming for the world championship title in 2000. Ten years ago, he had just arrived in Formula 1 and had to check in to the cheapest hotels. Those days are now long gone.

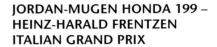

JORDAN-MUGEN HONDA 199 –
HEINZ-HARALD FRENTZEN
ITALIAN GRAND PRIX

Jordan-Mugen Honda 199

SPECIFICATION

- Chassis : *Jordan 199*
- Engine : *Mugen-Honda V10 MF 301 HD*
- Tyres : *Bridgestone*
- Wheels : *OZ*
- Fuel / oil : *Repsol*
- Brakes (discs) : *Carbone Industrie*
- Brakes (calipers) : *Brembo*
- Transmission : *Jordan 6 gears*
- Radiators : *Secan / Jordan*
- Plugs : *FIAMM / FIAMM*
- Electronic mgt : *TAG 2000*
- Shock absorbers : *Jordan*
- Suspensions : *push rods (ft/bk)*
- Dry weight : *600 kg, driver included*
- Wheelbase : *3050 mm*
- Front track : *1500 mm*
- Rear track : *1418 mm*

TEAM PROFILE

- Address : *Jordan Grand Prix Ltd. Buckingham Road, Silverstone, Northants NN12 8TJ United Kingdom*
- Telephone : *(44) 1327 850 800*
- Fax : *(44) 1327 858 120*
- Web : *www.jordangp.com*
- Established in : *1981*
- First Grand Prix : *USA 1991*
- General director : *Eddie Jordan*
- Technical director : *Gary Anderson*
- Team-manager : *Trevor Foster*
- Chief mechanic : *Tim Edwards*
- Nber of employees : *110*
- Sponsors : *Benson & Hedges, Repsol*

STATISTICS

- Number of Grand Prix : 146
- Number of victories : 3
- Number of pole-positions : 2
- Number of best laps during the race : 2
- Number of drivers' world titles : 0
- Number of constructors' titles : 0
- Total number of points scored : 213

POSITION IN WORLD CHAMPIONSHIP

1991 : 5th – 13 points	1996 : 5th – 22 points
1992 : 11th – 1 point	1997 : 5th – 33 points
1993 : 10th – 3 points	1998 : 4th – 34 points
1994 : 5th – 28 points	1999 : 3rd – 61 points
1995 : 6th – 21 points	

Heinz-Harald Frentzen and Eddie Jordan seem to have developed a taste for victory. At Monza, they clinched their second win of the season.
▽

The big time at last

Don't be fooled by it. His comic appearance and a reputation for never taking anything seriously are simply a weapon in Eddie Jordan's armoury. They were effective enough to hoist his team into third place in both the championship and even put Heinz-Harald Frentzen into a four way battle for driver honours, up until the final round. Who would have thought the nutty Irishman would one day be heading a team capable of harrying the mighty Ferrari and McLaren. This was all the more remarkable, given he did it without the support of a major engine manufacturer, although having the undivided attentions of Mugen-Honda has definitely brought dividends which those teams using Supertec power would like to have had. This year, Jordan finally made it into the premier division of those teams who win and are here to stay. It scored its first win in 1998 and racked up two more in '99 and there is every sign that this upward trend will continue. The biggest disappointment for Eddie Jordan was that Honda chose to make its return to grand prix racing with the BAR team, rather than his own outfit. However, with BAR's atrocious performance in 1998, Honda will no doubt be equally keen to see the Mugen-Honda engines do well in the back of the Jordans. Eddie Jordan can be admired for what he has achieved; not just on the track, but also away from it. He has proved it is still possible to be successful and look as though you are having some fun at the same time.

SUCCESSION OF DRIVERS 1999

- Damon HILL : *all Grands Prix*
- Heinz-H. FRENTZEN : *all Grands Prix*

Benetton-Playlife

9. Giancarlo FISICHELLA

DRIVER PROFILE

- Name : FISICHELLA
- First name : Giancarlo
- Nationality : Italian
- Date of birth : January 14, 1973
- Place of birth : Roma (I)
- Lives in : Monte Carlo (Monaco)
- Marital status : single
- Kids : -
- Hobbies : skiing, fishing, football, tennis
- Favourite music : disco music, Zucchero
- Favourite meal : pasta, pizza, steaks and fish
- Favourite drink : orange juice
- Height : 172 cm
- Weight : 69 kg

STATISTICS — PRIOR TO F1

• Nber of Grand Prix :	57	1984-88 :	Karting
• Victories :	0	1989 :	World Champion-ship Karting (4th)
• Pole-positions :	1		
• Best laps :	1	1991 :	F. Alfa Boxer; karting (EUR) (2nd)
• Accident/off :	13		
• Not qualified :	0	1992-94 :	F 3 (ITA),
• Laps in the lead :	35		champion in1994
• Km in the lead :	172	1995 :	DTM/ITC Alfa
• Points scored :	49		Romeo

F1 CAREER

1996 : Minardi / Ford. 0 point.
1997 : Jordan / Peugeot. 20 points. 8th of championship.
1998 : Benetton / Playlife. 16 points. 9th of championship.
1999 : Benetton / Playlife. 13 points. 9th of championship.

10. Alexander WURZ

DRIVER PROFILE

- Name : WURZ
- First name : Alexander
- Nationality : Austrian
- Date of birth : February 15, 1974
- Place of birth : Waidhofen (AUS)
- Lives in : Perchtoldsdorf
- Marital status : engaged to Karin
- Kids : -
- Hobbies : mountain biking, skiing
- Favourite music : Beatles, Pink Floyd, Rolling Stones
- Favourite meal : pasta and meat
- Favourite drink : apple juice with mineral water
- Height : 187cm
- Weight : 74 kg

STATISTICS — PRIOR TO F1

• Nber of Grand Prix :	35	1986 :	BMX worldchampion
• Victories :	0	1989 -90 :	kart (AUS) (2nd)
• Pole-positions :	0		Middle East KW (4th)
• Best laps :	1	1991 :	FFord 1600 (AUS)(1st)
• Accident/off :	5	1992 :	FFord 1600 (D)(1st)
• Not qualified :	0	1993 :	F3 (AUS) champion
• Laps in the lead :	0	1994 :	F3 (D) (2nd)
• Km in the lead :	0	1995 :	F3 (D) (6th)
• Points scored :	24	1996 :	Le Mans 24h (1st)

F1 CAREER

1997 : Benetton / Renault. 4 points. 14th of championship.
1998 : Benetton / Playlife. 16 points. 9th of championship.
1999 : Benetton / Playlife.3 points. 13th of championship.

Neat, tidy and trendy, Giancarlo Fisichella and his film star looks made him the ideal candidate for the flashy Benetton team. Sadly, he has joined a team which is in a serious decline and was rarely able to show his true natural talent, apart from his second place finish in Canada. There is no doubt the young Roman has the ability to be a winner, if not a champion, but he is still young enough to need guidance and a good car. He has therefore not really progressed since his Jordan days. A team-mate who pushed him harder might also be useful. Now we must wait and see if Benetton can supply him with a car that is nearer the mark than the B199. It could hardly be worse.

There is no doubt that Alexander Wurz is a quick driver. You don't lose your speed from one day to the next, for no good reason. In a nutshell, he is simply too tall and too heavy for a modern F1 car. This problem was exacerbated in the early part of the season by the B199's Front Torque Transfer system, which carried a heavy weight penalty and achieved nothing. Without it the car improved, but Wurz's build does not allow him the luxury of moving ballast around in the car. On top of that, he has been criticised for spending too much time fine tuning his image rather than his car. But what is the point of looking for something to blame? Needs to try harder.

BENETTON-PLAYLIFE B199 –
GIANCARLO FISICHELLA
CANADIAN GRAND PRIX

Benetton-Playlife B199

SPECIFICATION

- Chassis : Benetton B199
- Engine : Supertec FB 01
- Tyres : Bridgestone
- Wheels : BBS
- Fuel / oil : Agip
- Brakes (discs) : Carbone Industrie
- Brakes (calipers) : Brembo
- Transmission : Benetton 6 gears
- Radiators : Benetton
- Plugs : Champion
- Electronic mgt : Magneti Marelli
- Shock absorbers : Dynamics
- Suspensions : push rods (ft/bk)
- Dry weight : 600 kg (with driver)
- Wheelbase : 2900 mm
- Front track : 1490 mm
- Rear track : 1405 mm

TEAM PROFILE

- Address : Benetton Formula Ltd.
  Whiteways Technical Centre
  Enstone, Chipping Norton
  Oxon OX7 4EE
  United Kingdom
- Telephone : (44) 1608 67 80 00
- Fax : (44) 1608 67 86 09
- Web : www.jtnek.ad.jp/www/JT/event/
  F1/welcome.html
- Established in : 1970 (under the name Toleman)
- First Grand Prix : Italy 1981
- General director : Flavio Briatore / David Richards
- Technical director : Pat Symonds
- Team-manager : Joan Villadelprat
- Chief mechanic : Mike Ainsley-Cowlishaw
- Nber of employees : 175
- Sponsors : Mild Seven, Fed Ex, Korean Air,
  Akai

STATISTICS

- Number of Grand Prix : 283
- Number of victories : 26
- Number of pole-positions : 16
- Number of best laps during the race : 38
- Number of drivers' world titles : 2
- Number of constructors' titles : 1
- Total number of points scored : 846.5

POSITION IN WORLD CHAMPIONSHIP

1981 : not classified	1991 : 4th – 38,5 points
1982 : not classified	1992 : 3rd – 91 points
1983 : 9th – 10 points	1993 : 3rd – 72 points
1984 : 7th – 16 points	1994 : 2nd – 103 points
1985 : not classified	1995 : 1st – 137 points
1986 : 6th – 19 points	1996 : 3rd – 68 points
1987 : 5th – 28 points	1997 : 3rd – 67 points
1988 : 3rd – 39 points	1998 : 5rd – 33 points
1989 : 4th – 39 points	1999 : 6th – 16 points
1990 : 3rd – 71 points	

After Flavio Briatore and David
Richards, it is the youngest
Benetton, Rocco, who has taken
over the reins of the team.
▽

Chasing after the past

What can one make of Benetton? This team
remains a mystery and there have to be doubts
about its ability to get back on top as long as
its relying on the technical talents of Nick
Wirth and Pat Symonds, while the other major
teams have a whole raft of engineers to design their creations. There are some who reckon the team is simply being kept running
with the aim of selling it on. Benetton appears
to be pinning much of its hopes for the future on persuading Renault to return to the fold,
when it might have done better to put its own
house in order. In fact, this process is now
underway, with the young, inexperienced, but
enthusiastic and level headed Rocco Benetton
revamping his management structure. The car
has proved capable of some good performances,
especially in the hands of Giancarlo Fisichella.
Much of the early part of the season was was-
ted in trying to get new technologies like the
Front Torque Transfer system to work. It was
supposed to be a revolutionary aid to improving cornering speed, but it turned into a was-
te of time and a weight handicap.

TEST DRIVER 1999
- Laurent REDON

SUCCESSION OF DRIVERS 1999
- Giancarlo FISICHELLA : all Grands Prix
- Alexander WURZ : all Grands Prix

Sauber-Petronas

11. Jean ALESI

DRIVER PROFILE

- Name : *ALESI*
- First name : *Jean*
- Nationality : *French*
- Date of birth : *June 11, 1964*
- Place of birth : *Avignon (F)*
- Lives in : *Nyon (CH)*
- Marital status : *married to Kumiko*
- Kids : *two daughters (Charlotte & Helena)*
- Hobbies : *skiing, tennis, golf, water skiing*
- Favourite meal : *pasta*
- Favourite drink : *Vichy Menthe*
- Height : *170 cm*
- Weight : *75 kg*

STATISTICS

		PRIOR TO F1
Nber of Grand Prix :	167	1981-82 : *Karting*
Victories :	1	1983-84 : *Renault 5 Turbo*
Pole-positions :	2	1985 : *F. Renault of France*
Best laps :	4	*(5th)*
Accident/off :	29	1986 : *F. 3 of France (2nd)*
Not qualified :	0	1987 : *French Champion of*
Laps in the lead :	239	*F. 3*
Km in the lead :	1113	1988 : *F. 3000 (10th)*
Points scored :	236	1989 : *Champion F. 3000*

F1 CAREER

1989 : *Tyrrell / Ford. 8 points. 9th of championship.*
1990 : *Tyrrell / Ford. 13 points. 9th of championship.*
1991 : *Ferrari. 21 points. 7th of championship.*
1992 : *Ferrari. 18 points. 7th of championship.*
1993 : *Ferrari. 16 points. 6th of championship.*
1994 : *Ferrari. 24 points. 5th of championship.*
1995 : *Ferrari. 42 points. 5th of championship.*
1996 : *Benetton / Renault. 47 points. 4th of champ.*
1997 : *Benetton / Renault. 36 points. 4th of champ.*
1998 : *Sauber / Petronas. 9 points. 11th of champ.*
1999 : *Sauber / Petronas. 2 points. 16th of champ.*

12. Pedro DINIZ

DRIVER PROFILE

- Name : *DINIZ*
- First names : *Pedro Paulo*
- Nationality : *Brazilian*
- Date of birth : *May 22, 1970*
- Place of birth : *São Paulo (BRE)*
- Lives in : *Monte Carlo, São Paulo*
- Marital status : *single*
- Kids :
- Hobbies : *traveling, reading, tennis*
- Favourite music : *soft rock, Sade*
- Favourite meal : *spaghetti alla crudaiola*
- Favourite drink : *mineral water*
- Height : *174 cm*
- Weight : *69 kg*

STATISTICS

		PRIOR TO F1
Nber of Grand Prix :	82	1987-88 : *Karting*
Victories :	0	1989 : *F. Ford Brazil*
Pole-positions :	0	1990 : *F. 3 South America*
Best laps :	0	1991 : *F. 3 GB*
Accident/off :	16	1992 : *F. 3 GB*
Not qualified :	0	1993-94 : *F. 3000*
Laps in the lead :	0	
Km in the lead :	0	
Points scored :	10	

F1 CAREER

1995 : *Forti / Ford. 0 point.*
1996 : *Ligier / Mugen. 2 points. 15th of championship.*
1997 : *Arrows / Yamaha. 2 points. 17th of championship.*
1998 : *Arrows. 3 points. 13th of championship.*
1999 : *Sauber / Petronas. 3 points. 14th of championship.*

He might be one of the longest serving grand prix drivers, but Jean Alesi has kept all the enthusiasm of a novice. Despite a career littered with missed opportunities, Jean would no more think of retiring than he would consider the possibility of simply cruising round to the flag. Next year, he begins his eleventh season in grand prix racing and right up to the last inch of his last race for Sauber he gave his all. And that "all" is a lot; a lot of talent, heart, speed and an incredible level of experience. At 35 he is the oldest man on the track, or he will be now that Damon Hill has gone. But at that age, the Piquets, Mansells and Prosts and Laudas were fighting it out for world championships. Why could this not happen to him? At Sauber, any hopes of being in with a chance were soon kicked into touch, but a Swiss-German and a Franco-Sicilian were never going to hit it off. It just took them two years to work that out.

After stints with Forti, Ligier and Arrows, Pedro Diniz pursues his journeyman progress through the F1 ranks with the Sauber team, who should have provided greater opportunities than Arrows. That indeed happened, but it was more down to Arrows retrograding than Sauber progressing. Whatever the situation, Pedro has still got something to prove, before being considered a true grand prix driver. That is a task he is tackling with diligence; finishing races and picking up points and learning as he goes. At one point he was doing better than Jean Alesi, to such an extent that Ferrari was rumoured to be interested in his services around the middle of the season. No doubt, Marlboro would have liked a Brazilian driver, which they now have in the shape of Barrichello and Michael Schumacher probably liked the idea of an amenable Number Two, who would provide no threat at all. But Diniz will continue plying his trade with Sauber, alongside Mika Salo in 2000. He beat his team-mate at Arrows a few times and if Sauber progresses, so will he.

Determination, energy and passion: you can see it all in the eyes of Jean Alesi. ▽

SAUBER-PETRONAS C18 –
JEAN ALESI
SPANISH GRAND PRIX

Sauber-Petronas C18

SPECIFICATION

- Chassis : *Sauber C18*
- Engine : *Petronas SPE 03A*
- Tyres : *Bridgestone*
- Fuel / oil : *Petronas*
- Brakes (discs) : *Carbone Industrie*
- Brakes (calipers) : *Brembo*
- Transmission : *Sauber 6 gears longitudinal*
- Radiators : *Behr/Secan*
- Plugs : *Champion*
- Electronic mgt : *Magneti Marelli*
- Shock absorbers : *Sachs*
- Suspensions : *push rods (ft/bk)*
- Dry weight : *600 kg, driver included*
- Wheelbase : *2980 mm*
- Front track : *1470 mm*
- Rear track : *1470 mm*

TEAM PROFILE

- Address : *Red Bull Sauber AG*
  Wildbachstrasse 9
  8340 Hinwil
  Switzerland
- Telephone : *(41) 1 938 83 00*
- Fax : *(41) 1 938 83 01*
- Web : *www.redbull-sauber.ch*
- Established in : *1972*
- First Grand Prix : *South Africa 1993*
- General director : *Peter Sauber*
- Technical director : *Leo Ress*
- Team-manager : *Beat Zehnder*
- Chief mechanic : *Urs Kuratle*
- Nber of employees : *90*
- Sponsors : *Red Bull, Petronas,*
  Dassault Systèmes

STATISTICS

- Number of Grand Prix : 113
- Number of victories : 0
- Number of pole-positions : 0
- Number of best laps during the race : 0
- Number of drivers' world titles : 0
- Number of constructors' titles : 0
- Total number of points scored : 83

POSITION IN WORLD CHAMPIONSHIP

1993 : 6th – 12 points	1997 : 7th – 16 points
1994 : 8th – 12 points	1998 : 6th – 10 points
1995 : 7th – 18 points	1999 : 8th – 5 points
1996 : 7th – 11 points	

△
*Peter Sauber, the quiet
man of Formula 1,
smokes a cigar under the
motorhome awning. Yet
another season has gone
by with no more success
than its predecessors and
probably the future ones.*

Patience is a virtue, but there are limits

Just like the 1998 car, the Sauber C18 was well born. But also just as in 1998, it was the brainchild of the team's technical dictator, Leo Ress. There is no denying his talent, but it is also a sad truth that he is an immovable and omnipotent despot and refuses to adopt the current and evidently effective fashion for collective design. His staff twiddle their thumbs and the car's development crawls to an early halt, or almost. Ferrari offered to supply its complete '98 car rear end but Sauber turned it down. Naturally, the drivers lost their cool and their patience. In the case of Pedro Diniz, there were no public outbursts, when it came to the explosive Alesi the results were noisy and nasty. After a run of unpleasant surprises, the Frenchman abandoned his car, having run out of fuel and announced he would leave the team at the end of the season. In the current climate and given he had no contracts from other teams in his pocket, this smacked of the usual Alesi bravado. In the end, Sauber came away with a few sixth places, three for Diniz and one for Alesi, hardly fitting for a team of this status. With a Ferrari '98 spec engine, it should have been possible to have the legs of the likes of Benetton and Williams with their Supertec engines. As for 2000. Sauber will keep Diniz and the same organisational structure. Mika Salo might yet end up pulling his hair out.

SUCCESSION OF DRIVERS 1999

- Jean ALESI : *all Grands Prix*
- Pedro DINIZ : *all Grands Prix*

Arrows

14. Pedro de la ROSA

DRIVER PROFILE

- Name : de la ROSA
- First names : Pedro
- Nationality : Spanish
- Date of birth : February 24, 1971
- Place of birth : Barcelona (ESP)
- Lives in : Barcelona (ESP)
- Marital status : engaged to Maria
- Kids : -
- Hobbies : karting, mountain bike
- Favourite music : Mecano
- Favourite meal : paella, pasta
- Favourite drink : mineral water
- Height : 177 cm
- Weight : 75 kg

STATISTICS

		PRIOR TO F1
• Nber of Grand Prix :	16	since 86 : Formule Fiat -
• Victories :	0	F.3 - F.3000
• Pole-positions :	0	1997 : 3rd of champion-
• Best laps :	0	ship Spark Plug
• Accident/off :	4	World Drivers
• Not-qualified :	0	
• Laps in the lead :	0	
• Km in the lead :	0	
• Points scored :	1	

F1 CAREER

1998 : Jordan. Test driver
1999 : Arrows. 1 point. 17 of championship

15. Toranosuke TAKAGI

DRIVER PROFILE

- Name : TAKAGI
- First names : Toranosuke
- Nationality : japanese
- Date of birth : February 12th 1974
- Place of birth : Shizuoka (JAP)
- Lives in : Shizuoka (JAP)
- Marital status : single
- Kids : -
- Hobbies : snowboarding, karting
- Favorite music : Pop, Spice Girls
- Favorite meal : pasta, indians and chinese meals
- Favorite drinks : mineral water
- Height : 180 cm
- Weight : 61 kg

STATISTICS

		PRIOR TO F1
• Nber of Grands Prix :	32	1986-88 : Karting
• Victories :	0	1989 : Kart A2, Japan (1st)
• Pole-positions :	0	1990 : Kart A2, Japan (1st)
• Best Laps :	0	1992 : Formula Toyota
• Accident/off :	6	1993 : All Japan F3 (10th)
• Not-qualified :	0	1994 : All Japan F3 (5th)
• Laps in the lead :	0	1994 : Japan F3000 (7th)
• Km in the lead :	0	1995 : Japan F3000 (2th)
• Points scored:	0	1996 : Japan F3000 (4th)

F1 CAREER

1997 : Tyrrell / Ford. Test driver
1998 : Tyrrell / Ford. 0 point
1999 : Arrows. 0 point.

Pedro does not fit any of the usual stereotypes for grand prix drivers. The former Japanese F3000 champion has an air of calm about him which belies his sporting abilities. It would be a mistake to judge him by his appearance. He is an accomplished sportsman, who is a great squash player as well as being a very quick driver. The only proof of that is that he did score Arrows' one and only point last season. And that was in his very first grand prix in Brazil, something previously achieved by the likes of Alain Prost. Comparing these two might be a bit premature, but Pedro is strong in the head and makes few mistakes. He also has a powerful personal sponsor in the shape of Spanish oil company Repsol, who share his ambitions. Team-mate Takagi's talents might be hidden, but his are clear to see.

This year Tora-san made a huge step forward. He managed to say a few words, he had his hair cut and he managed the occasional smile. Behind the wheel though, it is harder to see any signs of progress. He is reckoned to be capable of the odd exploit during qualifying, but is criticised for a lack of determination and stamina over the length of a grand prix. That has certainly been born out by his results, or lack of them when compared to team-mate Pedro De La Rosa. Writing anything about Tora Takagi is difficult. Nothing is known about him and talking to Japanese people does not offer any clues. At the time of writing, even his future is in doubt. Either way, he still has a lot to prove.

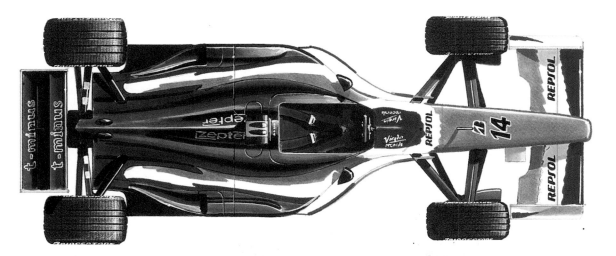

**ARROWS A20 –
PEDRO DE LA ROSA
AUSTRALIAN GRAND PRIX**

Arrows A20

Prince Malik ado Ibrahim brought a splash of colour to the Formula 1 paddocks. The Nigerian took his role with Arrows very seriously. It came to nothing and he did not last long, leaving his bills unpaid.

SPECIFICATION

- Chassis : *Arrows A20*
- Engine : *Arrows V10 A20E*
- Tyres : *Bridgestone*
- Wheels : *BBS*
- Fuel / oil : *Repsol*
- Brakes (discs) : *Carbone Industrie*
- Brakes (calipers) : *AP Racing*
- Transmission : *Arrows 6 gears*
- Radiators : *Secan*
- Plugs : *NGK / FIAMM*
- Electronic mgt : *TAG 2000*
- Shock absorbers : *Dynamics*
- Suspensions : *push rods (ft/bk)*
- Dry weight : *600 kg, driver included*
- Wheelbase : *2950 mm*
- Front track : *1465 mm*
- Rear track : *1410 mm*
- Total length : *5140 mm*

TEAM PROFILE

- Address : *Arrows Grand Prix Int. Ltd.*
  Leafield Technical Centre
  Leafield
  NR Witney
  Oxon OX8 5PF
  United Kingdom
- Telephone : *(44) 1993 87 10 00*
- Fax : *(44) 1993 87 10 87*
- Web : *www.arrows.co.uk*
- Established in : *1977*
- First Grand Prix : *Brazil 1978*
- General director : *Tom Walkinshaw*
- Technical director : *Roger Silman*
- Team-manager : *Rod Benoist*
- Chief mechanic : *Stuart Cowie*
- Nber of employees : *170*
- Sponsor : *Bridgestone, Repsol, Zepter,
  BAAN*

STATISTICS

- Number of Grand Prix : 337
- Number of victories : 0
- Number of pole-positions : 1
- Number of best laps during the race : 0
- Number of drivers' world titles : 0
- Number of constructors' titles : 0
- Total number of points scored : 157

POSITION IN WORLD CHAMPIONSHIP

1978 : 9th – 11 points	1989 : 7th – 13 points
1979 : 9th – 5 points	1990 : 9th – 2 points
1980 : 7th – 11 points	1991 : *not classified*
1981 : 8th – 10 points	1992 : 7th – 6 points
1982 : 10th – 5 points	1993 : 9th – 4 points
1983 : 10th – 4 points	1994 : 9th – 9 points
1984 : 9th – 6 points	1995 : 8th – 5 points
1985 : 8th – 14 points	1996 : 9th – 1 point
1986 : 10th – 1 point	1997 : 8th – 9 points
1987 : 6th – 11 points	1998 : 7th – 6 points
1988 : 4th – 23 points	1999 : 9th – 1 points

The art of accommodating the left overs

Mike Coughlan used to be John Barnard's right hand man and the team's former technical boss had designed a splendid car over the winter of 97/98. Many people reckoned the A20 was the prettiest car on the grid, being more elegant and thoroughbred than the rather bitty Ferraris and the nondescript McLarens. But that was two years ago. John Barnard left Arrows to go and work for Prost Grand Prix and Mika Coughlan took over his master's mantle and did the best he could. Matters took a turn for the worse over the winter as the budget took a dive. On top of that, both drivers were pretty much debutants, as Takagi's time at Tyrrell hardly counted as race experience. Then there was the phantom Nigerian Prince who did not deliver on his promises. Prince Malik Ado Ibrahim brought the Morgan Grenfell bank to the party and announced a dodgy marketing gambit billed as "T-Minus." He promised a lot and delivered little, while wasting the team's precious time. However, Pedro De La Rosa scored his first point in the season opener in Australia, giving team boss Tom Walkinshaw cause for optimism. Alas, it was a false dawn. Walkinshaw then sold his Ixion car dealerships to buy back Arrows and treat himself to a supply of Supertec V10 engines for 2000.

SUCCESSION OF DRIVERS 1999

- Petro de la ROSA: *all Grands Prix*
- Toranosuke TAGAKI: *all Grands Prix*

Stewart-Ford

16. Rubens BARRICHELLO

DRIVER PROFILE

- Name : *BARRICHELLO*
- First names : *Rubens Gonçalves*
- Nationality : *Brazilian*
- Date of birth : *May 23, 1972*
- Place of birth : *São Paulo (BRA)*
- Lives in : *Monte Carlo (Monaco)*
- Marital status : *married to Silvana*
- Kids : *-*
- Hobbies : *jet-ski*
- Favourite music : *pop, rock*
- Favourite dish : *pasta*
- Favourite drink : *Pepsi*
- Height : *172 cm*
- Weight : *71 kg*

STATISTICS | PRIOR TO F1

- Nber of Grand Prix : 113 | 1981-88 : Karting (5 times
- Victories : 0 | Brazilian
- Pole-positions : 2 | Champion)
- Best laps : 0 | 1989 : F. Ford 1600 (3rd)
- Accident/off : 17 | 1990 : Champion Opel
- Not qualified : 0 | Lotus Euroseries
- Laps in the lead : 75 | 1991 : Champion F. 3 (GB)
- Km in the lead : 333 | 1992 : F. 3000
- Points scored : 71

F1 CAREER

1993 : Jordan / Hart. 2 points. 17th of championship.
1994 : Jordan / Hart. 19 points. 6th of championship.
1995 : Jordan / Peugeot. 11 points. 11th of championship.
1996 : Jordan / Peugeot. 14 points. 8th of championship.
1997 : Stewart / Ford. 6 points. 13th of championship.
1998 : Stewart / Ford. 4 points. 12th of championship.
1999 : Stewart / Ford. 21 points. 7th of championship.

17. Johnny HERBERT

DRIVER PROFILE

- Name : *HERBERT*
- First name : *Johnny*
- Nationality : *British*
- Date of birth : *June 27, 1964*
- Place of birth : *Romford (GB)*
- Lives in : *Monte Carlo (Monaco)*
- Marital status : *married to Rebecca*
- Kids : *two daughters (Amelia, Chloe)*
- Hobbies : *golf, squash, fishing*
- Favourite music : *rock, pop*
- Favourite drink : *apple juice*
- Height : *167 cm*
- Weight : *65 kg*

STATISTICS | PRIOR TO F1

- Nber of Grand Prix : 144 | 1984-85 : F. Ford 1600
- Victories : 3 | 1986 : F. Ford 2000
- Pole-positions : 0 | 1987 : GB F. 3 Champion
- Best laps : 0 | 1988 : F. 3000
- Accident/off : 22 | 1989 : Benetton / Ford &
- Not qualified : 3 | Tyrrell / Ford. 0 point.
- Laps in the lead : 44 | 1990 : Lotus /
- Km in the lead : 226 | Lamborghini. 0 point (only
- Points scored : 98 | 2 GP).

F1 CAREER

1991 : Lotus / Judd. 0 point.
1992 : Lotus / Ford. 2 points. 14th of championship.
1993 : Lotus / Ford. 11 points. 8th of championship.
1994 : Lotus / Honda. 0 point.
1995 : Benetton / Renault. 45 points. 4th of champ.
1996 : Sauber / Ford. 4 points. 14th of championship.
1997 : Sauber / Petronas. 15 points. 10th of champ.
1998 : Sauber / Petronas. 1 point. 11th of champ.
1999 : Stewart / Ford. 15 point. 81th of champ.

The Brazilian is another driver to undergo something of a renaissance at the moment, after his career took something of a dive back in 1996. Essentially, the move to the brand new Stewart team in 1997 saw a revitalised Rubens. He has continued to improve and this year, thanks to the Alan Jenkins- designed SF03 he has really been able to show off his talents, especially if the rain gods have come to his assistance. He has been a consistent front runner, who has generally out-shone his team mate all year long. Although he has been in Formula 1 since 1993, he is still only 27; young enough to cope with partnering Michael Schumacher at Ferrari in 2000 and come out the other side unscathed.

Nothing seems to wipe a perpetual smile off Johnny Herbert's face. He is the eternal cheeky chappy of Formula 1 who can get away with murder and still be loved by one and all. Although he was generally out-qualified by Barrichello, he did not let this get him down, even when there were rumours the team wanted to dump him. Eventually, he shook off some of the bad luck which had contributed to his poor season and then, a little bit of good fortune came along and hey presto, Johnny pulled a win out of the bag in the European Grand Prix. It was the Stewart team's first and last Formula 1 win as the team will be re-named Jaguar next season. It will have given Herbert, one of the veterans of the field, a new lease of life before tackling the difficult task of partnering Eddie Irvine in the new team with the historic name.

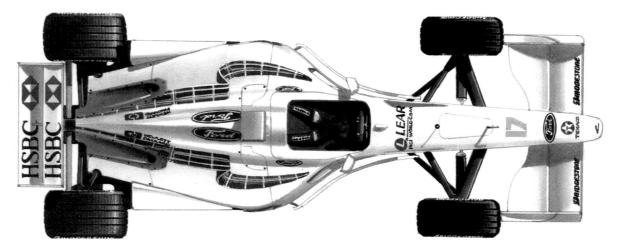

STEWART-FORD SF-3 –
JOHNNY HERBERT
EUROPEAN GRAND PRIX

SPECIFICATION

- Chassis : *Stewart Ford SF-3*
- Engine : *Ford Cosworth V10-CR1*
- Tyres : *Bridgestone*
- Fuel / oil : *Texaco*
- Brakes (discs) : *Carbone Industrie*
- Etriers : *AP Racing*
- Transmission : *Stewart / XTrac*
- Radiators : *Secan*
- Plugs : *Champion / FIAMM*
- Electronic mgt : *Ford*
- Shock absorbers : *Stewart / Penske*
- Suspensions : *push rods (ft/bk)*
- Dry weight : *600 kg, driver included*
- Wheelbase : *2900 mm*
- Front track : *1470 mm*
- Rear track : *1555 mm*

TEAM PROFILE

- Address : *Stewart Grand Prix*
  Stewart Building, Bradbourne Dr.
  Milton Keynes, MK7 8BJ
  United Kingdom
- Telephone : *(44) 1908 279 700*
- Fax : *(44) 1908 279 711*
- Established in : *1996*
- First Grand Prix : *Australia 1997*
- General director : *Jackie Stewart*
- Technical director : *Gary Anderson*
- Team-manager : *David Stubbs*
- Chief mechanic : *Dave Redding*
- Nber of employees : *75*
- Sponsors : *HSBC, Visit Malysia, Havoline,*
  Sanyo, Bridgestone, Ford, Texaco

Stewart-Ford SF-3

STATISTICS

- Number of Grand Prix : 49
- Number of victories : 1
- Number of pole-positions : 1
- Number of best laps during the race : 0
- Number of drivers' world titles : 0
- Number of constructors' titles : 0
- Total number of points scored : 47

POSITION IN WORLD CHAMPIONSHIP

1997 : 9th – 6 points	1999 : 4th – 36 points
1998 : 8th – 5 points	

Jackie Stewart achieved his objective; to build up an F1 team and sell it on to a major manufacturer for ten times the initial investment. Thanks Ford.

▽

Consigned to the history books

The outmoded Stewart team, clinging to strange anachronisms like tartan trousers and having an obsession with Rolex watches, will now be a thing of the past, as from 2000 onwards, Stewart is re-born as Jaguar Racing, albeit with Jackie and Paul Stewart still at the helm. At least Stewart will have made its mark on the F1 record books in its brief three year career. Rubens Barrichello had notched up three podium finishes for the team, but then came the crowning glory, with Johnny Herbert's magnificent if unexpected victory in the European Grand Prix. "It was the greatest moment of my career," said Jackie Stewart at the Nurburgring, "Maybe even of my life." The pretty little SF03 was impressive right out of the box and in a way, that first victory had always looked on the cards, but for the fact that, once the giants at McLaren and Ferrari had got into their stride, it got harder for anyone else to get a look in. As for the future, now that Ford/Jaguar has total control of the operation, it is bound to make rapid progress and could pose a threat to the establishment.

SUCCESSION OF DRIVERS 1999

- Rubens BARRICHELLO : *all Grands Prix*
- Johnny HERBERT : *all Grands Prix*

Prost-Peugeot

18. Olivier PANIS

DRIVER PROFILE

- Name : *PANIS*
- First names : *Olivier Denis*
- Nationality : *French*
- Date of birth : *September 2, 1966*
- Place of birth : *Lyon (F)*
- Lives in : *Grenoble (F)*
- Marital status : *married to Anne*
- Kids : *two chirldren (Caroline & Aurélien)*
- Hobbies : *bike, karting,*
- Favourite music : *Stevie Wonder*
- Favourite meal : *pasta*
- Favourite drink : *Coca Cola*
- Height : *173 cm*
- Weight : *76 kg*

STATISTICS | PRIOR TO F1

• Nber of Grand Prix :	91	1981-87 : *Karting*
• Victories :	1	1988 : *Champion Steering*
• Pole-positions :	0	*Wheel Elf Paul Ricard*
• Best laps :	0	1989 : *Champion F.*
• Accident/off :	12	*Renault of France*
• Not qualified :	0	1990 : *F. 3 of France (4th)*
• Laps in the lead :	16	1991 : *F. 3 of France (2nd)*
• Km in the lead :	53	1992 : *F. 3000*
• Points scored :	56	1993 : *Champion F. 3000*

F1 CAREER

1994 : *Ligier / Renault. 9 points. 11th of championship.*
1995 : *Ligier / Mugen. 16 points. 8th of championship.*
1996 : *Ligier / Mugen. 13 points. 9th of championship.*
1997 : *Prost / Mugen Honda. 16 points. 10th of champ.*
1998 : *Prost / Peugeot. 0 point. not classified*
1999 : *Prost / Peugeot. 2 point. 15th of championship.*

19. Jarno TRULLI

DRIVER PROFILE

- Name : *TRULLI*
- First name : *Jarno*
- Nationality : *Italian*
- Date of birth : *July 13th, 1966*
- Place of birth : *Pescara (I)*
- Lives in : *Franzavilla (I)*
- Marital status : *single*
- Kids : *-*
- Hobbies : *tennis, karting, swimming*
- Favourite music : *Vasco Rossi, Elton John*
- Favourite meal : *pizza*
- Favourite drink : *Coca Cola*
- Height : *173 cm*
- Weight : *60 kg*

STATISTICS | PRIOR TO F1

• Nber of Grand Prix :	59	1963-87 : *Karting*
• Victories :	0	1988-93 : *Karting 100*
• Pole-positions :	0	*6 times champ.(ITA)*
• Best laps :	0	*3 times 2nd in world*
• Accident/off :	9	*championships*
• Not qualified :	0	1994 : *Wordl Champ.125*
• Laps in the lead :	37	*FC and 100SA karting*
• Km in the lead :	160	1995 : *Champ. F3 (D), 4th*
• Points scored :	11	1996 : *Champ. F3 (D), 1st*

F1 CAREER

1997 : *Prost / Mugen Honda 3 points 14th of championship.*
1998 : *Prost / Peugeot. 1 point. 15th of championship.*
1999 : *Prost / Peugeot. 7 point. 11th of championship.*

Alain Prost in jokey mood. After a great end to the 1999 season, the Frenchman can look to 2000 with optimism.

John Barnard joined the Prost team at the end of 1998 to work his magic on the AP02 programme. A few months later and Alain Prost took on Alan Jenkins as well in the role of technical director.

Olivier Panis was lying third in the opening stages of the 1999 season finale in Suzuka, until his car expired. It might be his best memory of a grand prix career which is now over or at least stalled. Well before the end of the year, the only seats available for 2000 were those at Minardi and Arrows. Olivier has really never been the same since his Canadian GP accident of two years ago. He has won a grand prix and visited the podium, but those days seem a long way away now. In many ways he is seen as almost too French to fit in with a British team, but that seems a strange criticism of a driver who is known for his strength and tenacity. Like many before him, he has looked to CART for a possible future. Even before the year was over, he was given the chance to do some testing for McLaren, no doubt organised through the good offices of Keke Rosberg, who now manages what is left of the Frenchman's career. There was also talk of him kicking Zanardi out of his Williams drive.

Jarno Trulli's second year under the tutelage of Alain Prost was rich in experience but poor in terms of results. However, that experience gained will come in very useful as he switches to what is bound to be a more competitive Jordan in 2000. The promising Italian has only acquired ten points in the past two years and that cannot satisfy an aspiring world champion. He enjoyed a stormy relationship with his boss Alain Prost: "Nothing is ever Alain's fault," was his acidic comment. He was also accused by his boss of not putting in much effort once he had secured the Jordan drive. Prost did admit that "he is now ready to win races." There is no doubting his speed. The only question mark is how he will fare, partnering the far more experienced Heinz-Harald Frentzen. They are probably very evenly matched, which should make for a thrilling confrontation.

PROST-PEUGEOT AP 02 – JARNO TRULLI EUROPEAN GRAND PRIX

Prost-Peugeot AP02

SPECIFICATION

- Chassis : Prost AP02
- Engine : Peugeot Sport A18 V10
- Tyres : Bridgestone
- Fuel / oil : Total
- Brakes (discs) : Carbone Industrie
- Brakes (calipers) : Brembo
- Transmission : Prost-Peugeot 6 gears
- Plugs : NGK / FIAMM
- Shock absorbers : Dynamics
- Suspensions : push rods (ft/bk)
- Dry weight : 600 kg, driver included
- Wheelbase : 2795 mm
- Front track : 1600 mm
- Rear track : 1600 mm
- Total length : 4135 mm
- Total height : 948 mm

TEAM PROFILE

- Address : Prost Grand Prix
  7, Avenue Eugène Freyssinet
  78280 Guyancourt France
- Telephone : (33) 1 39 30 11 00
- Fax : (33) 1 39 30 11 01
- Web : www.prostgrandprix.fr
- Established in : 1997
- First Grand Prix : Australie 1997
- General director : Alain Prost
- Technical director : Bernard Dudot
- Team-manager : Jean Pierre Chatenet
- Chief mechanic : Robert Dassaud
- Nber of employees : 155
- Sponsors : Gauloises Blondes, Alcatel, BIC
  Dassault Systèmes, Total,
  Sodexho, Playstation, Canal Plus

STATISTICS

- Number of Grand Prix : 49
- Number of victories : 0
- Number of pole-positions : 0
- Number of best laps during the race : 0
- Number of drivers' world titles : 0
- Number of constructors' titles : 0
- Total number of points scored : 31

POSITION IN WORLD CHAMPIONSHIP

1997 : 6th - 21 points | 1999 : 7th - 9 points
1998 : 9th - 1 point |

TEST DRIVER 1999

- Stéphane SARRAZIN

SUCCESSION OF DRIVERS 1999

- Olivier PANIS : all Grands Prix
- Jarno TRULLI : all Grands Prix

The Peugeot bosses kept out of the spotlight this season. Here, Corrado Provera.
▽

Some slight progress

Difficult to know exactly what to say about this team, if not say pretty much the same as last year. Looking at the points tally and making an impartial analysis of their season, the team is progressing. Not only have the Prost Peugeots pulled off the odd surprise in qualifying, they have also managed to look good in the warm up sessions and post race lap times which put them in the top ten. In terms of points though, they have been less successful, with two sixth places for Panis and a sixth and second for Trulli. That was about it for the Blues, with the team's first podium ranking as the major achievement of their year, although but for a badly timed pit-stop, identical to Mika Hakkinen's tactical error, Olivier Panis might well have won the European GP. In motor racing there are so many different parameters, that trying to re-write history serves no useful purpose. However, add together all these little plus signs and it has to be said that Prost is moving forward as a team. As to finding out what level they are at, perhaps the team could be compared to Jordan in 1996. Now it needs to move forward more quickly, even if its budget is not one of the best.

Minardi-Ford

20. Luca BADOER

DRIVER PROFILE

- Name : *BADOER*
- First name : *Luca*
- Nationality : *Italian*
- Date of birth : *January 25, 1971*
- Place of birth : *Montebelluna (I)*
- Lives in : *Monte Carlo (Monaco)*
- Marital status : *single*
- Kids : *-*
- Hobbies : *snowbiking, motorsports*
- Favorite music : *italian pop*
- Favorite meal : *meat*
- Favorite drink : *orange juice*
- Height : *170 cm*
- Weight : *58 kg*

STATISTICS

		PRIOR TO F1
• Nber of Grands Prix :	50	1985-88 : *karting of Fiat*
• Victories :	0	*Abarth*
• Pole-positions :	0	1989-91 :*F.3 Italie*
• Best laps :	0	1992 : *Champion of*
• Accident/off :	2	*F.3000*
• Not qualified :	0	1993 : *Lola/Ferrari. 0 point*
• Laps in the lead :	0	1994 : *Minardi. Pilote essai*
• Km in the lead :	0	1995 : *Minardi/Ford. 0 pt*
• Points scored :	0	1996 : *Forti/Ford. 0 point*

F1 CAREER

1997 : *Ferrari : Test driver.*
1998 : *Ferrari : Test driver.*
1999 : *Minardi / Ford. 0 point.*

21. Marc GENÉ

DRIVER PROFILE

- Name : *GENÉ*
- First name : *Marc*
- Nationality : *Spanish*
- Date of birth : *March 29th 1974*
- Place of birth : *Sabadell (ESP)*
- Lives in : *Bellaterra (ESP)*
- Marital status : *single*
- Enfant : *-*
- Hobbies : *scuba diving, reading, cinema*
- Favorite music : *Dire Straits*
- Favorite meal : *pasta*
- Favorite drink : *mineral water*
- Height : *173 cm*
- Weight : *69 kg*

STATISTICS

		PRIOR TO F1
• Nber of Grands Prix :	15	1994-95 : *British F.3*
• Victories :	0	1996 : *1er Il Fisa Golden*
• Pole-positions :	0	*Cup Superformula*
• Best laps :	0	1997 : *F.3000*
• Accident/off :	3	1998 : *1er Open Fortuna*
• Not qualified :	0	*Nissan*
• Laps in the lead :	0	
• Km in the lead :	0	
• Points scored :	1	

F1 CAREER

1999 : *Minardi / Ford. 1 points. 18e of championship.*

A former F3000 star and a regular in a series of second rate Italian teams in the mid Nineties, Badoer made his F1 comeback this season. Once again it was with a second string Italian outfit in the shape of Minardi. He brought with him the kudos that hangs like a halo around any driver with a Ferrari connection, as he is the Scuderia's test driver. He readily admits that it is the testing role which is his main priority. Sadly, that seems to have become obvious every time he got behind the wheel of his weekend Minardi. He had to sit out a race with a broken wrist but eventually produced Minardi's best race performance in ages, when he almost finished fourth at the Nurburgring. Sadly he was forced to retire from the European GP with just twelve laps to go. This did a lot to restore confidence and morale.

The Catalan driver was the surprise late arrival. With just a few days to go before the opening round in Melbourne, Marc Gene was hired by Minardi. No one in the closed world of F1 knew what to make of this polite young man or where he came from. For his part, he did all he could to capitalise on his good fortune, or Fortuna, as he was the winner of the Spanish Nissan Fortuna series. He gave up studying economics to get fit, both mentally and physically and found himself a major Spanish sponsor. That was all it took and Gene and Telefonica signed up with Minardi. His best qualifying was a fifteenth place, but the young man with a lot to say has improved steadily throughout the year and he could do better in 2000 if the machinery at his disposal is up to the job.

Giancarlo Minardi still loves his motor racing. The fact his fellow team owners have all become millionaires does not bother him. He invests all he has in his team in the good old fashioned way.

MINARDI-FORD M01–
MARC GENÉ
EUROPEAN GRAND PRIX

Minardi-Ford M01

SPECIFICATION

- Chassis : *Minardi M 01*
- Engine : *Ford Zetec R-V10*
- Tyres : *Bridgestone*
- Fuel / oil : *Agip / Motul*
- Brakes (discs) : *Carbone Industrie*
- Brakes (calipers) : *Brembo*
- Transmission : *Minardi/ XTrac 6 vitesses*
- Radiators : *Minardi*
- Plugs / battery : *Champion / FIAMM*
- Electronique mgt: *Magneti Marelli*
- Shock absorbers : *Dynamics*
- Suspensions : *pushrods/coaxial spring (front/rear)*
- Dry weight : *600 kg, driver included*
- Wheelbase : *2900 mm*
- Front track : *1452 mm*
- Rear track : *1421 mm*

TEAM PROFILE

- Address : *Minardi Team SpA*
  Via Spallanzani 21 (Z.I.)
  48018 Faenza
  Italia
- Telephone : *(39) 0546 696 111*
- Fax : *(39) 0546 620 998*
- Web : *www.minardi.it*
- Established in : *1974*
- First Grand Prix : *Brasil 1985*
- Chairman : *Gabriele Rumi*
- General manager : *Gian Carlo Minardi*
- Technical manager : *Gustav Brünner*
- Chief mécanic : *Gabriele Pagliarini*
- Nber of employees : *85*
- Sponsors : *Fondmetal, Avex, Doimo, Roces*

STATISTICS

- Number of Grands Prix :   237
- Number of victories :   0
- Number of pole-positions :   0
- Number of best laps during the race : 0
- Number of drivers' world titles :   0
- Number of constructors' world titles : 0
- Total number of points scored :   28

POSITION IN WORLD CHAMPIONSHIP

1985 : *not classified*	1993 : *8th – 7 points*
1986 : *not classified*	1994 : *10th – 5 points*
1987 : *not classified*	1995 : *10th – 1 point*
1988 : *10th – 1 point*	1996 : *not classified*
1989 : *10th – 6 points*	1997 : *not classified*
1990 : *not classified*	1998 : *not classified*
1991 : *7th – 6 points*	1999 : *10th – 1 point*
1992 : *11th – 1 point*	

Did you say attractive?

"Attractive." That was the quality hit upon by Cesare Fiorio to describe Minardi this season. In one sense, the team's sporting director is correct, because from the start of the season it has made a good impression, or at least a better one than in recent years. As the season drew to a close, they were putting on a better show than the ageing Arrows, their direct rivals in the championship. Naturally, they have put the far wealthier BARs and its world champion driver in the shade. In all areas, Minardi has improved. Under the guidance of its technical director Gustav Brunner, the two cars have evolved as much as those at the top end of the grid, with a longer wheelbase version coming out in time for the European race and that is a major achievement. The drivers have also improved with the passage of time as they have humbly and diligently gone about their business. At the Nurburgring, the team's finest hour this year, Marc Gene scored a point and Luca Badoer just missed out on three, almost within sight of the flag. In short, this is a serious team, with Gene impressing, if Badoer has been somewhat disappointing. Above all, the team is happy, friendly and always smiling, something which does not cost much, but is nevertheless a rarity in Formula 1. Go for it Minardi!

TEST DRIVER 1999

- Gaston MAZZACANE

SUCCESSION OF DRIVERS 1999

- Luca BADOER : *15 Grand Prix*
- Marc GENÉ : *all Grand Prix*
- Stéphane SARRAZIN : *1 GP (Brazil)*

BAR - Supertec

22. Jacques Villeneuve

DRIVER PROFILE

- Name : *VILLENEUVE*
- First name : *Jacques*
- Nationality : *Canadian*
- Date of birth : *April 9, 1971*
- Place of birth : *St-Jean-sur-Richelieu, Quebec, CAN*
- Lives in : *Monte Carlo (Monaco)*
- Marital status : *single*
- Kids : *-*
- Hobbies : *skiing, computer, reading, guitar*
- Favourite music : *rock and pop*
- Favourite meal : *pasta*
- Favourite drink : *milk*
- Height : *171 cm*
- Weight : *63 kg*

STATISTICS

		PRIOR TO F1	
• Nber of Grand Prix :	64	1986 :	*Jim Russel School*
• Victories :	11	1987 :	*Driving school*
• Pole-positions :	13		*Spenard-David*
• Best laps :	9	1988 :	*Ital. Champ. Alfa*
• Accident/off :	11	1989-91 :	*F3 (-, 14th, 6th)*
• Not qualified :	0	1992 :	*F3 Japan (2nd)*
• Laps in the lead :	634	1993 :	*F. Atlantic (3rd)*
• Km in the lead :	2814	1994 :	*IndyCar (6th)*
• Points scored :	180	1995 :	*IndyCar (Champion)*

F1 CAREER

1996 : *Williams / Renault. 78 points. 2nd of championship.*
1997 : *Williams / Renault. 81 pts. **World Champion**.*
1998 : *Williams / Renault. 21 pts. 5th of championship.*
1999 : *BAR / Supertec. 0 point.*

23. Ricardo Zonta

DRIVER PROFILE

- Name : *Zonta*
- First name : *Ricardo*
- Nationality : *Brazilian*
- Date of birth : *March 23, 1976*
- Place of birth : *Curitiba (BRA)*
- Lives in : *Monte Carlo (Monaco)*
- Marital status : *single*
- Kids : *-*
- Hobbies : *water skiing, jogging*
- Favourite music : *The Corrs, Paralamas do sucesso*
- Favourite meal : *pasta*
- Favourite drink : *orange juice*
- Height : *172 cm*
- Weight : *64 kg*

STATISTICS

		PRIOR TO F1	
• Nber of Grand Prix :	12	1987 - 92:	*Karting*
• Victories :	0	1993 :	*Formula Chevrolet*
• Pole-positions :	0	1994 - 95:	*F3 (6 victories)*
• Best laps :	0	1996 - 97:	*F3000 avec*
• Accident/off :	1		*Super Nova*
• Not qualified :	0		*(Champion)*
• Laps in the lead :	0		
• Km in the lead :	0		
• Points scored :	0		

F1 CAREER

1997 : *Jordan. Test driver.*
1998 : *McLaren. Test driver.*
1999 : *BAR / Supertec. 0 point.*

The Canadian has probably forgotten what a chequered flag looks like after a disastrous 1999, but unlike that other world champion, retirement is not on Jacques Villeneuve's agenda. The exciting Villeneuve style was in short supply this year, mainly because of the dreadful reliability of his mount. It might have been beneath his dignity, but he faced his responsibilities with courage and without giving up. He had decided to move to BAR and he was determined to stick with it. Hopefully, all the work he put into the project will pay off in the future. Nothing has dented his fighting spirit and maybe the arrival of Honda in 2000 will help revive memories of his exciting driving style.

Ricardo Zonta did not choose the easiest of routes into the sport of grand prix racing. F3000 champion, GT World Champion, this graduate of the Mercedes talent school was taken on by an ambitious but novice outfit and so he was faced with the dual task of learning the job while trying to make a good impression. Not easy when he had to do all that in a team built around Jacques Villeneuve. But Zonta's talent did shine through occasionally, even beating his team mate now and again. However, there were teams when it all got too much for him and he seemed to give up. Sitting out four races after a big shunt in his home Brazilian GP did little for his confidence. However, he just about managed to do enough to persuade team boss Craig Pollock to keep him on for another year. He is a real hope with talent and an engaging character: a beginner who is already a world champion.

Managing Director Craig Pollock. A difficult role at the end of a disastrous 1999 season.
▽

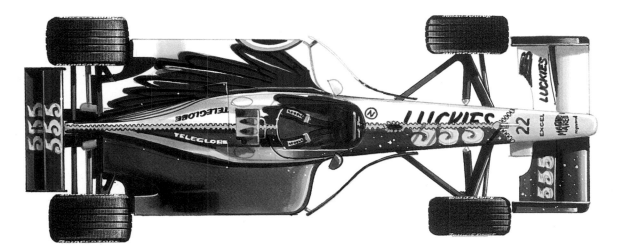

BAR-SUPERTEC 01
JACQUES VILLENEUVE
MONACO GRAND PRIX

BAR-Supertec 01

SPECIFICATION

- Chassis : *BAR PR01*
- Engine : *Supertec V10 -FB01*
- Tyres : *Bridgestone*
- Wheels : *OZ*
- Fuel / oil : *Petrobras/Castrol*
- Brakes (discs) : *Hitco carbone*
- Brakes (calipers) : *AP Racing*
- Transmission : *Boîte longitudinale 6 vitesses Reynard/Xtrac*
- Radiators : *Secan (water) / IMI (oil)*
- Plugs : *NGK*
- Electronic mgt : *Magneti Marelli*
- Shock absorbers :
- Suspensions :
- Dry weight : *600 kg, driver included*
- Wheelbase : *3020 mm*
- Front track : *1800 mm*
- Rear track : *1800 mm*
- Total length : *4470 mm*

TEAM PROFILE

- Address : *British American Racing Brackley, Northamptonshire NN13 7BD England*
- Telephone : *(44) 1280 84 40 00*
- Fax : *(44) 1280 84 40 01*
- Web : *www.britishamericanracing.com*
- Established in : *1997*
- First Grand Prix : *Australie 1999*
- General director : *Craig Pollock*
- Technical director : *Adrian Reynard*
- Team-manager : *Greg Field*
- Chief mechanic : *Steve Farrell*
- Nber of employees :
- Sponsor : *British American Tabacco (BAT)*

STATISTICS

- Number of Grand Prix : 16
- Number of victories : 0
- Number of pole-positions : 0
- Number of best laps during the race : 0
- Number of drivers' world titles : 0
- Number of constructors' titles : 0
- Total number of points scored : 0

POSITION IN WORLD CHAMPIONSHIP

1999 : *not classified*

TEST DRIVER 1999

- Patrick LEMAIRE

SUCCESSION OF DRIVERS 1999

- Jacques VILLENEUVE : *all Grand Prix*
- Ricardo ZONTA : *12 Grands Prix*
- Mika SALO : *4 GP (BRA-S.M-MON-ESP)*

Officially, Adrian Reynard was in charge of the technical aspects, but in practice he did very little and hardly ever came to the circuits.
▽

SSDD

"A win in our first grand prix? Sure, its an ambitious challenge, maybe even a presumptuous one. But why not set ourselves a high target to start with, as we are in this to win." That's what the team's chairman Adrian Reynard had to say at the team's launch. Certainly, he is the only one there who could come up with this sort of statement and still sound vaguely credible. From Formula Ford to Indycar, via F3000, all Reynard's cars have won first time out in a new category. Sadly, ten months after making this statement, Jacques Villeneuve had to wait until the Belgian Grand Prix to see a chequered flag. Adrian Reynard was put on the spot, accused by his Canadian driver of not investing enough time in the development of the car and in making it reliable.. On top of that, the press starting running the rumour that the man who created the team, Craig Pollock, was in danger of being shown the door to his own outfit. He had pulled of the coup of securing a supply of Honda engines, but apparently the problem lay, not with the motive power, but with the chassis. Craig Pollock's reply was to say that their next would be a BAR and not a Reynard. One day soon, this team has got to work. That's for sure.

ARROWS

F1-V10

SPECIFICATIONS

- Output: *715 hp at 15 000 rpm*
- Maximum revs : *16 400 rpm*
- Weight : *120 kilos*
- Capacity : *2996 cc*
- Configuration : *72 degrees V10*
- Material : *aluminium block*
- Valves : *4 per cylinder*

STATISTICS

• Number of Grand Prix :	32
• Number of pole-posotions :	0
• Number of constructors' titles :	0
• Number of victories :	0

RACE PROFILE

- First Grand Prix : *Australie 1998*
- Team 1999 : *TWR-Arrows*
- Nber of victories 1999 : *0*
- Nber of pole-positions 1999 : *0*

FERRARI

048

SPECIFICATIONS

- Output: *805 hp at 16 500 rpm*
- Maximum revs : *17 400 rpm*
- Weight : *118 kilos*
- Capacity : *2997 cc*
- Configuration : *80 degrees V10*
- Material : *aluminium block*
- Valves : *4 per cylinder*

STATISTICS

• Number of Grand Prix :	619
• Number of pole-posotions :	127
• Number of constructors' titles :	9
• Number of victories :	125

RACE PROFILE

- First Grand Prix : *Monaco 1950*
- Team 1999 : *Ferrari*
- Nber of victories 1999 : *6*
- Nber of pole-positions 1999 : *3*

FORD

CR-1

SPECIFICATIONS

- Output: *790 hp at 16 200 rpm*
- Maximum revs : *17 000 rpm*
- Weight : *105 kilos*
- Capacity : *2998 cc*
- Configuration : *72 degrees V10*
- Material : *aluminium block*
- Valves : *4 per cylinder*

STATISTICS

• Number of Grand Prix :	483
• Number of pole-posotions :	132
• Number of constructors' titles :	12
• Number of victories :	165

RACE PROFILE

- First Grand Prix : *USA 1963*
- Teams 1999 : *Stewart, Minardi*
- Nber of victories 1999 : *1*
- Nber of pole-positions 1999 : *1*

MERCEDES-BENZ

FO110H

SPECIFICATIONS

- Output: *810 hp at 16 200 rpm*
- Maximum revs : *16 800 rpm*
- Weight : *114 kilos*
- Capacity : *2998 cc*
- Configuration : *72 degrees V10*
- Material : *aluminium block*
- Valves : *4 per cylinder*

STATISTICS

• Number of Grand Prix :	109
• Number of pole-posotions :	36
• Number of constructors' titles :	1
• Number of victories :	28

RACE PROFILE

- First Grand Prix : *France 1954*
- Team 1999 : *McLaren*
- Nber of victories 1999 : *7*
- Nber of pole-positions 1999 : *11*

MUGEN-HONDA

MF 301 HD

SPECIFICATIONS

- Output: 765 hp at 15 800 rpm
- Maximum revs : 16 000 rpm
- Weight : 108 kilos
- Capacity : 2999 cc
- Configuration : 72 degrees V10
- Material : aluminium block
- Valves : 4 per cylinder

RACE PROFILE

- First Grand Prix :
  Afrique du Sud 1992
- Team 1999 : Jordan
- Nber of victories 1999 : 2
- Nber of pole-positions 1999 : 1

STATISTICS

- Number of Grand Prix : 130
- Number of pole-posotions : 1
- Number of constructors' titles : 0
- Number of victories : 4

PETRONAS

SPE 03A

SPECIFICATIONS

- Output: 790 hp at 16 500 rpm
- Maximum revs : 17 300 rpm
- Weight : 125 kilos
- Capacity : 2997 cc
- Configuration : 80 degrees V10
- Material : aluminium block
- Valves : 4 per cylinder

RACE PROFILE

- First Grand Prix : Australie 1997
- Team 1999 : Sauber
- Nber of victories 1999 : 0
- Nber of pole-positions 1999 : 0

STATISTICS

- Number of Grand Prix : 49
- Number of pole-posotions : 0
- Number of constructors' titles : 0
- Number of victories : 0

PEUGEOT

A18

SPECIFICATIONS

- Output: 785 hp at 15 700 rpm
- Maximum revs : 16 200 rpm
- Weight : 125 kilos
- Capacity : 2998 cc
- Configuration : 72 degrees V10
- Material : alliage léger
- Valves : 4 per cylinder

RACE PROFILE

- First Grand Prix : Brésil 1994
- Team 1999 : Prost Grand Prix
- Nber of victories 1999 : 0
- Nber of pole-positions 1999 : 0

STATISTICS

- Number of Grand Prix : 98
- Number of pole-posotions : 0
- Number of constructors' titles : 0
- Number of victories : 0

SUPERTEC

FB01

SPECIFICATIONS

- Output: 780 hp at 15 800 rpm
- Maximum revs : 16 600 rpm
- Weight : 117 kilos
- Capacity : 2999 cc
- Configuration : 71 degrees V10
- Material : aluminium block
- Valves : 4 per cylinder

RACE PROFILE

- First Grand Prix :
  Australie 1998
- Teams 1999 : Williams
                Benetton
                BAR
- Nber of victories 1999 : 0
- Nber of pole-positions 1999 : 0

STATISTICS

- Number of Grand Prix : 32
- Number of pole-posotions : 1
- Number of constructors' titles : 0
- Number of victories : 0

The engines

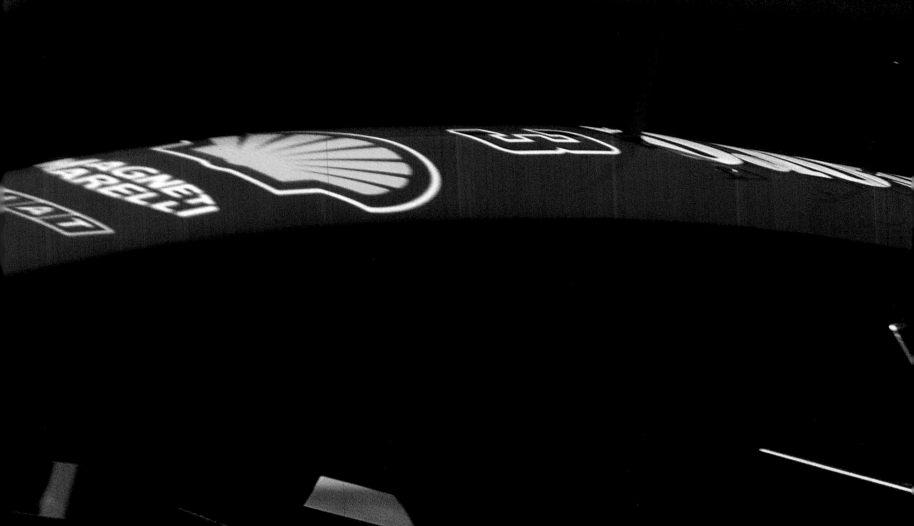

Spotlights

It is something of a tradition in "The Formula One Yearbook:" five of the best international journalist give their personal view of the season. From Germany to Japan, from Italy to England and Canada, a writer's passport affects gives a different perspective.

Ferrari: Worldchampion, at last

1999 : punto di vista Italiano

by Christiano Chiavegato
«La Stampa»

Ferrari sets out on the trail of the first world championship of the new millennium having yet again lost out on the Drivers' title at the final hurdle. However, the Scuderia did at least have the consolation of taking the Constructors' crown and that should serve as a base for trying yet again to take the prize that has eluded them since 1979, as they have consistently lost out to Williams, Benetton and above all McLaren. On the technical side Ferrari is very solid, although it will have to deal with a new element as Rubens Barrichello steps in to replace Eddie Irvine, who has switched to Jaguar Racing. As usual, the Maranello boys do not face an easy task. On top of facing up to its usual rivals, it will have to deal with the added challenge of the German company BMW, which returns to the sport to partner Williams and Honda, who now join forces with Jacques Villeneuve and British American Racing. It will be a tough assignment and the outcome is far from certain, unlike the team's determination to take the Driver's crown. It is clear that in order to succeed the Scuderia cannot afford to make the slightest mistake and must remain at full strength all year long, unlike 1999, when the accident at Silverstone deprived the team of its number one driver.

To tell the truth, even the previous season had begun in a mood of optimism.

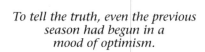

To tell the truth, even the previous season had begun in a mood of optimism. The team was solid, both technically and in terms of its management structure, while the drivers, on the track at least, worked in perfect harmony. Over the winter, Ross Brawn and Rory Byrne had tested various components fitted to a hybrid car before finalising the design of the F399, which was presented in its final version at the Fiorano track on 30th January. The new car, in theory derived from its predecessor, the F 300, had been completely revised: lower centre of gravity, weight down by about 20 kilos (in order to be able to shift the ballast around to improve the balance;) a completely redesigned engine with an 80 degree V, it was 6 kg lighter and 5 mm lower; a brand new rear end, with torsion bars and vertical springs as on the front; smaller cooling radiators. All the same, the engine, while reckoned to have improved driveability in all areas, did not appear, at least at the first race, to have significantly more power. The philosophy of Ferrari's technical department had been as always, to opt for maximum reliability, with a three stage development programme planned to be introduced in the course of the season.

In some respects, the first race of the year in Australia was disappointing in terms of performance. It was immediately apparent in qualifying at Melbourne, that the McLaren was much quicker and Schumacher had to settle for third place on the grid, while Irvine was only sixth. But the race had a pleasant

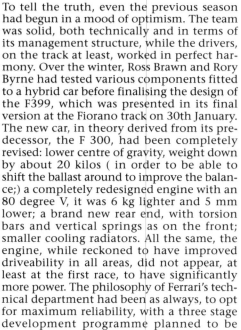

surprise up its sleeve. The German driver encountered electrical problems with the steering wheel and was further slowed with a puncture on his way to eighth place. Eddie Irvine was able to make the most of the problems encountered by both McLarens to take the first win of his Formula 1 career. The Irishman thus led the championship and kept the lead after the second race in Brazil, thanks to a fifth place, when Mika Hakkinen dominated in front of Michael Schumacher. That brought us to the start of the European leg of the season, with the classic San Marino Grand Prix at Imola. The home crowd were ecstatic over Schumacher's first win of the season and they were equally pleased with Hakkinen's retirement due to driver error. It meant that although Irvine was forced out with a broken engine - a very rare technical failure for the Scuderia this season - the Irishman retained his title lead. Ferrari went on to a triumphant Monaco with its drivers taking a glorious one-two finish. Leading both championships, it now seemed as though the Scuderia had the situation well under control. But the next round, the Spanish Grand Prix at the Montmelo circuit was a sudden and unwelcome cold shower: Hakkinen and Coulthard finished ahead of Schumacher and Irvine, who lost the lead of the championship although Ferrari hung on against the McLaren assault in the constructors' points tally.

At this time, the Maranello boffins were working on the first major modification to the F399, which had already undergone a few minor changes in the area of suspension geometry. But this first change did not bring the expected results and that lack of progress was compounded by errors in the pits and accidents. In Canada, Schumacher was leading, until under pressure from Hakkinen, he slammed into the concrete wall opposite the pits. Irvine now second, was run into by Coulthard and spun round. He continued in eighth place but mounted an inspired comeback to finish on the podium in third place. However, McLaren were now coming on strong with three wins from six starts and pulling out a lead in the championship. For the French Grand Prix, Brawn and Byrne were working on major bodywork modifications aimed mainly at improving air flow over the back of the car. However, these changes only seemed to produce an advantage on the slower tracks, so that for Monza and Hockenheim for example, the F399 reverted to its previous configuration, although the results did not follow. Black clouds, literal and metaphorical hung over the Maranello team at Magny Cours. The 048B engine appeared for the first time, with a smaller top end, but problems in the pits wiped out any advantage. The race was turned on its head by the rain and Irvine lost precious seconds when he pitted unexpectedly to change tyres and then lost more places after a spin when the Safety Car was out. Schumacher suffered his second steering wheel electrics problem of the season.

CHRISTIANO CHIAVEGATO,
58 years old, was introduced very young in journalism. He strated at "La Stampa" in 1959, while still attending various sporting events for "La Gazzetta dello Sport" for fifteen years. He has covered about ten Olympic Games, summer and winter, before concentring on motorsport at the end of the sixties. Since 1976, he has not missed a single GP and has written many books on Ferrari, and a biography of Niki Lauda.

The championship challenge looked compromised as the teams headed for the British Grand Prix at Silverstone. Worse was to come and Ferrari's title hopes took a serious knock. Schumacher was trying to pass Irvine on the opening lap on the fast run down to Stowe corner. Allegedly a brake bleed nipple failed, leaving the German with no retardation. Whatever the real cause, his Ferrari headed straight as an arrow for the tyre barriers. When the dust had settled, Schumacher was seen trying to get out of the cockpit. He could not because he had a double fracture to the right leg. The Scuderia was thrown into disarray as the lynchpin of its title challenge for the past four years was now out of action. The German's excellent levels of fitness helped his recovery, but for the need for further surgery and the suggestion he should take no risks and stay away until the following year, clouded the issue of his return to the cockpit, which after a final test at Maranello was eventually made in triumph in Malaysia.

In the meantime, Mika Salo was called in as a substitute and Eddie Irvine's luck changed as did his status from Number Two to Number One. He immediately won the next two races; in Austria he did it on his own and in Germany he learned what it was like to have someone working for him for a change, as Salo moved over to hand him the lead.

It was enough to put the Irishman back in the championship lead. From then on, the season slewed into a downward spiral of failure and farce. Hungary was a disaster, where the car failed to respond to set-up changes. Monza saw an equally mysterious lack of competitiveness, even if the double

---

*Eddie Irvine
immediately won the
next two races*

---

failure of the McLarens kept the Scuderia in the hunt for year end honours. By now, the latest C version of the 048 engine had turned up, with a new bottom end and further lightened, offering greater performance in terms of extra engine revs available for the races. The European race will be remembered for the missing wheel fiasco during Irvine's pit stop and then came the unbelievable events in Malaysia.

The return of Michael Schumacher appeared to galvanise the Scuderia to a return to form which gave hope that the ultimate prize was still up for grabs. The German drove an imperial race, handing it not once but twice to his team mate. The illegal barge board saga; the team's disqualification and reinstatement simply added some pep to the final

showdown in Suzuka as Irvine went to Japan leading by four points. The Ferraris were not as competitive as they had been two weeks earlier and Michael saw the theoretical advantage of starting pole position disappear in a cloud of tyre smoke from too much wheelspin. It was enough to let Hakkinen take the lead and his second consecutive title.

The Prancing Horse had to settle for the consolation prize in the shape of its ninth Constructors' Championship, which is puts it at the top of the table along with Williams as the teams who have taken the most titles. In Maranello, they were already working on the future.

Ross Brawn, Rory Byrne and engine chief Paolo Martinelli, who is using the newly-allowed if dangerous new material berilium, in the search for a performance advantage, have all insisted on a radical revision to the car with different technical solutions.

These include a centrally mounted oil reservoir, rather than fitting it between the gearbox and the engine. There will also be an aerodynamic design, which is revolutionary compared with the 1999 car and will feature a move away from the high nose to a lower one.

Will it be enough to give Ferrari that Drivers' crown in the first year of a new century?

△
Eddie Irvine did not manage to clinch the drivers' title this year. Black clouds hung over the Scuderia on several occasions, most notably at Silverstone, when Michael Schumacher had an accident which cost him his title hopes.

The Scuderia Family Photo at the Spanish Grand Prix
▽

Québec has its own team: BAR

1999 vu du Canada

by Réjean Tremblay
«La Presse»

There are some events that people never forget. On 26th October 1997, all of Quebec got up at seven in the morning to watch the European Grand Prix held at Jerez in Spain.

All the viewing figure records were broken and a huge collective cry went up when Jacques Villeneuve overtook Michael Schumacher and the German landed himself in the gravel after attempting a dubious blocking move to keep the Canadian behind him.

Two years later; a mere second in historical terms, a lifetime in Formula 1 and Jacques Villeneuve was desperately trying to pick up his first point of the season in the Malaysian Grand Prix. Canadian television viewing figures were good, but the massive local fervour had given way to patient resignation. Jacques Villeneuve might still be the local hero, but the BAR team was a source of ridicule.

However, it was through the birth and difficult first steps of the British American Racing team that Canada followed the 1999 Formula 1 season. BAR is to Canada what Prost is to France and Sauber to Switzerland; the national team, the local team.

This despite the fact the outfit is more British than anything else. The factory is in Brackley, England and team boss Craig Pollock is a Scot, who taught in Switzerland, is now a Monegasque resident and who lived for a long time in Indianapolis in the United States.

BAR is its adoptive team and the team everyone has followed throughout this interminable and terribly disappointing season

---

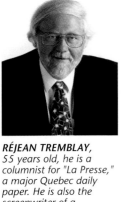

RÉJEAN TREMBLAY,
55 years old, he is a columnist for "La Presse," a major Quebec daily paper. He is also the screenwriter of a television series which has been seen in over fifty countries. He has covered the Olympic Games as well as major tennis tournaments. Like all natives of Quebec he is a keen follower of the "Canadien de Montreal" the local hockey team. But his great passion is Formula 1, because no other sport puts such a premium on the symbiosis of talent, courage and intelligence.

But no one cares about that in Quebec, as BAR is its adoptive team and the team everyone has followed throughout this interminable and terribly disappointing season.

Of course there is Jacques Villeneuve, but there is so much more as well. The story begins a few years back when Jacques Villeneuve came back from Japan after a year in Formula 3000. He went to find Craig Pollock, his former physical education teacher and asked him to be his manager, his agent and his big brother.

At this time in Canada, the country's leading cigarette brand, Players, had set up a bold programme to help the development of young racers. The Players boys were already shining in Formula 1600, Formula 2000 and in Formula Atlantic. And of course, the Villeneuve name was golden in Canada. So when Craig Polloc turned up in Montreal with a young guy in glasses and a pony tail, the Players men soon realised they were being offered an incredible deal.

Jacques Villeneuve quickly dominated the Atlantic series and thanks to backing from Players, he made the move to Formula Indy.

In his second season, he won the prestigious Indy 500 and the CART championship.

The hearts of all Canadians were beating for Villeneuve and they beat even faster when he made the move to Formula 1 and the Williams team.

But why the switch to BAR?

Because the links with Players had never really been severed. British American Tobacco owns forty percent of Imperial Tobacco, the

company which owns the Players brand. Since then, BAT has actually bought out all of Imperial Tobacco.

It was a Canadian and former marketing director at Imperial Tobacco in Canada called Tom Moser, who became international sponsorship director for BAT in London, who sold the Formula 1 team idea to his BAT bosses.

It was another Montreal-based company, Edelman's who picked up the public relations account for the BAR F1 project. In London, Jean-Claude Torquia, also from Quebec was put in charge of F1 communications and another Quebec company, PPGI who secured the rights to broadcast television images in Asia; a vital BAT market.

To round off the Quebec influence in the minds of racing fans, the main sponsor for this team which had promised to deliver wins in

its first season was the multinational, Canadian based Teleglobe company. Teleglobe, which is a fibre optics and satellite communications company is well known in Canada thanks to the charisma of its president, Charles Sirois. Everything was thus in place for BAR to become Canada s and Quebec's "local" team.

The Canadian press turned out in force in Brackley for the unveiling of the BAR cars. Every single paper and every single television newscast carried photos of the magnificent blue and gold car for Ricardo Zonta and the red, white and black one for Jacques Villeneuve. Craig Pollock's rebel stance, facing off FIA and FOA and F1's power broker, Bernie Ecclestone and his former employee Max Mosley, went down well with the North Americans, who knew nothing of F1's aristocracy.

However, while the fans were delighted with this turn of events and were already placing bets on when Jacques Villeneuve would score his first podium finish, the media was already picking holes in the triumphant scenario played out in Brackley.

The car had run very little, the first crash tests had been a disaster and the first live images transmitted from Melbourne were enough to upset even the most partisan supporters of Villeneuve and BAR. Seeing a Formula 1 car's rear wing fly off at 300 km/h does little to inspire confidence.

The anxiety level increased when it was discovered that Adrian Reynard had not bothered travelling to Australia to see his chassis. He was in Homestead, a few kilometres from Miami, Florida, for the start of the Formula Indy season and the Cart championship.

Reynard's and Pollock s explanations were not very convincing and the Quebec press was already talking of discord in the BAR camp.

It was the same scenario in Brazil, where the tatty paddock and Ricardo Zonta's accident threw a dark shadow over the weekend.

But that was only the start of it. In Montreal, where feverish preparations for the Canadian Grand Prix were underway, people were encouraged by Villeneuve's fifth place on the grid at Imola and there was talk of maybe having something to celebrate after one of the most atmospheric races of the season.
The Canadian Grand Prix has a special atmosphere. Like Monaco it takes place in a city centre, except that the city centre is on a beautiful island, slap bang in the middle of the Saint Laurent river. The Grand Prix is also the sign that summer has arrived after the never-ending Canadian winter.

The Grand Prix is also the sign that summer has arrived after the never-ending Canadian winter

After the race comes the Jazz Festival, the Comedy Festival, the French Festival and hundreds of thousands of tourists hit town.
The teams invade the hotels in the city centre and the streets are packed all week long. Everyone is an F1 expert, everyone loves the drivers, even Michael Schumacher, but the heart of Quebec beats for its Jacques Villeneuve. This year, he turned up a day earlier than usual because his social diary was so full: a major Teleglobe press conference, scores of television interviews and autographs and handshakes wherever he went.
But Villeneuve has rarely left his admirers satisfied with the Canadian Grand Prix and 1999 was no exception. Just before the long pit straight, there is a tight chicane, which forces the drivers to brake at the very last fraction of a second, before brushing against a wall bearing the legend: "Bienvenue au Quebec," (Welcome to Quebec!) The local hero, in good company with Michael Schumacher and Damon Hill, finished his race in the wall. The other disappointment was Heinz-Harald Frentzen's accident, caused by brake failure, when lying second. The German is popular in Montreal, because he was Villeneuve's team-mate at Williams.
People started to have doubts come the mid-season. The BAR performances were ever more catastrophic, the car did not finish races, the drivers were in a bad mood, the rumblings of dissent in the team grew stronger, as did rumours that Craig Pollock was about to be given his marching orders. Disaster in France, disaster in England, Adrian Reynard's depar-

ture, Tom Moser's arrival on the financial side to find new sponsors: there was more going on in the motorhomes than on the track.
Through all this, Jacques Villeneuve and Ricardo Zonta, now back from injury after his accident at Interlagos in the Brazilian race, were still giving their all. The BAR cars could not go the distance and were unable to match the pace of the Mika Hakkinen and David Coulthard in those infernal McLarens. At least the Canadians could take some consolation from the fact that their little Jacques was doing all he could to get the car to the finish and maybe, finally, pick up a few points on the way.
They took hope from Ireland and Japan. Frentzen's win in Magny-Cours and the solid performance of the Jordan owed much to the Mugen-Honda engine and Craig Pollock had clinched a deal for an exclusive supply of factory Honda engines for 2000 for the BAR cars. By the time the circus got to the European Grand Prix, Frentzen was only ten points behind championship leader Hakkinen and then he qualified on pole at the Nurburgring. Even more encouraging was the fact that when he was forced to retire at the half distance, Frentzen was leading from the other championship contenders.
It was time to start dreaming again. At Williams, Villeneuve had been head and shoulders above Frentzen. With Honda and its Japanese engineers coming on the scene, one could hope the best was yet to come, but only in 2000.

One Saturday evening in Monza, Craig Pollock was trying to relax with a beer, before catching a few hours sleep before the next day's race. The young man with the eternal smile on his face, who used to walk slowly through the paddock, with a mobile phone glued to his ear, as he did deals for his driver Jacques Villeneuve, had transformed himself into a tired company boss,

with a weary look from having to fight on all fronts to get to the end of a disappointing season.
BAT above all, was looking for results. Hundreds of millions of dollars had been invested and with just a few races remaining, not a single point was on the table to cheer the company's 160,000 employees.
He had to face the FOA regulars, be it Ron Dennis, Eddie Jordan, Tom Walkinshaw, Alain Prost or Frank Williams, none of whom were prepared to give an inch or any of their other privileges.
He had to face the international press who picked the bones out of every last misery, big or small which befell British American Racing; the young team with the money which was supposed to be showing the old hands how to do it. That evening, tired, but far from beaten, Craig Pollock summed up his adventure with one short sentence: "We have created a Formula 1 team and brought together some of the best brains in the sport, as a result of a dream which began one morning in Indianapolis. We can be proud of what we have done, despite our problems and disappointments."
In Quebec, in the land of Jacques Villeneuve, everyone has stayed loyal to the cause. It is after all, "our" team.

△
Despite a desperate time on track, Jacques still managed to smile this season.

◁
With long time friend and now his boss Craig Pollock, there was a perfect understanding throughout the year. (opposite)

Michael Schumacher's murderous summer

by Anno Hecker
«Frankfurter Allgemeine Zeitung»

1999 aus deutscher Sicht

Would he race or would he not? Michael Schumacher put his fans through the wringer during the summer of 1999. His accident was not the end of the world as the man himself had suggested and everyone in Germany was relieved to see that was the case, shortly after his crash on 11th July at Silverstone. Michael Schumacher staged a comeback and boy was he quick! The Kid from Kerpen has a reputation as a perfectionist and a quick one at that. It must have irked him seeing his less than perfect right leg after the accident. He had to be the best, not just in the car, but out of it as well. Pushed by this need to be the best, Michael Schumacher plans everything down to the minutest detail and always tries to undercut the time required to get things done.

But bones take time to heal, especially when they are broken! The German did not want to believe it. Against the best medical advice, he pushed his cardiovascular and muscular training in order to come back as quickly as possible. As far as the outside world was concerned, the Ferrari driver's entourage wanted to give the impression that Schumacher was living through this enforced lay-off in great good humour and was relaxed about it. In fact, impatience reigned. The accident threw him off the merry-go-round of success, before going through false hopes and great disappointment. And then, right at the end, just a few days before making his comeback in Malaysia, he relived that old chestnut in Germany; was Schumi cheating yet again?

Even the most partisan Schumi watchers could not help but notice the odd anomaly in the different press statements issued by the greatest racer of his era.

His first comeback attempt at Mugello was leaked to the press and caused a surprise. Had not the great man told everyone, via the giant TV screens at the German Grand Prix, that his injury was more serious than was first thought? His heel was also injured and the tissue around the bone was damaged because of the high speed of the impact. It would take time to heal, he said.

Then, just a few days later, he jumped into his Ferrari and got down to business, just like in the good old days. *"It was to boost my confidence,"* he explained. It also served to show Eddie Irvine, that even on crutches, he was still the king. The limping Schumacher had proved to himself and to his team-mate who was pumped up after two back-to-back wins who was boss. The

ANNO HECKER,
36 years old, worked first as a physical education instructor befor turning to journalism in 1986. After working as a political correspondent for a Bonn news agency, he joined "Frankfurter Allgemeine Zeitung" in 1991 to cover motor sports. He specialised in stories combinig politics and sport.

tabloid press did not need to be asked twice and they heralded the return of the injured hero, who would still be back in time to fight his own corner in the 1999 world championship. Even the more serious publications, even those close to him and even F1 experts now predicted an early return for the great man. It was predicted to take place at Spa, the kid from Kerpen's favourite track, venue for his F1 debut, his first

F1 win in 1992 and all of this just 80 kilometres from his home town. It was all absolute nonsense. Those who saw Schumacher limping at his second test at Monza, felt sorry for him; he needed crutches. His face was contorted with pain. He had to pull himself up the bannister leading to the media centre to announce after just 15 laps that he was giving up on the idea: *"I need more time."*

Indeed his injuries did need more time to heal properly. But more than the leg, Schumacher was suffering because he had exaggerated his own abilities. He had pushed himself to the limit, when he was used to extending his limits. The Monza test had not been a public relations exercise, but a vain attempt to keep his championship hopes alive.

Schumacher was unable to make a good start. But apparently, he did not want to believe it or hear it and he had to feel it for himself. *"From now on, I will do what the doctors tell me,"* he declared with a bitter look in Monza. It was the first time Schumacher had bowed to circumstances. But probably insurance became an issue. Who would foot the bill if an injured Schumacher was rendered incapable of doing his job?

The whole accident incident allowed everyone to see just how stubborn the 30 year old could be.

His manager Willi Weber is no longer as close to his charge as he would like to have people think. Almost every time Weber announced a comeback or a setback, Schumacher would issue a contradictory statement. All this toing and froing led to an argument with Ferrari President Luca di Montezemolo. Since then, Weber has kept away from the red motorhomes.

At the same time, the relationship linking Schumacher with Ferrari, especially with Jean Todt had become much more intense. But even the Frenchman could not stem

his driver's ambition. As before, in the days of the Sauber-Mercedes team and the sports car world cup, Schumacher worked harder than he needed to. *"Michael's enthusiasm for learning everything, for always wanting to improve everything produced a tension which worked against him,"* recalls Leo Ress, Sauber's Technical Director. Knowing that he is pretty much superior to all the other drivers when it comes to his mental and physical strength, pushed his training programme to the limit, even though he was injured, to the point where he almost collapsed from exhaustion. It was all for nothing and in fact it made matters worse and his knees, which had given him trouble in the past, played up again. At the time, he had required surgery after pushing his training too hard.

Nearly all the decisions and counter-decisions surrounding the Ferrari driver's future bore a direct relation to his state of health. However, logic had nothing to do with the last missive from Dr. Schumacher.

M. Schumacher wanted to come back at all costs

Several weeks earlier, when he was still in with a chance of the championship, he wanted to come back at all costs. But now, with just a few weeks of the series left to run, he decided to opt out of taking part in Malaysia and Japan under the pretext of a lack of fitness. This was a body blow for the Ferrari management, but they reacted with cunning. They made a short statement which raised just one question with everyone who read it: why wouldn't a fit driver race? Schumacher no longer needed crutches, but he said he was not capable of

racing. The next day however, he managed to set a new lap record at the Scuderia's test track. In Germany he was accused of being egocentric and the Italian media hinted at treason.

Ferrari would normally have reacted. But this time it simply kept quiet and waited. President Luca di Montezemolo is a true pro when it comes to dealing efficiently with the media. But he was also forced to put some indirect pressure on his driver. Because Schumacher's game looked like an insult or at least an affront. Would a German dare make fun of the Ferrari management? If Enzo Ferrari had known about it, he would have turned in his grave.

Di Montezemolo had to be firm and used the press to achieve his aims. Schumacher, who claims to rarely read the papers, especially the Italian ones and who has little interest in the history of the sport was finally convinced to climb back in the cockpit, despite not being happy with his fitness training. It only took one simple suggestion; that the credit for a Ferrari success in the final stages of the championship would be layed squarely at his feet. After the outcry in Germany, he had nothing to lose and everything to gain. It was a great opportunity to polish up a tarnished image.

Tension at Mercedes

There were rumours of a power struggle at Mercedes and a possible change in the role of motor sport boss. The comfortable world of the men from Stuttgart showed signs of fragility during the 1999 season. Norbert Haug, DaimlerChrysler's charismatic motorsport boss was showing signs of irritability at the penultimate race of the season in Sepang. It was as if he knew there was something going on in the corridors of power. Insiders spoke of a change at the top. Niki Lauda was rumoured to be coming in "alongside" Haug and that eventually, the Austrian triple world champion would take over the reins from the former journalist from Pforzheim. *"What's that? What's that rumour,"* countered Haug's boss, Jurgen Hubbert. *"That's ridiculous,"* added the DaimlerChrysler board member on the morning of the Malaysian race. He could not say anything else of course because Haug had caught him discussing the Lauda rumour with a couple of journalists. It proved one thing, that the Mercedes motor sport boss needed support, because he no longer felt sure of his position.

Having been at the top for almost all of Mercedes' recent motor sport history, "Mister Mercedes" had survived a near-miss when DaimlerChrysler had come within a whisker of catastrophe at the Le Mans 24 Hours.

We will never know what would have happened if one of the GT cars had flown over the barriers and fallen into the crowd when three of them somersaulted that weekend. Haug had been against racing the cars after one flipped in

practice, but he had to give in to his masters' wishes and put up with the criticism after the accidents. *"How will the boss get to the next race if there's an airline strike?"* went the joke in the paddock. *"He'd fly Mercedes GT Air of course!"* was the witty reply. Haug, despite his occasional fits of temper, does have a sense of humour and he might have been able to laugh this off, but for the failures in Indycar racing. Roger Penske took matters into his own hands, dumping Mercedes in favour of 1999 champions' Honda engine for next season.

Penske has been a Mercedes partner for years now and changing engines was a big decision. Just like Mercedes itself, the American entrepreneur owns 25 percent of the Ilmor engine builder and supplier to McLaren. As head of motor sport, Haug has to accept responsibility for the failures, at least to the outside world. Haug certainly did not have to justify himself to McLaren's Ron Dennis. There had never been a real answer as to why DaimlerChrysler invested so much money in Formula 1 without even having a decisive influence over its choice of drivers. His critics say Haug always sided with Dennis to avoid confrontation. But the McLaren man would discuss matters with Haug's master, Hubbert. This impression was strengthened after the race at the Nurburgring.

When Haug commented on the avoidable failure on television, saying that Mika Hakkinen had made the bad call to come into the pits, Hubbert sent him back to deny it. Dennis corrected Haug in front of the cameras: *"Excuse me Norbert, but it's the team which calls the shots, not Mika."* Since then, Hubbert does not hide the fact he asks journalists the reasons for success or failure in front of Haug, as though his motor sport man does not know the answers...

◁
(left page)
Michael's wife Corinna came to support her husband at the last two grands prix of the season.

(opposite)
Always relaxed, the German was on top form this season. He drove some of the best races of his career, notably in Monaco and especially in Kuala Lumpur.

"The curtain finally goes up"

1999 wo hurikaeru

by Kunio Shibata
«GPX Press», Tokyo

Honda returns and Toyota says its coming. These are certainly the two single biggest items of news from Japan as we head for the third millennium. But at the moment no one can be too sure what these companies are planning.

Having changed its mind several times, Honda finally opted to partner British American Racing, starting in 2000. However, there is still some hesitancy and some unanswered questions. How long should the collaboration with this team last, given how uncompetitive it is at the moment? Would Jordan not have been a better choice?

For their part, Toyota has not given a clear answer as to exactly when it is going to join the party, or how. Is this down to their traditional caution, or does it indicate a lack of clear direction?

Where do these two Japanese giants want to go?

A long and winding road

In this article last year, I wrote about "The Honda Spirit." Honda Spirit is a phrase the employees of this company love to bandy about. Personally, I am not sure if this spirit still exists, as it did way back in the Sixties.

At the time it was something of a synonym for the kamikaze mentality, as they launched an F1 project without any in-house know-how nor trained personnel. The final result added up to two wins in five years. Not a great record, but one that Mr. Nakamura and his team took pride in for the individual way they went about achieving it.

Then, in 1999, Honda was going to kick off the third project, ten years after it had enjoyed total success as an engine supplier. This time, they had opted for a return as a complete team, with some European assistance. Former Tyrrell men were taken on board. Harvey Postlethwaite designed the car and Dallara built it.

The first tests, between December 1998 and February 1999, produced very encouraging results. Not only did the car turn in respectable lap times, with test driver Jos Verstappen at the wheel, it was also very reliable.

Despite this, a major drama unfolded at the end of April. The Japanese company's directors announced that the whole project was being wound up, in favour of simply supplying BAR with engines.

A few days earlier, Dr. Postlethwaite died suddenly at a test session. But there is no link between his death and Honda's decision. It was not his death which led the project being canned. Honda had already signed a deal with BAR back at the beginning of March and Postlethwaite had written to them, trying to get them to change their minds. It was in vain.

It was mainly down to some political in-fighting between two rival factions within Honda.

KUNIO SHIBATA,
43 years old, he left Japan, giving up his joy in journalism in 1982 to move to Paris and study Political Science. He became a freelance producer for Japanese television and having always been interested in motor racing, he began covering the Grands Prix for a press agency in 1987 when Satoru Nakajima arrived on the scene. He has written for the specialist Japanese magazine «Grand Prix Xpress» since 1991

There was an "extremist" group, which wanted to keep the total-team idea alive at all costs. Then there was the "moderate" group, which was not necessarily against the F1 project, but wanted to see a balance between expenditure and profit.

In 1998, when the company's new president, Mr. Yoshino announced the F1 comeback, he did not go into any detail, as there was no detail available to announce. But the extremist group made the most of this declaration and very quickly built a prototype and started

running it, thinking that if the car was a real entity, then Honda would be obliged to go down that route. But in the end, it was the moderates who won the day and the board decided that the project would be too costly.

Honda versus Mugen

But having buried the whole-car project, why did Honda choose BAR?

Their official answer is as follows: "The team has plenty of future. Furthermore, it is willing to accept that our engineers are involved in the development of the chassis."

However, there are many teams with "plenty of future" and there are many team who would be willing to accept Honda engineers in their midst, if they came with a free engine.

In the end, BAR was Honda's only option. They had been in discussion with Benetton, who decided to stick with Supertec. Williams and Stewart were already tied in with other engi-

ne companies. Sauber? Unless Honda was willing to buy the entire team, there was little future in being involved with a team based outside the UK.

So what about Jordan? It would have been a very interesting alternative. And it remains so for Honda, as the Irish team has finally delivered on its long term promise, taking third place in the championship, ahead of Williams and Stewart. On top of that, Heinz-Harald Frentzen was in the running for the Drivers' title up until the fourteenth race of the series.

Their performance is pretty much the major exploit of the year. Jordan would be an ideal partner for Honda, especially when BAR failed to score a single point.

But this pretty Irish flower has a thorn. Jordan works with Mugen, a company built up by Hirotoshi Honda, only child of the late Soichiro, the founder of Honda Motors. And Hirotoshi is still one of the main Honda shareholders. This makes Mugen pretty much untouchable and Honda cannot kick Mugen out of its Jordan deal.

But Hirotoshi is not totally in agreement with this. "As 40% of my company now belongs to Honda, Honda can have a say in what I do. Our relationship is comparable to the one linking Mercedes and Ilmor. Maybe with a bit more independence, but similar. In fact, I am only a small shareholder in Honda, with less than 10%. My father hated this sort of inheritance and so do I actually. On top of that, being the son of the founder counts for little in this company."

It would seem that Honda would like to supply Jordan with engines, but Hirotoshi would never accept that and because of this, people reckon the Honda - Mugen relationship is suffering. But Hirotoshi denies this allegation.

"Given BAR's performance, it is easy to understand why Honda is looking for a more competitive team. Their engineers have also helped us a lot in designing the Mugen engine. But I would remind you I am the major shareholder in my company and I want the Mugen name to have a long future in F1."

In other words, he wants both a technical and financial dependence on Honda and inde-

pendence for his own brand. This is a delicate situation. Because it is quite likely that next year, Jordan will be far more competitive than BAR and that the works Honda engine will be slower than the semi-works unit.

But will Honda stay faithful to BAR despite this? I doubt it. The anglo-american team has been disappointing since the start of the 1999 season, in terms of its results and in terms of Craig Pollock's management, who has virtually sacked his partner Adrian Reynard. A bad move, as Honda probably had more faith in Reynard than in Pollock.

Jordan will be far more competitive than BAR and that the works Honda engine will be slower than the semi-works unit

---

It is quite likely that Honda will try and form a partnership with Jordan, by chasing Mugen away. Hirotoshi Honda certainly does not deny that possibility. "Of course Jordan is an attractive proposition for Honda. Because, with BAR they will take at least three years to get a first win. Jordan took 8 years and even Mercedes had to wait 5. It would therefore be much easier for Honda to work with Jordan. But, we will survive.

Honda will fulfill its first year's obligation with BAR. But after that? Everything will depend on the results achieved in 2000.

Toyota - the timid giant

Toyota, that giant among car companies is planning to tackle F1 for the first time in its history and its debut is scheduled for 2003. Given that Honda first put its toe in the F1 water back in 1964, Toyota will be joining the party almost forty years later.

The founders of Toyota and Honda were both born in the same region of Japan, about 50 kilometres apart. It is a pure coincidence and just about the only thing the two companies have in common.

In Japan, Toyota is referred to as the "Shopkeeper from Mikawa," the area where the company was started. It is of course used as a derogatory term, because this shopkeeper is above all, very careful.

"One must tap a stone bridge before crossing it," says an old Japanese saying, but Toyota will tap the bridge and still not cross. Thanks to this mentality, this company has absolutely no debts. Indeed, it is worth around twenty billion dollars, hence its nickname, "The Bank of Toyota."

Then, in the era of former president, Mr. Okuda, the company did an about face. Apart from in the USA, Toyota had never been very bold when it came to foreign investments. Okuda set out to conquer the European market. A huge factory is currently under construction in the north of France, which will build the latest Yaris model, to go head to head with the Clio and 206. However, unlike in the States, where it has some prestige, Toyota has a reputation for reliability but little else in Europe. Hence the need to compete in Formula 1.

Several options

Early in 1999, the new president, Fujio Cho officially announced the F1 project which, in complete contrast to Honda, will involve building up its own team. Up until now, Toyota has been involved in three international motor sport projects: Indy, WRC and Le Mans.

In '99, TTE (Toyota Team Europe) made a huge effort to win Le Mans. But two cars retired, leaving only the third one run by a Japanese team to finish second. There were mixed feelings of relief and disappointment, followed by Toyota giving up on Le Mans.

TTE also looks after the World Rally Championship, as it has done for 28 years. Its boss, Ove Anderson and Toyota respect one another, but when the F1 project was announced, many experts predicted the end of the rally programme.

Despite denials from Anderson, it seemed ever more likely and in September, Anderson told his two drivers, Carlos Sainz and Didier Auriol to look elsewhere for work, even though they had a TTE contract up to the end of 2000. Then, on 10th October at the San Remo Rally, Anderson officially announced the retirement of his team.

That leaves Toyota with Indy as its only racing programme. Given then importance of the American market and the fact the team has yet to finish on the podium, it is likely to be kept going for a while yet. The rally programme has been sacrificed on the altar of F1 participation. Although that is due to launch in 2003, it would not be much of a surprise if the debut was brought forward to 2001 or more likely 2002.

Despite the fact that Toyota has been advertising heavily for F1 experienced staff, there is still talk of the Japanese company buying out an existing team, rather than shell out the 48 million dollar deposit required from a new team. Sauber and Minardi, both in financial difficulties, could be targeted. However, it seems that TTE will have a strong involvement. According to one of its engineers, this company would be involved in the chassis development as well as the engine and it is also trying to recruit experienced engine personnel.

Whatever happens, Toyota will have to jump into the F1 business and that means having to take quick decisions without endless preambles. To do that, the usually timid Toyota will have to change the habits of a corporate lifetime, if it wants to succeed in F1.

△
This year, Toranosuke Takagi was the only Japanese driver in Formula 1 and his performance can best be described as average. Very quick in some corners, there were also a lot of errors. At the moment, no one knows if Tora-san is part of Honda or Toyota's future plans.

McLaren and the 1999 championship

1999: a British point of view

by Nigel Roebuck
«Autosport»

The day after the Australian Grand Prix, David Coulthard was all smiles. True, neither he nor McLaren-Mercedes team mate Mika Hakkinen had finished the race, but the prognosis for the season was good indeed. *"If anything,"* David said, *"I reckon we've got an even bigger performance advantage than we had last year..."*

If if Coulthard's impressions were right, there was reason enough to contemplate what looked like a very boring season, with 20 drivers fighting for third place each weekend, behind the McLarens.

Not everyone in the team was quite as optimistic as DC, however. *"This new car, the MP4-14,"* one senior team member said to me, *"is undoubtedly a big step over last year's car. Security being what it is these days, it's unlikely you will ever get to see it with its rear bodywork off, but, believe me, Adrian Newey has produced an absolute work of art. The packaging is unbelievably neat - the whole thing looks like the inside of a Swiss watch...*

"However," he went on, *"I think that could be a problem in itself. Obviously, you want to build a car as light as you can, so that you have as much ballast as possible to bring it up to the minimum weight limit; that way you can play with the weight distribution, putting the ballast where it's going to do the most good, according to the demands of a particular circuit.*

"This car is very light, and while that's obviously good in one way, in another it's bad, for it means there is less mass to absorb vibrations, and so on. As I say, the packaging is extremely tight, and there's a pretty good chance that vibrations are going to give us reliability problems this year."

"The other thing," he concluded, *"is that this is a much more complex car to work on than last year's MP4-13. An engine change, for example, is going to take much longer than before. We may well have a performance advantage, but I don't necessarily think we're going to dominate the season in the way that some people believe..."*

His words have proved uncannily accurate. While no one would dispute that the McLaren-Mercedes has been the fastest car of the year, its reliability has been no match for Ferrari. Add in that there have been unforced driving errors by both Hakkinen and Coulthard, and that McLaren, long considered operationally the best team in the paddock, have made too many mistakes, both technically and strategically, and you have a season's results which are a shadow of what they might have been.

In Australia, Mika and David began impressively, qualifying first and second, but race day was by no means as straightforward. Coulthard was obliged to take the spare car, when his own suffered hydraulics problems, and as early as lap 14 he was out, stuck in sixth gear.

Hakkinen did not last too much longer.

NIGEL ROEBUCK,
52 years old, decided to quit his industrial job and enter journalism at the age of 24. In 1971, he starts writing for the American magazine «Car & Driver», before joining the British weekly motorracing magazine «Autosport» in 1976. He is covering Formula One since 1977, while working for the «Sunday Times», for «Auto week» and the Japanese magazine «Racing On».

Although he led comfortably from the start, his advantage was wiped out by the Safety Car, sent out after an accident to Jacques Villeneuve. On the restart, Mika tried to accelerate, but a fault in the throttle linkage meant there was no response.

With both McLarens out, Eddie Irvine went on to score his first victory, for Ferrari.

In Brazil, though, McLaren seemed to be on their way. Once again Hakkinen and Coulthard commandeered the front row, and Mika went on to win the race. It was not, though, a day without problems, for David burned out his clutch on the grid, and stal-

led. Later he retired with gear selection problems - and Mika, too, was momentarily troubled in the same way. While leading on the fourth lap, he found himself unable to get fifth gear, and believed his race over. *"Then,"* he said, *"the gears came back, and I never had the problem again, but it was a worrying race..."*

Imola was worrying, too, but for a rather different reason. After building a 12-second lead, and looking unapproachable, Hakkinen unaccountably lost control at the last corner on lap 18. The McLaren hit the barrier hard, and Mika confessed he had simply dropped it.

Coulthard was afterwards criticised for a dif-

ferent reason. After Hakkinen's accident, he led easily enough from Schumacher's Ferrari - and perhaps he should have gone harder, for he lost the lead to Michael on the pit stops, and afterwards lost a huge amount of time while lapping backmarkers. David, although collecting six points, had not, in the opinion of most observers, been assertive enough.

In Spain, though, the McLaren-Mercedes drivers delivered their first 1-2 of the season, and it was rather more conclusive than qualifying had suggested, for Hakkinen snatched pole position, from Irvine's Ferrari, only in the dying seconds of the session, and Coulthard had to settle for third on the grid. Away from the start, though, David passed Eddie, and thereafter the McLarens were untouchable.

They shone at Monte Carlo, too - but only in qualifying. At the end of a remarkably dramatic session, Hakkinen beat Schumacher to pole position, and Coulthard vaulted past Irvine, to line up third.

All the hard work, though, was thrown away in the first 10 seconds of the race. Unlike Ferrari, McLaren had decided on a one-stop strategy, which meant that their cars went to the grid 'heavy'. When the lights went out, the red cars got away faster than the silver, and at this place, more than anywhere else, track position is everything.

Coulthard disappeared on lap 36 (gearbox problems again), and Hakkinen lost second place to Irvine when he had to take to the escape road at Mirabeau after encountering oil put down by Takagi's Arrows.

After the race, in which he finished third, Mika said his car had suffered from heavy steering, as well as inconsistent handling, but investigations revealed nothing untoward, and team members privately suggested that perhaps their driver had simply 'gone to sleep'. They were to say the same of him later in the year, at the Nurburgring.

Hakkinen won at Montreal, though, a circuit at which he had never previously been successful. He was agreeably surprised, too, for in practice he struggled to find a balance in the McLaren, and was beaten to pole position - for the first time in 1999 - by Schumacher. In the race he was unable to stay with the Ferrari, but after 30 laps Michael crashed out of the lead, just as Mika had done at Imola.

Coulthard had a wretched race in Canada. On the restart (following a Safety Car period, after Schumacher's accident), David tried to pass Irvine at the first corner, but they had a coming-together, after which the McLaren came in for a quick inspection. All was well with the car, but DC then misread the pit exit lights - and that led to a stop/go penalty. In the end, he was seventh.

So to Magny-Cours, where the weather was awful. On qualifying day, rain began to come down before the session, but it was not particularly hard, and some teams deemed it a good idea to get out early, in case the weather worsened. Both McLaren drivers were keen to do this, but the team management decided otherwise, and it was fortunate for them that Ferrari made the same mistake. By the time the two leading teams took to the

track, conditions were awful, with cars spinning all over the place, and visibility appalling. In the circumstances, Coulthard did remarkably well to set fourth fastest time, but Hakkinen never found a clear lap, and was down in 14th. On the front row were Rubens Barrichello's Stewart-Ford and Jean Alesi's Sauber.

It rained on race day, too, and, had his luck been good, Coulthard would probably have won with ease, for he was into the lead by lap six, and then pulled out seven seconds over Barrichello in a matter of three laps. That, though, was as far as he was going. *"Some sort of electrical failure,"* he said. *"The engine just turned itself off..."* Seven races into the season, David had finished only three times. Hakkinen, in the meantime, turned in a magnificent drive. From the seventh row of the grid, he was up to sixth place by lap five, all his overtaking moves clean and decisive. There was a spin at half-distance, but he recovered from that, and actually got into the lead at one point; in the end, beaten by Heinz-Harald Frentzen's one-stop strategy,

Mika finished second. At that stage of the game, he led Schumacher in the World Championship, by 40 points to 32, with Irvine next up, on 26.

Then came Silverstone, where Michael crashed on the first lap, and put himself out of racing for - at the very least - several weeks. On the face of it, Mika now looked to be shooting at an open goal.

He scored nothing in the British Grand Prix, though. From pole position, he led easily - until his first pit stop. Immediately after it, he was back in for attention to a loose left rear wheel, and a few laps later the replacement wheel came off.

In the end, Hakkinen's car was withdrawn 'on safety grounds', and although Coulthard went on to win, from Irvine, there was cause for concern at McLaren. Insiders suggested that 'finger trouble' had been responsible for Hakkinen's problem, and that, from a team long considered operationally the best in Formula 1, was unexpected, to say the least.

At the A1-Ring, Coulthard had what he himself described as *"every driver's worst nightmare"*. On the opening lap, at the second corner, he made an ill-judged attempt to pass Hakkinen - and nudged his team mate into a spin.

Although Mika's car was essentially undamaged, he was now at the back, and although he then drove a sensational race to third place, a certain victory had been lost. Worse, Irvine won, having taken the lead from Coulthard on the stops, and then held off a late challenge from the Scot.

The victory put Eddie within two points of Hakkinen, but still Mika behaved with admirable composure after the race. Assuredly he had words with Coulthard in private, but on the surface McLaren's 'team image' remained watertight.

Germany was altogether a mess. As usual, Hakkinen was on pole, and led, but his pit stop was slow (thanks to a stuck valve on his refuelling rig), and he dropped to fourth, behind the Ferraris of Irvine and Mika Salo and the Jordan of Frentzen. Heinz he dealt with quickly, but then his right rear tyre

exploded, at around 340km/h. After a series of terrifying spins, the McLaren nosed into a tyre barrier, Hakkinen emerging quite unhurt, but understandably upset.

It was a poor race for Coulthard, who finished fifth, after tangling with Salo, stopping for a new nose, then incurring a stop/go penalty for cutting part of a chicane.

And Irvine won again, Salo - now playing Eddie's traditional 'slave' role at Ferrari - dutifully moving over to let him by. At the top of the table it was Irvine on 52, then Hakkinen on 44.

In Hungary the rot was stopped, even if only temporarily, for Mika led all the way, and David - after a bad start - came through to finish second. Although Irvine was third, his lead was down to two points, and what McLaren clearly needed was another 1-2 at Spa.

In fact, Hakkinen and Coulthard finished 2-1 in Belgium, for Mika, although on pole, made a hesitant start, and was beaten to the first corner by DC. Thereafter, he made no effort to challenge his team mate, and the suggestion was that there had been a pre-race agreement: whoever leads out of the

David Coulthard watches his team leader go by. Once again the Finn totally dominated the Scotsman this season. ◁

A difficult season but the Mika Hakkinen and his boss still enjoy an excellent relationship. ▽

The cruel tifosi jump for joy at the sight of Mika Hakkinen crashing out of the Italian Grand Prix.

first corner wins the race. Afterwards Hakkinen was clearly angry: although he led the championship again, it was by only a single point.

Unlike Ferrari, McLaren do not routinely impose team orders on their drivers, and while this policy is to be admired, it is not without risk, for inevitably the drivers will take points from each other over the course of a season.

Although he didn't say as much, Hakkinen clearly felt that, given that the season was coming down to a crucial point, it was time for Dennis to insist that the team concentrate on him, the McLaren driver with the best chance of becoming World Champion. Ron Dennis, reacting to this suggestion, said that no, the time for that had not yet come.

Given Hakkinen's reputation for keeping his emotions to himself, many were surprised by his obvious displeasure at Spa, but perhaps he felt that, all things being equal, this was a championship he should have had virtually locked away by now. If the pressure upon him was mounting, it was not because of mistakes he himself had made.

There were tears this time, and from rage at himself

At Monza, though, he could blame no one else. After leading for 30 laps, he made a novice's mistake at the first chicane, changing down to first, rather than second, gear, locking up the back wheels and spinning into retirement. There were tears this time, and from rage at himself.

It was more than fortunate for Mika that Irvine finished only a poor sixth, putting them level on 60 points, but a new factor in the equation was Frentzen, who won, and was now only 10 points adrift of them.

Heinz should have won at the Nurburgring, too, for he beat Coulthard and Hakkinen to pole position, and led the dry-wet-dry race until retiring at half-distance.

By then Mika's afternoon was already in pieces. Early in the race, it began to rain on the far side of the circuit, and while most teams opted to keep their drivers out there, McLaren overreacted to the new conditions, and brought Hakkinen in for wet tyres.

The rain abated almost immediately - and four laps later he was back in for more dry tyres. Now back in 14th place, and lapped, he drove with a notable lack of enthusiasm through the middle section of the race, and

An "off" in practice. Proof that Mika Hakkinen was on the limit all season long.

came to life only when the track dried out again. At this stage, he began running record laps, and pressured Irvine into a mistake, which put him fifth. Again, though, Mika was very fortunate that Eddie was even in range; this was so only because of a disastrously slow tyre stop by Ferrari.

Coulthard, meantime, threw victory away. On lap 38, leading comfortably, he spun into a tyre barrier, and that was the end of any championship hopes he may have had. From now on - finally - he would be playing a supporting role to Hakkinen.

At Sepang David undoubtedly did his best. The returning Michael Schumacher, having handed the lead to Irvine, was intent on delaying Eddie's championship rivals as much as possible, but Coulthard passed him on lap five, and in remarkably assertive fashion. He then began to close on Irvine, only to pull off with low fuel pressure.

Thereafter, there was little hope for Hakkinen, for it was now two Ferraris against a lone McLaren, and he duly finished third. For six days, following the disqualification of Irvine and Schumacher, that became first,

and brought with it a second World Championship, but then an FIA Court of Appeal reinstated the Ferraris, and Mika was off to Suzuka, four points behind Irvine, and needing to win.

Whatever the outcome of the Japanese weekend, this was not a season of which McLaren could be particularly proud. True, the MP4-14 was the best car of the year, and Ilmor's latest Mercedes-Benz V10 had probably more power than any other engine, but the fact remains that the team did not get the most out of what they had.

All things being equal, Hakkinen - particularly in the absence of Schumacher - should have had the title secure long before the end of the year, and the same was true of the team in the Constructors' Championship.

After 15 races, both Hakkinen and Irvine had four wins apiece - but Mika started 11 times from pole position, Eddie not once. On laps led, Hakkinen beat Irvine by 333 to 133, but significantly, the Ferrari driver had completed 930 laps, the McLaren man only 798. To finish first, like the man said, you first have to finish...

Simulation tools, an invaluable aid

When it comes to braking, performance is the permanent concern of Carbone Industrie. Its engineers spend hours working in front of their screens, to find the right result; a result which will be validated or not after just two minutes of track testing.

Formula 1 teams do not have much time during practice do decide on what braking material to use. The choice is vital as it can decide the outcome of a grand prix. In order to meet these demands, Carbone Industrie (a division of Messier-Bugatti) has developed its own simulation programme, designed specifically for Formula 1.

A combination of bench testing and computer simulation makes it easier to tackle the testing of new braking materials on the cars.

This combination serves to discover the optimum operating temperature and thus advise the teams and drivers what they can expect from the brakes as they work to get them up to temperature.

---

if braking performance is very different to the norm, the driver might decide to pit

---

This is an important phase in terms of the driver's confidence and that confidence itself is an important performance factor. In some cases, if braking performance is very different to the norm, the driver might decide to pit, without even getting the brakes up to the working temperature. He can then decide the new material is less effective than the standard and the test is at an end.

Simulation is one of three key elements of developing braking systems used in Formula 1, along with a static test bed and, of primary importance, track testing.

Each of these elements helps provide a better understanding of the other two, all aimed at improving the performance of the car.

Simulation can also help when new parameters are thrown into the equation. For example, some changes to the regulations not directly linked to braking, can impact on this part of the package. Thus, simulation allows any problems to be anticipated and solutions prepared in advance. It should be remembered that it can take months to prepare the carbon and simulation therefore allows something to be tried out well before it has to be tested on the track with the car set up

to deal with a modification to the rules. This avoids any last minute surprises.

Simulation takes place in three completely separate stages. The first involves collecting data at the actual grands prix, which is why the race team has an important role to play in the process. Data is gathered via telemetry and also from comments of the drivers. This data is then added to by those who supply the teams. All this information is then relayed to the Carbone Industrie staff.

The second part of the simulation can then begin. Performance in terms of speeds, pressures, deceleration and brake temperatures are all analysed at the Carbone Industrie facility near Lyon in France.

Specific and general analyses are carried out. General, because research into materials must move forward and specific because analysis is carried out on each different car.

For this, Carbone Industrie uses DAISY (Dynamometer for the Automobile and Investigation of the Systems.) From this, material graphs are produced showing the definition of the various parameters of friction tested on the bench.

The test bed is full scale and can test a variety of areas: materials, brakes and braking systems. These are all dedicated specifically to Formula 1.

The test bed can simulate the weight of the vehicle using inertia. Electrically it can also reproduce the relationship between the wheel and the track. It can alter the braking pressure and torque and acceleration/deceleration forces. It can also reproduce different climatic conditions. DAISY reproduces several driving modes: automatic by programmed cycles, circuit simulation taken from data off the cars. DAISY can also be adapted for different configurations. By lengthening the testing process it is possible to analyse the numerical data acquired during track testing

and racing. That involves the third step which uses a computer specifically dedicated to F1 simulation. First the parameters are defined which will be used as a reference point. This allows a study of problems on the car, such as instability under braking. To date, all problems encountered have been successfully solved with this computer. The analysis extends to determining the influence of the parameters on the balance of the car as well as the wear rate of the brakes. Virtual simulation takes into account the parameters of the material type and the braking configuration on a car, always referred back to results on the bench.

During simulation, the major variation is always in temperature. This allows the pressure required to be calculated. The results passed to each team means it can decided on a choice of material and an idea of what set-up to use on the car. This all saves time and means the car is as ready as possible to face the challenge of the circuit being used.

In 1999, the best example of this came at the Canadian Grand Prix where simulation helped define SA3.7, a carbon/carbon material as the right one to use. In the same way at the Malaysian Grand Prix, simulation allowed the teams to find the right material to use on this circuit they had never used before.

△
Jacques Villeneuve hard on the brakes as the carbon discs glow red. This year, it was thanks to the simulation programme that Carbone Industrie engineers were able to calculate what type of discs they would need for the brand new circuit outside Kuala Lumpur.

The simulation computer screen used by Carbone Industrie for Formula 1. On the horizontal, one can see the representation of a circuit (in this example Hockenheim) with the different parameters that can be observed: car speed, deceleration, brake pressure and disc surface temperature.

▽

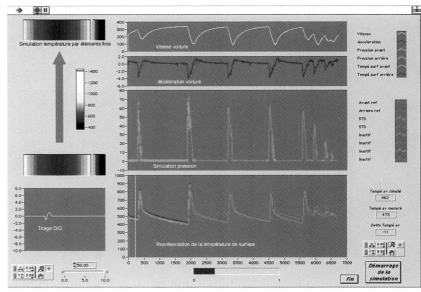

Bridgestone

The importance of Formula 1

When Bridgestone arrived in Formula 1 in 1997, its stated aim was to increase brand awareness for the company in Europe, where 12 races out of 16 are being held, and finally to increase sales.

It wanted to reach the target of a 20% market share of global tyre sales.

"We want to be the clear leader in tyre sales around the world and to increase our actual share to 20%," declared Yoichiro Kaizaki, President, Chairman of the Board and Chief Executive Officer of Bridgestone Corporation.

A television audience of around 5.4 billion people around the world watch Formula 1 on an accumulated yearly basis, especially in Europe and South America, but also in Japan, North America and Australia. According to Bridgestone, participation in F1 constitutes an excellent method of improving the marque's visibility and brand awareness.

And it is working: In 1997 and 1998 Bridgestone commissioned a market research survey to see how well known its name was among the general public.

In Germany, Great Britain, France, Italy and Spain, the five biggest European markets, the unaided or prompted brand awareness of the Bridgestone brand in 1998 at least doubled or even tripled in some of these markets, compared with 1996.

At the same time, sales of Bridgestone tyres in the replacement market for road cars increased by more than 20% from 1996 to 1998. According to Bridgestone management, both these spectacular results can mainly be put down to F1.

"Our successful participation in Formula 1 has been particularly effective in improving brand awareness in Europe," confirmed Mr. Kaizaki. So, despite the huge amounts spent on F1, the investment has proved to be worthwhile for the Japanese company.

▷ As well as supplying all the F1 teams, Bridgestone has always run a vast circuit advertising campaign, with spectacular results as seen here in Melbourne.

△ Melbourne marked the start of a new relationship between Scuderia Ferrari and Bridgestone. Here, engineer Yoshihiko Ichikawa is in conversation with Jean Todt.

A complete tyre range

Bridgestone Corporation, with headquarters in Tokyo, is one of the leaders among the world's tyre companies, producing a complete line of tyres for passenger cars, trucks, off-road machines, motorcycles, aeroplanes and other vehicles which account for 79 per cent of its sales world wide. It also manufactures a wide range of diversified products which include industrial rubber and chemical products, sporting goods and others. These products are sold in more than 150 countries and territories around the world.

TYRE RANGE

Passenger car tyres:
    Turanza (grand touring)
        ER20 and ER30
    Potenza (sport)
        S-02 pole-position
        RE720 (new in 1999)

General use
    B330
    Winter
        Winter radial WT-12, WT-17
        Blizzak MZ-02
        Blizzak LM-22 Studless

4x4 Tyres
    Dueler H/P 680, H/T 689, A/T 693
        M/T 673
    Winter
        Dueler DM-Z2

Truck and bus tyres

Off the road tyres

Motorcycle tyres.

How does a Formula One involvement benefit road tyre development?

Bridgestone Motorsport's Technical Manager, Yoshihiko Ichikawa explains how the tyre company exploits the lessons it learns from motor racing to improve the tyres it produces for road cars.

There is a huge difference between a road tyre and a race tyre. You don't need to be an expert to see that a competition tyre uses a much softer rubber than a road tyre and also that the wheel width is much bigger.

These differences do not prevent the Bridgestone engineers from making the most of their high level involvement in motor racing, in Formula 1 and CART, to develop new products destined for the road.

- What are the main differences in developing a race tyre and one for the road?

Yoshihiko Ichikawa: In the case of competition tyres, there is no need to worry about notions of comfort from the tyre, or the noise it makes or its effect on fuel consumption; all criteria that have to be studied in the case of a road tyre. However, a racing tyre must give a very high level of grip. Basically, they are two very different types of tyre. For us, competition is a test bed. If we come across a solution that seems good in theory, we can try out in racing and not just in Formula 1 either. That way we can find out if it works.

- How do you carry out these tests?

Yoshihiko Ichikawa: When we discover a new type of material or a new type of construction, or a new tread pattern, etc... we can test these elements in a competition environment. All the data we gather can then be forwarded to our research department, so that there is a constant flow of information between the research and competition departments. After every race and every test session, we send all the data back to Tokyo. Sometimes we also send back tyres themselves so that they can be analysed. On occasion, engineers from the research department attend private test sessions.

- Is it easy to adapt the new technologies found during testing and racing to road cars?

Yoshihiko Ichikawa: No and in fact, development never goes directly from racing to the road. Before any new discovery can be used for road cars, it has to be re-examined from different angles. For example, for a new polymer, we have to look at how it will stand up to the demands of a road tyre and what effect it will really have on performance. We are always looking for a compromise. On top of that, racing is not the only area where we test new discoveries. The research department combines information acquired from several sources. On the other hand, racing allows us to test theoretical results very quickly.

- What happens when something new is tested in F1 and does not work?

Yoshihiko Ichikawa: These things can happen. Experiments are not always successful. In these cases, the teams are disappointed, but there is not much we can do about it. Racing tyres also need to improve and naturally that means experimentation and therefore the occasional error. When we try something new, sometimes we do it in Formula 1 and Indycar at the same time. But generally, everything works very well with the teams.

Yoshihiko Ichikawa

The story of a little Stone Bridge

Every company had a founding. And every company had a founder. But you won't find any company where people are more aware of their founding purpose than the people at Bridgestone are.

Shojiro Ishibashi was perfectly clear about his purpose when he started making tyres in 1931 in a little town on the island of Kyushu, in the south of Japan . Shojiro Ishibashi said he wanted to serve society by providing people with products of superior quality.

The founder was ambitious enough to dream that his quality products would earn the satisfaction of customers world-wide. Though Japan lagged woefully behind the West in industrial development, he dreamed that his company would become a global enterprise

Shojiro Ishibashi even christened his fledging venture with an English variation of his name. "Ishi" of the surname Ishibashi translates "stone" and "bashi" translates as "bridge". So, the surname "Ishibashi" translates as "stone-bridge". He was getting ready for something international. But even Shojiro Ishibashi could not have known how spectacularly his company would fulfil his hopes.

From a family concern, Bridgestone has grown today to a point where it is one of the biggest tyre companies in the world and posted in 1998 a turnover of over 17 billion dollars.

Together with two main competitors –Goodyear and Michelin, Bridgestone dominates the world tyre market, leaving only a few crumbs for the other brands.

In 1988, Bridgestone bought Firestone, which had been the second largest American company after Goodyear.

Today, Bridgestone has 94 tyre and non-tyre factories in 23 countries and it employs over 97.000 people world wide.

Bridgestone/Firestone global organisation comprises 3 regional Head Quarters: one in Tokyo -Japan, a second in Brussels-Belgium and a third in Nashville, USA.

Furthermore, Bridgestone/Firestone owns 3 technical centres and 7 proving grounds, located all over the world.

Both Bridgestone and Firestone tyres are now original equipment on almost all major car manufacturers, from Volkswagen Group, GM, Fiat, Ford, Japanese brands, BMW to high performance models from Porsche, Ferrari and Aston Martin.

The" little bridge of stone" has become a giant viaduct....

▷ *Bridgestone's motor sport boss, Hiroshi Yasukawa.*

Making the most of its F1 involvement.

For Nicolas, the customer is king

From his days as a ski instructor, Nicolas retains his athletic build. At the circuits, he can be spotted from a long way off, but getting to talk to him is not so easy as he is usually welded to his mobile phone. During the Monaco Grand Prix, he once got through four batteries in three hours!

Everyone's friend and ever smiling despite his heavy work load, he is one of the best known faces in the paddock. When Nicolas comes out with his usual reply: "*I'll be with you in five minutes,*" you know you are going to have to wait for an hour before he turns up!

This is because he is a busy lad. What with welcoming guests to the Paddock Club, bringing the drivers along, looking after the Bridgestone merchandising at the circuits and dealing with other F1 sponsors, he certainly has no time to get bored at a grand prix. "*Usually, I get up around six in the morning to get to the circuit at seven,*" he explains. "*First of all, I call in at our unit in the Paddock Club, to make sure everything is in order and to speak to the caterer. I also inform the security staff as to which drivers will visit our unit that day. At Monza for example, we welcomed Giancarlo Fisichella on Saturday, Alessandro Zanardi came on Sunday morning and the two Ferrari drivers at lunchtime. As I am the only representative of Bridgestone/Firestone Europe in the Paddock Club, it is my job to meet our guests and drivers.*"

The rest of the day is no quieter. "*I organise pit tours for our most important guests. At a busy grand prix, there can be up to fifteen different tours a day, which involves a lot of juggling with the passes.*"

On top of this, as Manager, Motorsport Promotions, Nicolas is also responsible for building special links with the other companies involved in Formula 1, in order to mount joint promotions. "*Together, we put on various events in between the grands prix, such as karting evenings or golf tournaments,*" explains Nicolas. "*I also have to coordinate all our F1 linked promotions, such as our "local hero campaign," a series of posters and driver figurines adapted for each country - Jean Alesi in France, Eddie Irvine for Ireland and so on.*" Through these contacts, all sorts of links have been forged, such as fitting (Benetton Group Sport Divigent) Rollerblades with Bridgestone tyres.

The Bridgestone shop at the circuits is yet another big responsibility. "*I have to organise the show cars with the teams, make sure everything is in place and that our full product range is layed out, be it road or truck tyres, or those for four by fours and motorcycles.*"

In between the grands prix, his telephone does not get much chance to rest. This is when Nicolas has to organise mailing out the Paddock Club tickets to the various subsidiary companies. "*Often we have over 100 guests per race. Spa is our busiest weekend of the European season and 145 people turn up.*" All in all, Nicolas is away from home for 200 days of the year. "*My private life is confidential,*" he jokes, while adding that his biggest fear is the unknown and unpredictable. "*Anything can happen at a grand prix,*" he claims. "*Two years ago at Monza, two helicopters collided on take off. Sometimes, guests bring their children without warning us. Others lose their documents, fall ill or cannot find their way back to their hotel. It's permanent stress. Thankfully, most of our guests are delighted with their weekend. They particularly like visiting the paddock and the Bridgestone work*

areas, where they can see what happens to the tyres."

It is a varied, but very demanding job. The telephone is ringing again and it is time for this interview to end and for Nicolas to head back to the Paddock Club. He was supposed to have been there over half an hour ago...

Nicolas Duquesne hosts an Eddie Irvine visit.

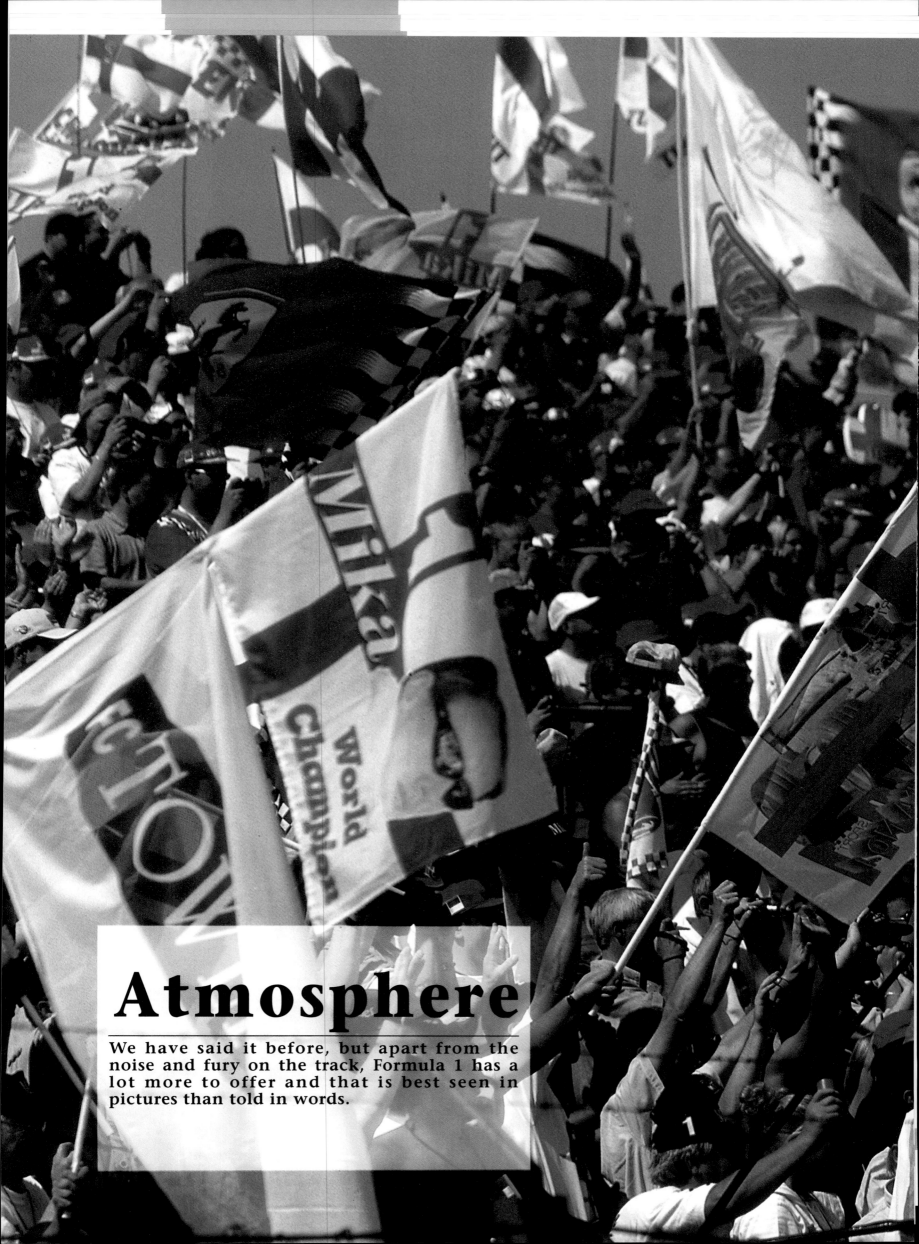

Atmosphere

We have said it before, but apart from the noise and fury on the track, Formula 1 has a lot more to offer and that is best seen in pictures than told in words.

The feminine touch

There is no more macho atmosphere to be found than that in a Formula 1 paddock. There are very few female mechanics or engineers and there are no women drivers. Luckily, a few charming young ladies are more than willing to brighten up the paddocks of the world.

BARRICHELLO

16

ATMOSPHERE

Consolation prize

Third time unlucky again. Ferrari is definitely out of luck when it comes to the final race of the season with the championship at stake. At least this time, the Scuderia can console itself with having won the Constructors' Championship. It might not be as prestigious as the Drivers' title, but it does mean that, despite Michael Schumacher's seven race absence, Ferrari has beaten the mighty McLaren-Mercedes at something. No mean feat.

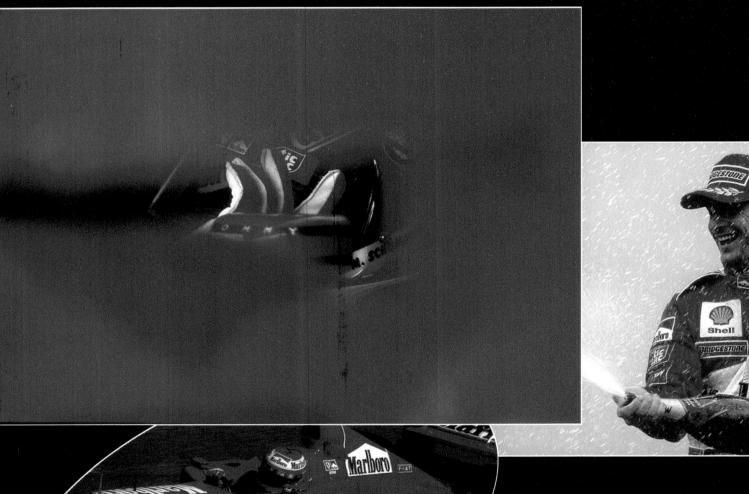

ATMOSPHERE

Style on the nose

Formula 1 cars are not exactly aesthetically pleasing with their ungainly air intakes and deflectors everywhere. However, their nose sections, thanks to aerodynamic dictates are beautifully pure in form. Thanks to the sponsors, their colours are pretty too.

The third force

The Jordan team has had its best ever season in Formula 1, despite the fact Eddie Jordan was virtually running a one car team for Heinz-Harald Frentzen. Dejected at being out-paced by the German, Damon Hill soon gave up the struggle. Luckily for the team, "HH" was in great form. Thanks to him, with the exception of Stewart's win at the Nurburgring, Jordan was the only outfit to break the McLaren-Ferrari stranglehold taking two victories. Eddie Jordan can be proud of what he has achieved. He now claims to be aiming for the championship. That will be a tougher challenge.

ATMOSPHERE

ATMOSPHERE

IN GEAR

A new broom

The Prost team spent much of the season waiting for a decision from its engine supplier, Peugeot. Would it leave at the end of 1999 or respect its contract to the end of 2000 or have a long term future in the sport? These doubts did not help the team effort. However, the team improved in comparison to the previous year with the arrival of B3 Technologies and technical director Alan Jenkins. These elements began to shine through at the end of the year as evidenced by Olivier Panis running third in the first part of the Japanese Grand Prix.

ATMOSPHERE

ATMOSPHERE

The eyes of the stars

Piercing or clear, aggressive or tired, the drivers eyes often say more about their determination than any press conference declarations, tempered by political correctness.

The 16 Grands Prix

16 grands prix, 16 venues and 16 races of different shades: some made, some logical, some memorable and some forgettable. But, and that is their attraction; all different, one from the other.
In its fiftieth year, the Formula 1 championship was so surprising that no scriptwriter would have dared come up with so many changes of fortune. Thanks to all this excitement, "The Formula 1 Yearbook" reads more like a novel.

Eddie's first!

Few would have bet on an Eddie Irvine victory in the Australian Grand Prix. But the Irishman did indeed take the first grand prix win of his career after an incident and retirement-packed race.

It all went wrong for McLaren; both cars retiring at almost the same moment. It was no better for Michael Schumacher, who started the 1999 season the way he ended the 1998 year, by stalling on the grid

QANTAS AUSTRALIAN GRAND PRIX
MELBOURNE

Both McLarens on the front row.

△
David on the attack. Over the winter, the Scotsman had claimed that he would be quicker this season in order to beat his team-mate. Well, he was wrong. In Melbourne, Mika snaffled the first of a series of poles off him.

▷

Mika Hakkinen's big shunt on the first day of practice was a portent of a difficult season ahead for the reigning champions.

Sunset over Sydney Harbour with its Opera House and city is a nightly spectacle. Only a few hours drive from Melbourne, it is a good excuse for a photo!

▽

Mika, David and Ron: all smiles and confidence....

Mika Hakkinen had evidently enjoyed his four month winter lay-off, judging by his unnaturally laid back attitude in the Melbourne paddock: *"Personally I feel in top form and ready to defend my world championship title"*, declared the Finn with previously unseen confidence.*"I have worked hard since last year and I have also learned a lot. In 1999 I will have a better understanding of how to channel my energy to win races. Of course, we must wait until Sunday afternoon to see exactly how competitive we can expect to be this year, but I am sure the huge amount of work the team has done over the winter will bring the rewards."*

McLaren boss Ron Dennis was singing off the same hymn sheet as his driver: *"Mika has changed since last year"*, was his analysis. *"That's understandable. He's already much richer ! (laughs)He seems happier to me; lively and more self-confident. When a driver reaches his ultimate goal and wins the world championship, it's normal that he should feel more sure of himself. I am sure that is the case with Michael (Schumacher,) Jacques (Villeneuve) and Damon (Hill)"*

Ron Dennis will not favour either one of his drivers

Victory in the previous year's championships has not sated Dennis' thirst for victory. *"We have got through an enormous amount of work this winter. Everyone at the factory is exhausted"*

he claimed. *"Our motivation comes from failure and the fear of failure. I don't think we can afford to be too optimistic at the start of this season. The regulations have not changed since 1998, which inevitably has allowed other teams to close the gap to us in terms of performance. In this situation, some teams like Williams for example, could produce a surprise"*. Last year, Mika Hakkinen quickly emerged as the favourite, to the detriment of David Coulthard. For this season, Ron Dennis said there would be no favouritism: *"We want to win as a team. I don't care whether it is Mika or David who wins the championship"*. This position would create a few problems several months later in Belgium.

...slightly dented!

With thirteen minutes remaining in the first day of practice of the season, Mika Hakkinen really wanted to show everyone what a newly crowned world champion was capable of. In the first sector of his lap he certainly did just that, beating his own best time by a huge six tenths of a second.

With just the last corner to negotiate, the Finn was a touch over optimistic. His McLaren MP4/14 got out of shape and he was unable to catch it. It was not the type of mistake we were used to from Mika as he had not committed a

similar error since Monaco in 1997.

There was no escape road at this point on the track and the car slammed into the tyres placed in front of the barriers. The McLaren was a mess: both right hand wheels, the gearbox and the engine were all smashed, but the driver got away unharmed: *"At least now I know where the limits of the car are,"* was the driver's uncharacteristically jokey response when he got back to the pits. *"Up until that point, the car felt very quick and efficient in the corners. I'm sure we'll be on the front row tomorrow".*

BAR does not deliver on its promise

By the end of the first day of practice, there were a lot of wry smiles in the paddock. On 2nd December 1997, when the BAR team was launched, technical director Adrian Reynard had lightheartedly suggested his cars would start their first grand prix from the front row of the grid.

From that day on, the team had created a rod for its own back, a rod which all the other teams were ready to beat it with as soon as they got to Melbourne.

The inevitable happened and the BARs did not make it to the front row of the grid. However, those who had thought to mock, kept their thoughts to themselves as the BAR performance level was not as bad as all that. Despite an off-track excursion and a radio failure between car and pit, Jacques Villeneuve qualified in eleventh place, although he looked to have the potential to have been on the second or third row. Not bad for a first public appearance. The Canadian tempered this with the thought that their problems stemmed from lack of experience. For his part, his boss Craig Pollock was all smiles.

Ferrari blames the settings

Although it was a bit early in the season to be grubbing around under the seat for a parachute, Ferrari was already trying to justify its less than convincing performance with some very unconvincing arguments.

Michael Schumacher had qualified third, but over a second down on the McLarens, which brought back unhappy memories of the start of the 1998 season. The German looked in a filthy mood as he stepped from the cockpit. *"I did not expect such a big gap"*, he admitted. *"We will have to get down to work next week. We do not know the cause of our problems, but I am sure we will find it. It is far too early to say our season is over".*

In Melbourne, the Scuderia never found the right set-up and whatever they did, the cars were all over the road. *"I do not want to go into technical details"*, continued the German. *"But the problem we have experienced here is one we never came across over the winter, when our car had shown enormous potential".*

One hypothesis put forward by the Italian team's engineers was that Mugello, Fiorano and Barcelona, , the circuits used for the development of the F399, were quicker tracks than the Melbourne street circuit, which required higher levels of downforce. It seemed the F399 was well adapted to the former but not to the latter.

Ferrari's Sporting Director Jean Todt had another theory, which did not seem to hold water. *"It seems that those teams which had already worked with Bridgestone last year had an advantage today. These new tyres are very hard. Mika Hakkinen used only one set throughout qualifying, while we fitted three to Michael's car. Only then did we realise the tyres got better the more laps they did".*

Ferrari had been pre-season favourites for the title, but the Melbourne set back put one in mind of 1998 when McLaren lapped the field. F1 it seemed never changed from year to year.

Alex plans to be aggressive

1997 and 1998 Indycar champion Alessandro Zanardi is back in Formula 1, having taken part in 25 grands prix from 1991 to 1994. He felt the sport had changed out of all recognition. *"It would be easier for me to say what is still the same"*, he said with a smile in the Melbourne paddock.

In the States, he built a reputation as an aggressive driver; more than that, a true killer who would push his opponents off the track if needs be. It was an attitude he had every intention of maintaining in F1. *"I am not sure what is meant by aggressive"*, he commented. *"I try and grasp every opportunity. If I think I can overtake, I am not paid to hang around and wait for an extra lap".*

△
A historic moment: Jacques Villeneuve is about to take to the track for the BAR team's first official session. From the pit wall, Craig Pollock exchanges a conspiratorial wink with his driver.

▷
"I think Formula 1 is going to suit me just fine!" Alex Zanardi rediscovers the charms of F1 in Melbourne.

STARTING GRID

		Mika HÄKKINEN 1'30"462	
David COULTHARD 1'30"946	-1-		
		M. SCHUMACHER 1'31"781	
R. BARRICHELLO 1'32"148	-2-		
		Heinz-H. FRENTZEN 1'32"276	
Eddie IRVINE 1'32"289	-3-		
		G. FISICHELLA 1'32"540	
Ralf SCHUMACHER 1'32"691	-4-		
		Damon HILL 1'32"695	
Alexander WURZ 1'32"789	-5-		
		Jacques VILLENEUVE 1'32"888	
Jarno TRULLI 1'32"971	-6-		
		Johnny HERBERT 1'32"991	
Pedro DINIZ 1'33"374	-7-		
		Alessandro ZANARDI 1'33"549	
Jean ALESI 1'33"910	-8-		
		Toranosuke TAKAGI 1'34"182	
Pedro de la ROSA 1'34"244	-9-		
		Ricardo ZONTA 1'34"412	
Olivier PANIS 1'35"068	-10-		
	-11-	Luca BADOER 1'35"316	

The atmosphere of the Albert Park circuit with its lake and concrete
walls. For Damon Hill, seen here during practice, this first grand prix
was not a good omen for the rest of the season: the Englishman
qualified behind team-mate Heinz- Harald Frentzen, didn't manage
a single lap in the warm-up and crashed on the first lap. In this
situation it is best to say better next time.

QANTAS AUSTRALIAN GRAND PRIX

...r also means new cars and that involves finding new ...lence the high number of off-track excursions during practice.

▷

"You have to believe me, it wasn't even frightening." Villeneuve's huge accident was of interest to all the media.

First grand prix and first point for Pedro De La Rosa. Few drivers in the history of the sport have managed to score points in their first world championship event. In recent times, this exploit has been achieved by Eddie Irvine, Jean Alesi, Alain Prost and Jacques Villeneuve. Did we have another star in the making?

▽

And there goes the rear wing!

Jacques Villeneuve had more excitement than he bargained for in the race. The Canadian's rear wing flew off, sending him into a frightening high speed spin. He was lucky to walk away from the wreck.

This was the second time that a BAR01 had lost a rear wing, which was worrying for the team and especially for the drivers! *"We still do not know if the two failures were caused by the same problem,"* said Craig Pollock, the team's boss, immediately after the incident. *"But we are going to have a good look at the problem as soon as we get back to the factory."*

Flexible wings

The failure rekindled the heated discussion on the subject of rear wing failures in F1. During winter testing, they were the cause of several accidents, most notably for Ferrari, Benetton, BAR and Stewart.

It transpired that some teams had actually designed the rear wings to bend back at high speeds, in order to reduce their aerodynamic drag down the straights. It was a dangerous idea which could have been responsible for the failures.

"The wings must withstand heavy vibration. Their supports also need to have a degree of flexibility. But using that feature so that they deliberately bend back makes them a moveable aerodynamic device, which is forbidden by the regulations. It is up to FIA to define the limit of what is permissible." Thus spoke Ron Dennis, insisting that McLaren had not adopted this design.

Prost on the right road

Sure, Jarno Trulli had benefited from the retirements at the head of the field, but seeing his car running third on lap 18 was enough to get the blood coursing in the Prost-Peugeot pit.

La compétitivité qui avait tant fait défaut l'an dernier était là. Et bien là, puisque l'Italien roulait alors à moins de trois secondes de la tête de la course.

It seemed that the competitiveness which had been missing the previous year had now arrived, given that the Italian was running less than three seconds behind the leader.

Joy was short-lived however. Just as the Safety Car came out for the second time, Trulli decided to make a pit stop. A problem with the refuelling nozzle on the car meant he had to come back into the pits a second time, when his mechanics had to force open the filler, losing precious time. As he went back out onto the track, Trulli was caught up in Spaniard Marc Gene's spin. He could not avoid the accident and ended up in the wall at the end of an action packed race. *"I hurt myself,"* he said after the race. *"As the steering wheel spun back it twisted my left wrist. I had a total of three accidents in this grand prix. At the first start, I touched Hill, then Fisichella ran into the back of me, breaking my diffuser. Then at the end, I could not avoid Gene. But at least I proved today that the car is competitive. I was able to pass Benettons and Williams and I could keep up with Frentzen easily."*

Olivier Panis retired on lap 24. During his pit stop, a wheel nut refused to budge. But for that, the Frenchman might have finished in the points.

PRACTICE TIMES

No	Driver	Car/Engine/Chassis	Practice Friday	Pos.	Practice Saturday	Pos.	Qualifying	Pos.	Warm-up	Pos.
1.	Mika Häkkinen	McLaren/Mercedes/MP4 -14/1	1'31"985	2°	1'30"324	1°	1'30"462	1°	1'32"670	2°
2.	David Coulthard	McLaren/Mercedes/MP4 -14/2	1'31"971	1°	1'30"969	2°	1'30"946	2°	1'32"560	1°
3.	Michael Schumacher	Ferrari/Ferrari/F399/190	1'33"576	7°	1'32"722	6°	1'31"781	3°	1'33"638	3°
4.	Eddie Irvine	Ferrari/Ferrari/F399/191	1'34"595	14°	1'32"994	10°	1'32"289	6°	1'35"241	16°
5.	Alessandro Zanardi	Williams/Supertec/FW21/01	1'33"951	9°	1'35"444	19°	1'33"549	15°	1'34"556	6°
6.	Ralf Schumacher	Williams/Supertec/FW21/03	1'33"957	10°	1'33"323	15°	1'32"691	8°	1'34"747	8°
7.	Damon Hill	Jordan/Mugen-Honda/199/04	1'33"420	6°	1'32"661	4°	1'32"695	9°	16'57"718	22°
8.	Heinz-Harald Frentzen	Jordan/Mugen-Honda/199/03	1'33"029	4°	1'32"876	8°	1'32"276	5°	1'35"085	14°
9.	Giancarlo Fisichella	Benetton/Playlife/B199/04	1'34"135	12°	1'32"975	9°	1'32"540	7°	1'35"013	12°
10.	Alexander Wurz	Benetton/Playlife/B199/02	1'34"046	11°	1'33"110	12°	1'32"789	10°	1'34"973	11°
11.	Jean Alesi	Sauber/Petronas/C18/03	1'34"541	13°	1'33"305	14°	1'33"910	16°	1'34"805	10°
12.	Pedro Diniz	Sauber/Petronas/C18/01	1'35"253	17°	1'32"999	11°	1'33"374	14°	1'34"460	4°
14.	Pedro de la Rosa	Arrows/Arrows/A20/04	1'35"756	19°	1'34"194	17°	1'34"244	18°	1'35"135	15°
15.	Toranosuke Takagi	Arrows/Arrows/A20/02	1'35"699	18°	1'34"386	18°	1'34"182	17°	1'35"568	18°
16.	Rubens Barrichello	Stewart/Ford/SF3/01	1'32"947	3°	1'32"828	7°	1'32"148	4°	1'35"046	13°
17.	Johnny Herbert	Stewart/Ford/SF3/03	1'33"166	5°	1'32"569	3°	1'32"991	13°	1'34"707	7°
18.	Olivier Panis	Prost/Peugeot/AP02/3	1'34"693	15°	1'34"129	16°	1'35"068	20°	1'34"518	5°
19.	Jarno Trulli	Prost/Peugeot/AP02/2	1'33"870	8°	1'33"252	13°	1'32"971	12°	1'34"784	9°
20.	Luca Badoer	Minardi/Ford/M01/02	1'37"958	21°	1'35"839	20°	1'35"316	21°	1'37"289	20°
21.	Marc Gené	Minardi/Ford/M01/03	1'36"481	20°	1'36"848	21°	1'37"013	NQ	1'38"471	21°
22.	Jacques Villeneuve	BAR/Supertec/BAR01/3	1'34"695	16°	1'32"717	5°	1'32"888	11°	1'35"676	19°
23.	Ricardo Zonta	BAR/Supertec/BAR01/2	1'38"075	22°	1'48"227	22°	1'34"412	19°	1'35"294	17°

MAXIMUM SPEEDS

No	Driver	P1 Qualifs	Pos	P1 Race	Pos	P2 Qualifs	Pos	P2 Race	Pos	Finish Qualifs	Pos	Finish Race	Pos	Trap Qualifs	Pos	Trap Race	Pos
1.	M. Häkkinen	282,1	1°	275,5	3°	295,3	1°	286,2	15°	293,7	1°	287,9	10°	307,6	1°	301,2	7°
2.	D. Coulthard	279,6	2°	277,7	1°	292,5	2°	290,9	4°	291,3	2°	290,0	3°	306,0	2°	301,6	5°
3.	M. Schum.	275,2	5°	276,0	2°	287,3	11°	290,5	6°	285,1	9°	290,5	1°	299,4	10°	304,6	1°
4.	E. Irvine	273,9	10°	273,9	8°	289,8	3°	290,5	7°	288,0	4°	289,8	5°	303,6	3°	304,1	2°
5.	A. Zanardi	273,6	12°	266,7	18°	288,1	8°	286,6	13°	283,9	13°	287,7	11°	297,1	14°	289,0	19°
6.	R. Schum.	274,1	8°	274,1	7°	288,1	9°	284,8	17°	284,5	11°	286,2	14°	300,3	6°	300,0	10°
7.	D. Hill	277,1	3°	NQ	-	288,0	4°	NQ	-	286,7	5°	NQ	-	302,0	5°	237,8	20°
8.	H. Frentzen	277,0	4°	275,4	4°	289,7	5°	287,4	11°	288,1	3°	290,0	4°	302,0	4°	301,4	6°
9.	G. Fisichella	274,4	6°	272,7	10°	289,6	10°	290,3	9°	285,0	10°	283,9	17°	300,2	7°	299,8	11°
10.	A. Wurz	274,2	7°	269,5	14°	287,1	12°	286,6	12°	285,2	8°	285,0	16°	299,9	8°	298,5	13°
11.	J. Alesi	268,3	19°	NQ	-	283,2	18°	NQ	-	283,8	15°	NQ	-	299,0	11°	NQ	-
12.	P. Diniz	269,4	17°	273,4	9°	284,8	14°	293,8	2°	283,6	16°	290,4	2°	298,0	13°	300,9	8°
14.	P. de la Rosa	269,8	16°	268,6	15°	283,6	16°	285,2	16°	281,9	17°	288,4	9°	294,4	20°	296,6	15°
15.	T. Takagi	267,8	20°	270,4	13°	281,8	21°	288,8	10°	280,5	21°	286,2	13°	293,7	21°	298,9	12°
16.	R. Barrichello	273,7	11°	275,0	5°	288,6	6°	291,7	3°	286,4	6°	289,3	7°	296,5	16°	301,8	4°
17.	J. Herbert	273,0	13°	NQ	-	286,7	13°	NQ	-	286,0	7°	NQ	-	299,6	9°	NQ	-
18.	O. Panis	266,8	21°	267,6	16°	283,6	15°	286,3	14°	281,3	18°	285,2	15°	296,4	17°	293,7	16°
19.	J. Trulli	270,4	15°	274,1	6°	281,9	20°	290,4	8°	281,0	20°	288,4	8°	294,7	19°	300,8	9°
20.	L. Badoer	268,5	18°	267,5	17°	283,0	19°	282,9	19°	281,2	19°	281,2	18°	296,0	18°	291,2	18°
21.	M. Gené	264,5	22°	264,6	19°	278,5	22°	284,5	18°	275,2	22°	281,1	19°	291,1	22°	293,0	17°
22.	J. Villeneuve	274,1	9°	271,6	12°	283,5	17°	290,7	5°	284,2	12°	287,6	12°	297,1	15°	298,4	14°
23.	R. Zonta	272,5	14°	272,5	11°	288,5	7°	294,1	1°	283,8	14°	289,4	6°	298,4	12°	302,6	3°

CLASSIFICATION & RETIREMENTS

Pos	Drivers	Team	Time
1.	Irvine	Ferrari	in 1h35'01"659
2.	Frentzen	Jordan Mugen Honda	at 1"026
3.	R. Schum.	Williams Supertec	at 7"012
4.	Fisichella	Benetton Playlife	at 33"418
5.	Barrichello	Stewart Ford	at 54"697
6.	de la Rosa	Arrows	at 84"316
7.	Takagi	Arrows	at 86"288
8.	M. Schum.	Ferrari	at 1 lap

Lap	Drivers	Team	Reason
1	Alesi	Sauber Petronas	transmission
1	Hill	Jordan Mugen Honda	off
14	Villeneuve	BAR Supertec	breakdown aerofoil
14	Coulthard	McLaren Mercedes	gearbox
21	Zanardi	Williams Supertec	off
22	Häkkinen	McLaren Mercedes	electronic
24	Panis	Prost Peugeot	crewless wheel
26	Trulli	Prost Peugeot	accident/Gené
26	Gené	Minardi Ford	off
28	Diniz	Sauber Petronas	gearbox
29	Wurz	Benetton Playlife	suspension
42	Badoer	Minardi Ford	off
49	Zonta	BAR Supertec	gearbox

FASTEST LAPS

	Drivers	Time	Lap
1.	M. Schum.	1'32"112	55
2.	Barrichello	1'32"894	29
3.	Häkkinen	1'33"309	9
4.	Frentzen	1'33"378	33
5.	R. Schum.	1'33"407	32
6.	Irvine	1'33"560	29
7.	Coulthard	1'33"603	9
8.	Fisichella	1'33"657	34
9.	Diniz	1'34"748	13
10.	Zonta	1'34"756	13
11.	Villeneuve	1'34"771	12
12.	Trulli	1'34"980	21
13.	de la Rosa	1'35"220	39
14.	Takagi	1'35"877	50
15.	Panis	1'35"910	13
16.	Wurz	1'36"068	20
17.	Badoer	1'37"073	29
18.	Zanardi	1'37"146	20
19.	Gené	1'37"454	20

LAP CHART

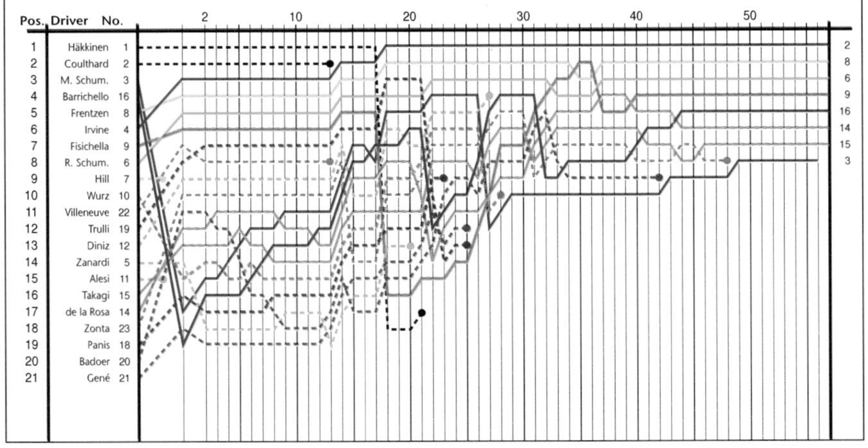

All results :
© 1999 Fédération Internationale de l'Automobile, 2 Ch. Blandonnet, 1215 Genève 15, Suisse

PIT STOPS

	Driver	Time	Lap	Stop n°
1.	Zanardi	23"512	13	1
2.	Diniz	24"711	15	1
3.	Zonta	34"918	15	1
4.	Badoer	46"637	15	1
5.	Fisichella	37"052	18	1
6.	Häkkinen	47"557	18	1
7.	Trulli	23"752	22	1
8.	Barrichello	25"027	22	1
9.	de la Rosa	23"919	22	1
10.	Gené	27"215	23	1
11.	Trulli	28"602	23	2
12.	Wurz	27"315	27	1
13.	M. Schumacher	41"287	27	1
14.	Barrichello	26"345	31	2
15.	Zonta	29"441	31	2
16.	Takagi	27"046	32	1
17.	Barrichello	26"335	32	3
18.	R. Schumacher	24"890	33	1
19.	Badoer	27"282	33	2
20.	Irvine	24"474	34	1
21.	Frentzen	24"630	34	1
22.	Fisechella	25"520	37	2
23.	M. Schumacher	11"371	37	2
24.	M. Schumacher	46"248	38	3
25.	de la Rosa	23"293	40	2
26.	Zonta	28"728	46	3

BRIDGESTONE

Quickest pit stop during the Australian Grand Prix, taking on fuel and four new Bridgestone tyres:

Pedro de la Rosa, Arrows, 23"293

CHAMPIONSHIP

(after one round)

Drivers :

1. Eddie IRVINE................................10
2. Heinz-Harald FRENTZEN.................6
3. R. SCHUMACHER............................4
4. Giancarlo FISICHELLA 3
5. Rubens BARRICHELLO.....................2
6. Pedro de la ROSA 1

Constructors :

1. Ferrari...10
2. Jordan Mugen Honda.....................6
3. Williams...4
4. Benetton Playlife............................3
5. Stewart Ford...................................2
6. Arrows..1

THE CIRCUIT

FIRST ROUND

QANTAS AUSTRALIAN GRAND PRIX, MELBOURNE

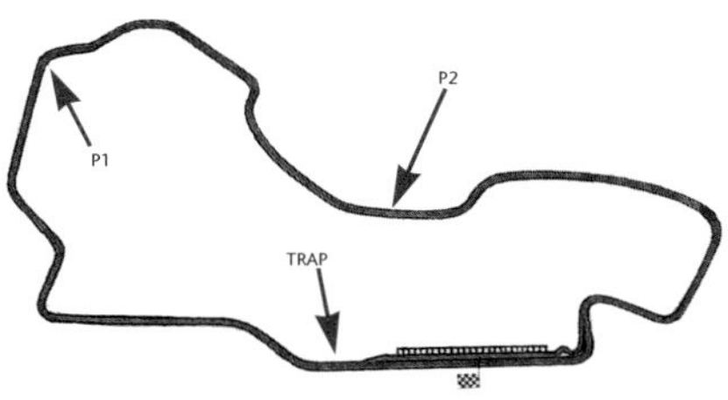

Date : March 7, 1999
Length : 5302 meters
Distance : 57 laps, 302.271 km
Weather : sunny, 19 °

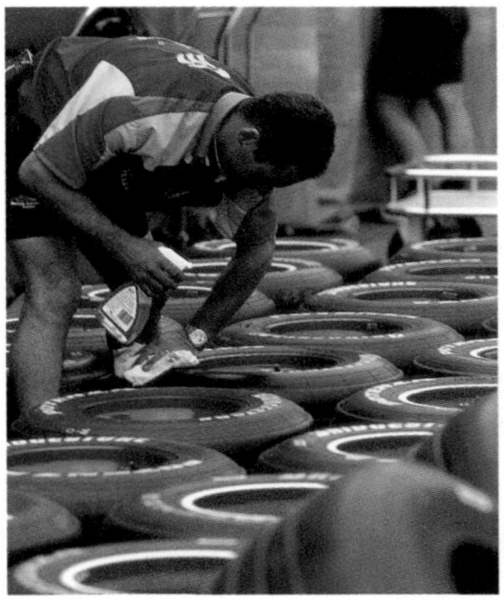

"Join up they said!" "You'll be doing delicate precision work they said!"
The life of a mechanic is not always as glamorous as one imagines.

RACE SUMMARY

- At the start, both Stewart-Fords catch fire on the grid. With just one spare, only Rubens Barrichello makes the re-start, behind the rest of the field. He has a brilliant race and finishes fifth despite a ten second penalty.
- At the first corner, Damon Hill goes off into the gravel and retires.
- Michael Schumacher fluffs the start and is swamped by the pack. The two McLarens clear off, with Mika Hakkinen out in front ahead of David Coulthard. Further back, Eddie Irvine leads Heinz-Harald Frentzen.
- On lap 14, Jacques Villeneuve's BAR loses its rear wing. The race is run behind the Safety Car until lap 17.
- One by one, both McLarens retire with gearbox problems. Eddie Irvine finds himself in the lead ahead of Heinz-Harald Frentzen, Ralf Schumacher and brother Michael.
- On lap 38, Michael Schumacher comes down the pit lane and goes out again without stopping. On the next lap he comes in for a new steering wheel. He finishes outside the points.

WEEKEND GOSSIP

• Schumi has no worries about his legs

Michael Schumacher fine tuned his physical condition by taking part in a friendly soccer match on Wednesday evening in Melbourne. "It was a bit strange," he observed. "Our opponents were so frightened of causing me an injury that they instantly moved out of my way when I had the ball. That meant I scored quite often, but it was not very interesting."

• Too sure of himself

Three drivers were making their F1 debut this season: the Brazilian Ricardo Zonta with BAR and the Spaniards, Pedro de la Rosa at Arrows and Marc Gene with Minardi. On the Friday, Gene explained, full of confidence, how easily he had adapted to Formula 1, adding he had only taken eight or nine laps to get the hang of the Melbourne track. He would have done better to keep quiet as he was the only driver who failed to qualify, as his best lap was over 107% of the pole time.

• What's this minus all about?

Suspense in the Arrows camp. On the cars in Melbourne was the message "T- 55." The number came down by one every day on the bodywork, in the garage and on the drivers' helmets. The "T" date corresponded to the Thursday prior to the San Marino Grand Prix. For the moment, it was a closely guarded secret at Arrows and even the mechanics did not know what it was all about. Rumours went around that it involved an announcement about an engine partner.

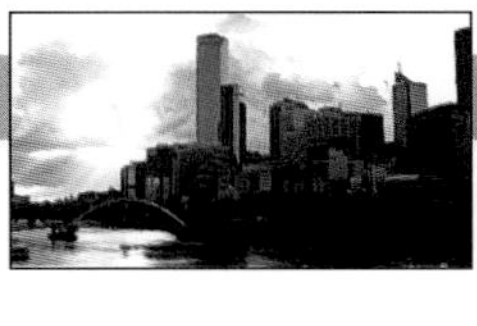

Mika, from a long way back

And there's one in the bag for Mika Hakkinen! But it had been a victory which could so easily have been a fiasco after events early on in the race. After the failure in Melbourne, the reliability problems of the MP4/14 had evidently not been solved. David Coulthard broke down on the grid and the Finn had his gearbox lock up briefly on lap four, which cost him two laps.

GRANDE PRÊMIO DO BRASIL
INTERLAGOS

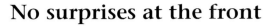

No surprises at the front

The front row at Interlagos was supremely predictable and the same as in Melbourne, with Mika Hakkinen ahead of David Coulthard.

However, the Finn was not completely happy with his car. *"We have tried all sorts of settings this weekend, which radically changed the car's handling and stopped me pushing to the limit. In fact, I never felt completely confident with the car until the very end of the session, when I was finally able to go quicker and quicker. But overall, being on pole is actually not too bad."*

His team-mate would have liked to have been able to say the same. Once again the Scotsman was no match for the Finn. However, he showed no signs of disappointment: *"Actually I am closer to Mika than I was last year on this circuit, so that is something."*

The disappointment continues

When the clocks stop at the end of the hour long qualifying session, there are always more malcontents than those who are satisfied. That was certainly the case with Michael Schumacher, only fourth on the grid and with Jacques Villeneuve at Interlagos.

While he had hoped to slightly close the gap to the McLarens, on Saturday, Michael Schumacher had to settle for fourth spot. *"To be honest, I did not expect to give away a whole second to the McLarens,"* said a surprised German. *"I thought we were going to be competitive from the start of the season and that is evidently not the case. We must carry on working at it."*

Ricardo Zonta's huge shunt

10h27 on Saturday morning. The second half of the session had only just begun when Ricardo Zonta's BAR suddenly flicked off line and crashed heavily into the barriers at Turn 6. There was no protective tyre barrier at this point on the circuit.

It was a very big accident. On this part of the track, the cars are doing 270 km/h and the damp grass did little to slow the Brazilian's progress. The driver's survival cell stood up well, the engine and gearbox were completely blown apart. Stunned and with severe pain in his left foot, Zonta was helicoptered to the Sao Paulo hospital.

At first the doctors reckoned he had a broken foot, but a second examination revealed that the Brazilian had no broken bones. However, he would not race a Formula 1 car again until the Canadian GP. He was replaced by Jacques Villeneuve's mate, Mika Salo, who drove at Imola, Monaco and in Spain.

Jacques Villeneuve's unhappy birthday

Nothing was going right for the BAR team during practice. After the first hour of practice on Friday morning, Jacques Villeneuve was credited with an unimpressive 19th place. Then in the afternoon, he did no running at all as there was a leak from the fuel cell, which proved difficult to repair. With the 1999 rules forbidding the use of the spare car on Friday, the Canadian wound up plum last.

This put him in a bit of tizzy - *"this is hell"* he told Canadian journalists, before heading off for his hotel before the session had even ended. More importantly, this meant he also missed out on the birthday cake the team had lovingly prepared to celebrate his 28th birthday that Friday; sadly the first day in his life that his name appeared on the bottom of a time sheet.

Things did not really improve on Saturday, the Canadian crawling up to 14th spot on the grid. "I lost a lot of time as I did not run much yesterday and so we missed out on set-up time," he complained. *"This morning, I had a problem with the fuel pump and again, I hardly went out on the track. On top of that, during qualifying I had problems with yellow flags at the end of the session. Everything has gone wrong this weekend and the car is desperately slow."*

"Rubinho" lights up Interlagos

"Vai fundo, Rubinho." The banners waved in the main grandstand at Interlagos that afternoon, recalling the joyous days of Brazilian motorsport when the object of the crowd's attention was a driver called Ayrton.

Since the death of the magician, the Paulistas (inhabitants of Sao Paulo) had lost their enthusiasm for the sport. The number of Brazilian journalists who followed the sport had fallen from thirty to .....two and the television viewing figures were in free-fall.

This year, it seemed that things were finally picking up again thanks to a young driver - he is only 26 -but already in his seventh season as a Formula 1 driver. Rubens Barrichello was born in Sao Paulo and his parents live oppo-

site the Interlagos circuit. Little *"Rubinho"* learned how to drive on the karting circuit which adjoins the home of the Brazilian Grand Prix. Up until now, driving first for Jordan and now for Stewart, he had done little to promote a passionate following among the crowd.

But after his Melbourne performance, when he qualified fourth and might have won the race, the ticket sales at Interlagos had gone into orbit. For the first time since the Senna era, the grand prix was a sell-out.

The crowd had already gone mad on Saturday, when *"Rubinho"* had snatched third place on the grid from Michael Schumacher.. *"Its true, the crowd was fantastic,"* admitted Barrichello

at the end of qualifying.«. *"I had told myself not to look at the grandstands during my last flying lap, but I couldn't help it. It was crazy seeing all these people cheering me on."*

The crowd did not affect the little Brazilian's concentration. *"I think today I drove the best lap of my career. I felt that way last year here, but then I was only 13th. That's all down to the difference between a good and a bad car."*

A win? Rubens Barrichello refused to discuss the possibility. *"We have to be realistic. I don't expect to win if the two McLarens are still on the track at the end of the race. But nothing is impossible and they could run into reliability problems. I hope to finish on the podium at least, which would be a great way of rounding off the weekend."*

Sao Paulo. Every year, the little world of Formula 1 arrives in the South American megalopolis with the same mix of fascination and revulsion. Nightmare traffic jams, pollution squalor and frightening poverty. Sao Paulo is a major shock after Melbourne.

▽

◁ *With the new ultra-compact engine produced by Ford for 1999, the Stewarts were transformed. After finishing fourth in Melbourne, "Rubinho" qualified third at home.*

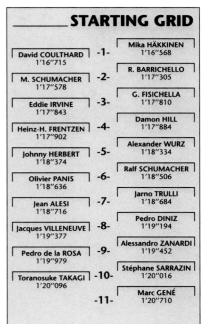

STARTING GRID

David COULTHARD 1'16"715	**-1-**	Mika HÄKKINEN 1'16"568
M. SCHUMACHER 1'17"578	**-2-**	R. BARRICHELLO 1'17"305
Eddie IRVINE 1'17"843	**-3-**	G. FISICHELLA 1'17"810
Heinz-H. FRENTZEN 1'17"902	**-4-**	Damon HILL 1'17"884
Johnny HERBERT 1'18"374	**-5-**	Alexander WURZ 1'18"334
Olivier PANIS 1'18"636	**-6-**	Ralf SCHUMACHER 1'18"506
Jean ALESI 1'18"716	**-7-**	Jarno TRULLI 1'18"684
Jacques VILLENEUVE 1'19"377	**-8-**	Pedro DINIZ 1'19"194
Pedro de la ROSA 1'19"979	**-9-**	Alessandro ZANARDI 1'19"452
Toranosuke TAKAGI 1'20"096	**-10-**	Stéphane SARRAZIN 1'20"016
	-11-	Marc GENÉ 1'20"710

A back-lit shot of Pedro Diniz. At Interlagos, the Brazilian was hoping for a good result in front of his fans and family. However, his race ended in a coming together with Toranosuke Takagi's Arrows on lap 44. Hence his black look as he walks back to the pits.

QANTAS AUSTRALIAN GRAND PRIX

Mika cracks, Michael wins

Mind you, the German would never have won if Mika Hakkinen had not made an error which sent his McLaren slamming into a concrete wall early in the race, when he was comfortably in the lead. From that moment on, all he could do was watch his team-mate David Coulthard fight it out with Michael Schumacher's Ferrari (photo.)

GRAN PREMIO WARSTEINER DI SAN MARINO
IMOLA

The three fastest qualifiers were covered by just two tenths

△ Missed again! David Coulthard misses out on pole by only 22 thousandths of a second.

Mika Salo replaced Ricardo Zonta injured in Brazil, in the BAR. ▽

Mika, David and Michael in the same breath

It really does seem as though David Coulthard is fated to be Mika Hakkinen's second. On Saturday, at Imola, a circuit which he admits to liking, where he won from pole position last year, the Scotsman lost out to the reigning world champion by just 22 thousandths of a second. That equates to 1.25 metres at the end of a lap which measures over 5 kilometres. *"I really enjoy driving here,"* explained David Coulthard. *"And today I felt right in the car. I had total confidence in it and I knew I was capable of getting pole. But bit by bit, I felt pole position slipping away from me."*

In the end, it was once again Mika Hakkinen who would start from pole position. *"This was a fantastic day for me,"* commented the Finn. *"The times are very close, it was very tense, but it all went alright in the end. It is an amazing feeling."*

Schumacher felt out of it

In third place, Michael Schumacher did not share that feeling. Despite four attempts, all to the accompaniment of the cheers from the partisan crowd at the Autodromo Dino e Enzo Ferrari, the German could not get his Ferrari round quicker than the two McLarens. But he came pretty close, as less than two tenths of a second separated his time from that of Mika Hakkinen.

That was the key point of the session as far as the German was concerned. *"After the Brazilian Grand Prix, I was frustrated to find that the gap to McLaren was still very big. I did not feel we were on the pace, but today I am quite satisfied. Such a small gap makes me quite optimistic, especially as two tenths is almost nothing and it is very difficult to do a 100% perfect lap on this circuit. I think if I had not made a small mistake on my final run, I could have got pole."*

Ferrari had traditionally gone better at Imola than just about anywhere else, so this return to form might not be seen again elsewhere. *"I don't see why we should be more competitive here,"* replied Michael Schumacher. *"We have done a lot of work since Brazil and we have some new parts which improve our performance. The car should also be more competitive on other circuits."*

STARTING GRID

David COULTHARD 1'26"384	-1-	Mika HÄKKINEN 1'26"362
Eddie IRVINE 1'26"993	-2-	M. SCHUMACHER 1'26"538
R. BARRICHELLO 1'27"409	-3-	Jacques VILLENEUVE 1'27"313
Damon HILL 1'27"708	-4-	Heinz.-H. FRENTZEN 1'27"613
Alessandro ZANARDI 1'28"142	-5-	R. SCHUMACHER 1'27"770
Johnny HERBERT 1'28"246	-6-	Olivier PANIS 1'28"205
Jarno TRULLI 1'28"403	-7-	Jean ALESI 1'28"253
G. FISICHELLA 1'28"750	-8-	Pedro DINIZ 1'28"599
Pedro de la ROSA 1'29"293	-9-	Alexander WURZ 1'28"765
Toranosuke TAKAGI 1'29"656	-10-	Mika SALO 1'29"451
Luca BADOER 1'30"945	-11-	Marc GENÉ 1'30"035

△ *"Someone could have told me it turned right here!"* Toranosuke Takagi in a spot of bother during practice. As Arrows team boss Tom Walkinshaw was keen to explain, the Japanese driver is very quick in the corners. Sometimes a touch too quick.

A historic victory for Ferrari on home soil.

Schumi shows 'em and Imola goes wild

16 years! For 16 years, the tifosi have been coming back to Imola hoping to see a red car win the San Marino Grand Prix. The last Ferrari victory dated back to 1983 when Patrick Tambay took the flag at the wheel of a 126C2 Turbo. The tifosi may have aged in that time, but their enthusiasm is as strong as ever. That at least is the conclusion one could draw from the mood of total delirium which welcomed Michael Schumacher after he won. He made a point of acknowledging their support with a very slow lap of honour. *"I really enjoyed that lap. I took the time to look at people's faces and to wave at them. After so many years without a win, their expressions were amazing."*
The win was all the more deserved as it had been far from predictable. On paper, McLaren

was stronger than Ferrari on this circuit and Michael owed this win to his talent and a daring race strategy. *"We wanted to be in a position to decide on strategy depending on how the race was going and we had several options planned. It was Ross (Brawn, the team's technical director) who decided what we should do. He decided to go for the extra stop and it was the right decision."*
It has to be said that at the start of the race Schumacher seemed totally powerless to stop Hakkinen flying away ahead of him. *"It seemed as though Mika had opted for a two stop strategy and so I did not want to push too hard. I was happy to keep a reasonable distance from David (Coulthard) and to wait for the right time."*
Once the Finn was out (see the Paddock section) the Ferrari strategists decided that the only

way to pass the Scotsman was to go for two stops. Taking less fuel on board would save time in the pit stop and allow for a greater pace with a lighter car. *"At the start of the race I was just looking after my tyres, but in the last thirty laps I was absolutely flat out. It was like doing 30 qualifying laps."*
It might have been a great win, but it was not enough to mask the evident superiority of the McLarens. Clever tactics would not be enough to win all the races for Ferrari. *"If I had only stopped once, I would not have won,"* admitted Schumacher. *"We took a risk and it paid off. But we have got closer to the McLarens. In qualifying, the gap was very small and it was the same in the race. That makes me optimistic for the rest of the season."*

△
First win of the season for Michael Schumacher. It could not have come at a better time. The fans had waited 16 years to see a Ferrari victory at Imola.

△
"I've wooooooon!" Michael Schumacher cannot contain his delight on the podium and risks falling off it on landing.

◁
A great shot. At Imola, the starting pack is always very photogenic. Here, the McLarens still seem to be in control. It will not last long.

GRAN PREMIO WARSTEINER DI SAN MARINO

Ralf Schumacher against the superb backdrop of Imola. The season had got off to rather a good start for the most famous little brother in F1. At least, unlike Heinz-Harald Frentzen the previous year, he felt totally at ease in the Williams camp.

GRAN PREMIO WARSTEINER DI SAN MARINO

McLaren makes mistakes

Everything had got off to a pretty good start for Mika Hakkinen at Imola. Having made the perfect start from pole, the Finn was flying along in front without a care in the world.

He was taking around a second a lap off his pursuers, led by team-mate David Coulthard. Hakkinen had the race in the palm of his hand when he went straight into the concrete wall at the start of lap 18. It was quite simply down to driver error. The back end of his car stepped slightly out of line, but there was no bringing it back. "I made a mistake. It's as silly as that," he said once back in the garage, without going into great detail.

Now McLaren was down to one man and David Coulthard had a four second lead over Michael Schumacher. He was at the wheel of the better car which should have allowed him to win the San Marino Grand Prix. However, he only finished second having been caught out by a surprising strategy from Scuderia Ferrari.

Coulthard blames backmarkers
This failure meant he did not look in the best of moods on the podium. "I should have won here," admitted the Scotsman after the race. "And I would have won if I had not lost so much time behind the backmarkers."

Coulthard had decided to lay all the blame fairly and squarely at the feet of these famous backmarkers, even though Michael Schumacher had also had to get past them. The German just swallowed them up, while the Scotsman was often timid in his approach, losing up to six seconds behind Olivier Panis. "My car was not perfect, but it was good enough to win," he continued. "I thought there was a rule stating that a driver must move over if he has been shown the blue flags, but it seems some drivers ignore the flags and just drive their own race. There is nothing wrong with my car or my driving and yet I haven't won." In short, the driver was blameless apparently. One wonders who is the backmarker here.

The 100th in the points ..... and on the grass

What a driver! Apart from the demonstration put on by Michael Schumacher, the San Marino Grand Prix witnessed yet another Jean Alesi festival. Three pit stops, three off-track excursions into the gravel and a point for sixth place to round off the day. A performance which drew the following remark from Peter Sauber: "scoring points in F1 is getting tougher than finding strawberries at the North Pole," he said with his usual phlegmatic approach.

It seemed the French driver had chosen to look for the strawberries in the grass. "Yes, I did go off a few times," he conceded. "As I didn't feel I was quick enough on the track, I thought I might be quicker on the grass!"

Jean Alesi had himself chosen his three stop strategy. After the race, he admitted it might not have been the best choice. "When you start from thirteenth on the grid, you have to try something. But with hindsight, these three stops were not the way to go." They did however get a point for the Sauber team in its 100th grand prix.

Rubens Barrichello shows his class

Rubens Barrichello could have won in Australia, if his car had not caught fire on the grid. He could have won again in Brazil, where he led for several laps before retiring.

But Formula 1 does not recognise "ifs" and Stewart had yet to deliver any solid results. That came at Imola with Rubens Barrichello on the podium and close to tears. "It is a very emotional moment, because I really believe this race marks a turning point in my career. For the first time in my Formula 1 career, I am driving a competitive car. I can finally show what I can do. Of course we are not yet in a position to beat McLaren and Ferrari, but I am sure we can be the best of the rest. In order to ensure we finished the race today, we limited the engine revs so as not to take any risks. It was still enough to get on the podium. I think we are going to do some great things this season."

results

PRACTICE TIMES

No	Driver	Car/Engine/Chassis	Practice Friday	Pos.	Practice Saturday	Pos.	Qualifying	Pos.	Warm-up	Pos.
1.	Mika Häkkinen	McLaren/Mercedes/MP4 -14/5	1'28"467	1°	1'26"750	2°	1'26"362	1°	1'28"838	3°
2.	David Coulthard	McLaren/Mercedes/MP4 -14/4	1'28"605	2°	1'26"509	1°	1'26"384	2°	1'28"642	1°
3.	Michael Schumacher	Ferrari/Ferrari/F399/193	1'29"534	5°	1'26"834	3°	1'26"538	3°	1'29"084	4°
4.	Eddie Irvine	Ferrari/Ferrari/F399/191	1'29"046	3°	1'27"193	4°	1'26"993	4°	1'28"749	2°
5.	Alessandro Zanardi	Williams/Supertec/FW21/02	1'29"614	6°	1'28"364	10°	1'28"142	10°	1'30"967	20°
6.	Ralf Schumacher	Williams/Supertec/FW21/04	1'29"630	7°	1'27"986	7°	1'27"770	9°	1'30"410	17°
7.	Damon Hill	Jordan/Mugen-Honda/199/4	1'29"452	4°	1'28"209	9°	1'27"708	8°	1'29"596	6°
8.	Heinz-Harald Frentzen	Jordan/Mugen-Honda/199/5	1'30"991	17°	1'28"196	8°	1'27"613	7°	1'29"683	8°
9.	Giancarlo Fisichella	Benetton/Playlife/B199/06	1'30"854	16°	1'28"569	15°	1'28"750	16°	1'30"303	16°
10.	Alexander Wurz	Benetton/Playlife/B199/05	1'30"830	15°	1'28"565	14°	1'28"765	17°	1'30"023	12°
11.	Jean Alesi	Sauber/Petronas/C18/05	1'30"182	11°	1'28"468	13°	1'28"253	13°	1'30"145	14°
12.	Pedro Diniz	Sauber/Petronas/C18/04	1'30"482	13°	1'28"447	12°	1'28"599	15°	1'29"703	9°
14.	Pedro de la Rosa	Arrows/Arrows/A20/07	1'31"257	19°	1'29"762	20°	1'29"293	18°	1'30"806	18°
15.	Toranosuke Takagi	Arrows/Arrows/A20/04	1'31"557	21°	1'29"300	19°	1'29"656	20°	1'30"904	19°
16.	Rubens Barrichello	Stewart/Ford/SF3/04	1'29"792	9°	1'27"429	5°	1'27"409	6°	1'30"191	15°
17.	Johnny Herbert	Stewart/Ford/SF3/05	1'31"046	18°	1'27"734	6°	1'28"246	12°	1'29"573	5°
18.	Olivier Panis	Prost/Peugeot/AP02/3	1'30"408	12°	1'28"956	18°	1'28"205	11°	1'30"036	13°
19.	Jarno Trulli	Prost/Peugeot/AP02/2	1'29"808	10°	1'28"405	11°	1'28"403	14°	1'29"615	7°
20.	Luca Badoer	Minardi/Ford/M01/01	1'31"547	20°	1'31"347	22°	1'30"945	22°	1'32"545	22°
21.	Marc Gené	Minardi/Ford/M01/04	1'33"529	22°	1'30"497	21°	1'30"035	21°	1'32"096	21°
22.	Jacques Villeneuve	BAR/Supertec/BAR01/3	1'29"765	8°	1'28"702	17°	1'27"313	5°	1'29"779	10°
23.	Mika Salo	BAR/Supertec/BAR01/2	1'30"569	14°	1'28"596	16°	1'29"451	19°	1'30"014	11°

MAXIMUM SPEEDS

No	Driver	P1 Qualifs	Pos	P1 Race	Pos	P2 Qualifs	Pos	P2 Race	Pos	Finish Qualifs	Pos	Finish Race	Pos	Trap Qualifs	Pos	Trap Race	Pos
1.	M. Häkkinen	294,1	2°	291,2	5°	224,2	2°	216,6	5°	173,0	6°	162,2	12°	303,2	1°	292,8	3°
2.	D. Coulthard	296,3	1°	295,2	1°	225,0	2°	219,6	1°	172,5	9°	160,9	17°	302,1	2°	293,3	2°
3.	M. Schum.	289,6	5°	292,8	4°	221,4	6°	216,1	7°	175,6	1°	163,4	7°	299,0	4°	295,8	1°
4.	E. Irvine	288,8	6°	289,5	6°	222,7	5°	215,2	10°	174,1	2°	162,9	10°	298,0	5°	290,0	8°
5.	A. Zanardi	282,5	17°	288,0	7°	217,3	15°	215,6	9°	171,6	14°	166,1	2°	290,2	18°	282,1	17°
6.	R. Schumacher	282,0	18°	280,2	18°	216,6	17°	211,1	17°	171,1	17°	161,7	16°	290,6	16°	286,1	12°
7.	D. Hill	291,7	4°	293,7	3°	219,9	8°	217,5	3°	174,1	4°	166,2	1°	294,1	10°	288,2	11°
8.	H.-H. Frentzen	292,4	3°	294,4	2°	221,0	7°	217,3	4°	172,6	8°	161,8	15°	299,8	3°	292,5	5°
9.	G. Fisichella	283,6	16°	284,2	14°	217,5	14°	212,7	14°	171,1	16°	162,9	9°	293,0	13°	290,2	7°
10.	A. Wurz	285,1	13°	279,2	19°	218,4	13°	208,6	19°	174,1	3°	159,1	19°	289,9	19°	265,5	20°
11.	J. Alesi	285,1	12°	286,1	10°	219,7	10°	216,0	8°	171,8	12°	162,9	8°	295,6	7°	292,7	4°
12.	P. Diniz	287,3	9°	285,7	11°	219,2	11°	215,1	11°	169,5	19°	164,1	5°	293,0	11°	288,3	10°
14.	P. de la Rosa	281,7	21°	280,6	16°	217,1	16°	211,2	16°	171,9	11°	164,7	4°	293,0	12°	267,7	19°
15.	T. Takagi	281,9	19°	283,0	15°	215,6	19°	211,6	15°	171,7	13°	165,7	3°	290,9	15°	290,2	6°
16.	R. Barrichello	286,4	10°	287,3	8°	223,1	4°	218,0	2°	172,2	10°	162,6	11°	297,1	6°	286,0	13°
17.	J. Herbert	287,6	7°	286,6	9°	223,5	3°	216,3	6°	171,4	15°	162,0	13°	294,9	9°	285,3	15°
18.	O. Panis	287,4	8°	285,4	12°	218,5	12°	214,2	12°	170,8	18°	163,9	6°	295,0	8°	289,2	9°
19.	J. Trulli	284,8	14°	NQ	-	216,3	18°	NQ	-	172,8	7°	NQ	-	290,2	17°	NQ	-
20.	L. Badoer	281,8	20°	278,5	20°	210,7	22°	208,0	20°	165,0	22°	159,5	18°	289,2	22°	285,4	14°
21.	M. Gené	280,2	22°	280,6	17°	210,8	21°	209,0	18°	166,6	21°	156,8	20°	289,4	21°	283,0	16°
22.	J. Villeneuve	285,7	11°	NQ	-	219,8	9°	NQ	-	174,0	5°	NQ	-	291,8	14°	NQ	-
23.	M. Salo	283,6	15°	285,4	13°	215,5	20°	212,8	13°	167,8	20°	161,8	14°	289,6	20°	280,6	18°

CLASSIFICATION & RETIREMENTS

Pos	Drivers	Team	Time
1.	M. Schum.	Ferrari	in 1h33'44"792
2.	Coulthard	McLaren Mercedes	at 4"265
3.	Barrichello	Stewart Ford	at 1 lap
4.	Hill	Jordan Mugen Honda	at 1 lap
5.	Fisichella	Benetton Playlife	at 1 lap
6.	Alesi	Sauber Petronas	at 1 lap
7.	Badoer	Minardi Ford	at 3 laps
8.	Gené	Minardi Ford	at 3 laps

Lap	Drivers	Team	Reason
1	Villeneuve	BAR Supertec	gearbox
1	Trulli	Prost Peugeot	accident
6	Wurz	Benetton Playlife	accident
6	de la Rosa	Arrows	accident
18	Häkkinen	McLaren Mercedes	accident
29	R. Schum.	Williams Supertec	engine
30	Takagi	Arrows	hydraulics
47	Frentzen	Jordan Mugen Honda	spin
47	Irvine	Ferrari	engine
49	Panis	Prost Peugeot	engine
50	Diniz	Sauber Petronas	spin
59	Zanardi	Williams Supertec	spin
59	Herbert	Stewart Ford	engine

FASTEST LAPS

	Drivers	Time	Lap
1.	M. Schum.	1'28"547	45
2.	Häkkinen	1'29"145	15
3.	Coulthard	1'29"199	52
4.	Irvine	1'29"726	45
5.	Panis	1'30"081	28
6.	Hill	1'30"140	37
7.	Frentzen	1'30"229	46
8.	Zanardi	1'30"254	55
9.	Alesi	1'30"442	39
10.	Barrichello	1'30"564	21
11.	R. Schum.	1'30"737	22
12.	Diniz	1'30"908	24
13.	Fisichella	1'30"977	33
14.	Salo	1'31"007	44
15.	Herbert	1'31"238	24
16.	Takagi	1'31"587	29
17.	Badoer	1'32"851	35
18.	Gené	1'33"175	38
19.	de la Rosa	1'33"328	3
20.	Wurz	1'33"337	3

All results :
© 1999 Fédération Internationale de l'Automobile, 2, Ch. Blandonnet, 1215 Genève 15, Suisse

LAP CHART

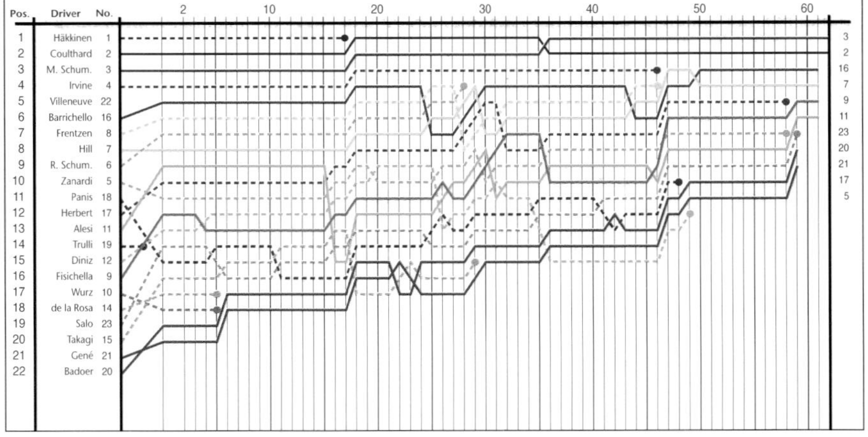

PIT STOPS

	Driver	Time	Lap	Stop n°
1.	Alesi	27"592	15	1
2.	Takagi	44"670	17	1
3.	Badoer	26"696	21	1
4.	Barrichello	26"368	24	1
5.	Takagi	26"934	23	2
6.	Gené	28"102	23	1
7.	Salo	27"599	24	1
8.	Diniz	29"834	25	1
9.	Panis	25"605	26	1
10.	Frentzen	25"181	27	1
11.	R. Schum.	26"007	28	1
12.	Irvine	25"237	29	1
13.	Hill	25"640	29	1
14.	Zanardi	25"406	29	1
15.	Alesi	25"879	30	2
16.	M. Schum.	23"922	31	1
17.	Herbert	30"613	31	1
18.	Coulthard	26"216	35	1
19.	Fisichella	28"793	35	1
20.	Diniz	3'09"684	35	2
21.	Panis	55"569	41	2
22.	Gené	25"865	41	2
23.	Diniz	26"956	40	3
24.	Barrichello	25"868	43	2
25.	Badoer	26"644	42	2
26.	M. Schum.	24"541	45	2
27.	Alesi	25"330	45	3
28.	Salo	26"048	45	2
29.	Zanardi	25"293	46	2
30.	Hill	24"360	49	2

BRIDGESTONE

Quickest pit stop during the Imola Grand Prix, taking on fuel and four new Bridgestone tyres:

Michael Schumacher, Ferrari, 23"922

CHAMPIONSHIP

(after three rounds)

Drivers :

1. M. Schumacher 16
2. E. Irvine 12
3. M. Häkkinen 10
   H.-H. Frentzen 10
5. R. Schumacher 7
6. D. Coulthard 6
   R. Barrichello 6
8. G. Fisichella 5
9. D. Hill 3
10. P. de la Rosa 1
    O. Panis 1
    J. Alesi 1

Constructors :

1. Ferrari 28
2. McLaren/Mercedes 16
3. Jordan/Mugen Honda 13
4. Williams/Supertec 7
5. Stewart/Ford 6
6. Benetton/Playlife 5
7. Arrows 1
   Prost/Peugeot 1
   Sauber/Petronas 1

THE CIRCUIT

THIRD ROUND

GRAN PREMIO WARSTEINER DI SAN MARINO, IMOLA

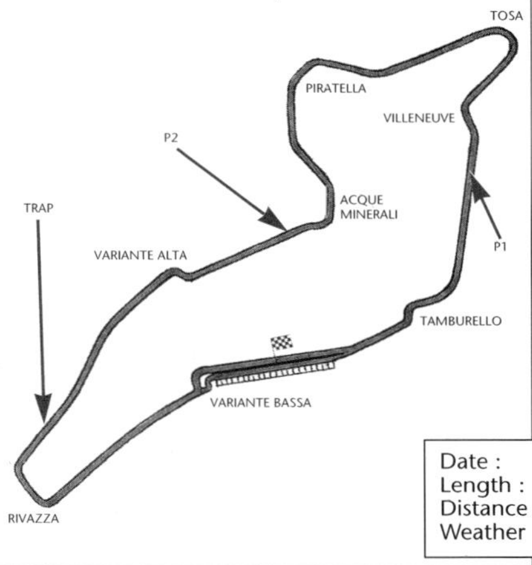

Date :	May 2, 1999
Length :	4927 meters
Distance :	62 laps, 305.428 km
Weather :	sunny, 22°

RACE SUMMARY

- At the start, Mika Hakkinen gets the better of David Coulthard and Michael Schumacher. Jacques Villeneuve is left stuck on the grid.
- By the end of the first lap, Hakkinen already has a 1.7 second lead over Coulthard. By the end of lap 17 he had stretched that lead to 12.4 seconds.
- On lap 18, Hakkinen crashes, Coulthard leads Michael Schumacher by 4.1 seconds.
- Schumacher closes in on Coulthard. On lap 30, the Ferrari is just 1.1 seconds behind the McLaren.
- Schumacher refuels on lap 31 in 6.2 seconds. Once back on the track he beats the lap record, while Coulthard remains stuck behind Panis. Ron Dennis asks Alain Prost to intervene.
- Lap 35 and Coulthard refuels in 9.2 seconds. He comes out of the pits behind the Ferrari. His race is lost.

WEEKEND GOSSIP

• Disappointment at Arrows

Although the Arrows team had made a song and dance about counting down the days on the cars, the drivers' helmets and in the pit garages (T-minus 55, 54 etc.) on the day, the Thursday before the race, it was all a bit of a damp squib. All that happened was the announcement of the "T-Minus" brand which would be affixed to high class consumer products. It was yet another mountain out of a molehill.

• Benettonland has landed

"From the days of the Pharaohs" is how the Italian daily paper "Corriere dello Sport" described the Benetton's new paddock hospitality unit. Less charitably it was also known as the "Bouncy Castle." The team had created a platform between its two motorhomes which was then closed in as one complete unit. With a castle-like entrance, the area contained every conceivable luxury available as the century came to a close: plasma TV screens, a bar area and ultra modern offices. Until now, the height of luxury was Ron's World, McLaren's double decker bus. Rumour had it that Ron Dennis was so jealous of the new arrival that he planned to close the entrance to his own vehicle with a portcullis and surround it with a moat filled with crocodiles.

• The death of Harvey Postlethwaite

Harvey Postlethwaite, the former Tyrrell engineer and technical director of the Honda F1 project died of a heart attack two weeks before the San Marino Grand Prix, while at a Barcelona test session. His death seemed to have prompted the Japanese company to finally announce its decision to withdraw plans to enter a complete Honda team, building both chassis and engine in 2000. Instead, it would settle for supplying engines to an existing team.

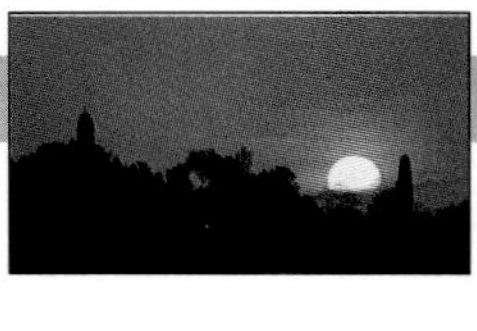

Schumacher cruises round the harbour

Only the greatest drivers win at Monaco. Ayrton Senna had won the Monegasque race six times, Graham Hill, father of Damon, five times and Alain Prost four.

In 1999, Michael Schumacher put his name on the trophy for the fourth time. He might have missed out on pole by a whisker, but nobody was allowed to challenge him in the race. Leading from start to finish, the German was simply peerless in the Principality.

With Eddie Irvine second, the Scuderia thus recorded its first one-two finish at the 46th attempt in Monaco.

GRAND PRIX DE MONACO
MONTE-CARLO

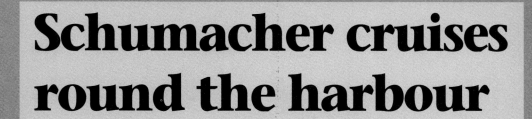

Ferrari lose pole after flag fall

Michael Schumacher flies along between the yachts and the grandstands. His efforts would be rewarded with a front row grid position.

It all went down to the wire. At the second when the stop watch called time on the qualifying session, the two Ferraris of Michael Schumacher and Eddie Irvine were still topping the time sheets. It looked as though the Scuderia had as good as clinched an all-red front row.

But at that point, Mika Hakkinen who had been trailing by six tenths of a second put in an outstanding lap to snatch pole by 64 tiny thousandths of a second.

At the same time, David Coulthard also found a clear track ahead of him and managed to get the other McLaren up to third on the grid.

It had been a costly final minute for Ferrari, who had been relegated to second and fourth spots.

As they walked back down the track from the pits to the paddock, the Scuderia's engineers looked stony faced and Michael Schumacher was not very happy either. *"It was a shame that I was held up by Pedro Diniz's Sauber on what would have been my quickest lap,"* commented the German. *"Especially as he had already slowed down and had plenty of room to move over."*

Schumacher in the spare

Michael Schumacher had a major moment in the morning's free practice session when he gave the guard rail at Ste. Devote a good whack. His race car was too badly damaged and he had to qualify in the spare car. *"The spare was not as good as my race car, but it was only a small difference."* All the same, it was enough to lose those vital 64 thousandths of a second which were to cost him pole position.

To put it bluntly, Schumi was in a bad mood on Saturday afternoon. *"No, I am not at all pleased to have lost pole. Having said that, the car worked well all week-end and I am confident for the race."*

Pedro Diniz pushing hard and sliding his Sauber-Petronas. Once again the Brazilian would demonstrate that he was a fair match for Jean Alesi in qualifying. He qualified 15th, just behind the Frenchman.

Obviously, Mika Hakkinen was delighted with his day's work in outfoxing his main championship rival. At one point it seemed as though the Finn was going to have his best time cancelled, having set it under yellow flags, but eventually, the Monegasque Stewards decided to let it stand. *"I clearly saw the yellow flag, but it was stationery and not waved, which means you just have to be careful. Yes I set my quickest time on that lap, but I showed that I had acknowledged the flag."* *"With Mika Hakkinen on pole and Michael Schumacher alongside him on the front row, the Monaco GP looked set to be a classic tussle-flag."* "itha Hakkinen on pole and Michael Schumacher alongside him on the front row, the Monaco GP looked set to be a classic tussle.

The Monaco paddock is still the place to meet the stars. This year Val Kilmer was one of many who escaped the Cannes Film Festival for a few hours to pose in the paddock.

Olivier Panis: early optimism proved founded

On Thursday, smiles were back on the agenda in the Prost team. In Brazil, Olivier Panis scored points for the first time in two years, having drawn a complete blank in 1998.

At Imola, two weeks prior to this race, he had managed to hang onto Giancarlo Fisichella's coat tails, before colliding with the Benetton. Then, on Thursday, on a track he is particularly fond of, having won in Monaco in 1996, the Frenchman was third quickest on the first day, which was no mean feat.

At the end of the day, enjoying a drink - non-alcoholic of course! - at the bar of the Beach Plaza Hotel, Olivier Panis was in optimistic mood. *"We did a really good job today. I took Alain's (Prost) advice and I started the day driving steadily, before attacking at the end of the ses-sion."* However, he did admit his car tended to understeer and that there was still a lot of work to do to get it right before Saturday's qualifying.

On Saturday, all that well founded enthusiasm frittered away. Olivier could do no better than eighteenth place, which was a major catastrophe on a track where overtaking is a risky business at the best of times. *"It was really bad luck,"* he moaned afterwards. *"I went straight on at Ste. Devote and the marshals pushed my car to move it out of the way. That was normal, because I was in a position that was very dangerous for the other cars. But the rules are merciless in this situation and my best time of the session was cancelled. It's a shame, because I think we could have got both cars into the top ten."*

Schumacher leads the first practice session

On the Wednesday prior to the grand prix, Michael Schumacher along with several other drivers took part in a charity football match organised by Prince Albert.

▽

New developments pay off for Ferrari

The spectacle is as mind-blowing as ever. Seeing and especially hearing the cars come out of the tunnel in a shower of sparks is still one of the most unforgettable and unique experiences of the season. To drive round Monaco with eight hundred horse-power under your right foot and at an average speed of 146 kilometres per hour (as did Michael Schumacher) owes more to the highwire repertoire than it does to racing. Thursday's practice times do not count for the grid, but watching trackside that afternoon, you could believe the entire outcome of the world championship depended on that day's times, given the level of commitment from the drivers. On Saturday however they would crank it up a notch, most of them knocking two to three full seconds off their previous best: the track would have picked up more sticky rubber off the tyres and the cars' settings would have improved.

Therefore, that first day only served to give a rough idea of the pecking order, which revealed that Ferrari was on top form on this circuit. *"The F399 are fitted with a new rear wing and various other aerodynamic modifica-*tions," explained Claudio Berro, the team's press officer. McLaren had not been idle either and there were various new bits on the MP4/14, most notably a new front wing. After a long duel with Mika Hakkinen, it was Michael Schumacher who stopped the clocks in the shortest space of time, despite a heavy crash in the morning. *"It was a bit frightening: a steering arm broke and I found myself in the middle of the corner with only one wheel turning,"* explained the German. *"But apart from that, it was great to be driving here in Monaco again."*

Heinz-Harald gets his finger stuck!

Heinz-Harald Frentzen had enjoyed a great start to the season and was lying fourth in the championship. He was still on form in Monaco as he qualified sixth.

However, the session was more action packed than he would have wished for. *"On my first run, I came up behind Pedro De La Rosa going very slowly on the racing line at the top of the climb to the Casino. He was doing at least 200 km/h less than me and I only just managed to avoid him. On my second run, I went over the kerb at the swimming pool and my car just took off. It was a miracle that I didn't hit anything. Then, at my third attempt, I got my finger stuck between the gear change paddle and the inside of the cockpit. That had never happened to me before and it stopped me from turning the wheel as much as I needed to get round the corner. That little incident must have cost me a few tenths."*

In the other Jordan, his team-mate Damon Hill did not have a good day, as the Englishman was only quick enough for 17th place on the grid.

"At least you can't get your finger stuck with a pen!" Heinz-Harald was pleased with the way qualifying had gone, even if the strange stuck finger incident had cost him a few tenths.

STARTING GRID

		Mika HÄKKINEN 1'20"547
M. SCHUMACHER 1'20"611	-1-	
		David COULTHARD 1'20"956
Eddie IRVINE 1'21"011	-2-	
		R. BARRICHELLO 1'21"530
Heinz-H. FRENTZEN 1'21"556	-3-	
		Jarno TRULLI 1'21"769
Jacques VILLENEUVE 1'21"827	-4-	
		G. FISICHELLA 1'21"938
Alexander WURZ 1'21"968	-5-	
		Alessandro ZANARDI 1'22"152
Mika SALO 1'22"241	-6-	
		Johnny HERBERT 1'23"333
Jean ALESI 1'22"354	-7-	
		Pedro DINIZ 1'22"659
R. SCHUMACHER 1'22"719	-8-	
		Damon HILL 1'22"832
Olivier PANIS 1'22"916	-9-	
		Toranosuke TAKAGI 1'23"290
Luca BADOER 1'23"765	-10-	
		Pedro de la ROSA 1'24"260
Marc GENÉ 1'24"914	-11-	

Ferrari scores a historic one - two

A race win in six photos. From top to bottom and left to right: an impeccable start (note the bird on the track). It would fly off just in time as the cars got to it; the solitary break, the total concentration needed to avoid the barriers; the lap of honour; the champagne and the podium. A perfect day.

Schumacher and Irvine are the Princes of Monaco

After Michael Schumacher had won two weeks earlier in Imola, the tifosi were on a roll and turned out in droves in Monaco.

The fans were not to be disappointed on the day as Ferrari managed to notch up a memorable one-two finish for the first time in 46 attempts in the Principality.

It was a total triumph after a faultlessly clean performance, which owed absolutely nothing to luck and was down t o the abilities of man and machine. Essentially, apart from the very last moments of qualifying on Saturday, Michael Schumacher had proved to be quicker than Mika Hakkinen throughout the weekend. Therefore it was no surprise that the German had the legs of the Finn in the race. *"We did expect to be quicker than the McLarens,"* confirmed Schumacher. *"It certainly helped that I got a good start. It was nice to be able to lead the race and pull away easily. We had planned that I would get away behind Mika, in which case we would have adopted a different strategy and even with that one, I think I would have been in with a chance of winning. But of course, it was much easier for me, getting away at the front of the field."*

Time to relax

Michael Schumacher ran a regal race, pulling away seemingly at will from the pursuing Mika Hakkinen, who was himself coming under pressure from the second Ferrari, driven by Eddie Irvine. The German though was under no pressure. *"I was very glad not to have had to push from start to finish,"* he continued. *"My neck still hurts from my accident on Saturday morning and it would have been tough to go flat out all the way. After the pit stop, I was even able to relax a bit."* In these cir-

cumstances the hardest thing to do is maintain concentration at the wheel. *"That's true, but I am used to racing out on my own. In that situation I try to control my own race and run at the pace I set myself."*

Thanks to this great win, Michael Schumacher was heading the world championship table with a comfortable 12 point lead over Mika Hakkinen. However, the German was not counting his championship chickens. *"Monaco is a special case and there are several circuits coming up which will not suit us so well. But it is good to come up to these races with a bit of a margin. It means you can drive within your limits rather than beyond them."* Prophetic words indeed!

Enthusiastic supporters, Luca di Montezemolo and Gianni Agnelli.

Would 1999 be Ferrari's year?

"This could be the gone one," said Gianni Agnelli, the honorary president of Fiat. He let slip this little hope at Monaco and it showed just how impatient the Ferrari bosses were for a taste of success.

The famous Scuderia had not won the drivers' world championship for twenty years; twenty years that the mighty Fiat group had demonstrated largesse with its cheque book towards the Italian team, in the hope of seeing it triumph. This time, as Agnelli was quick to point out, it had started rather well. The Scuderia had indeed won three of the season's first four races, whereas in the previous three seasons, the team had always been left for dead at the start, only to fight back later in the year.

The Scuderia bosses were keen to see this as some sort of sign. *"I said after the Australian Grand Prix that Eddie's win was a favourable omen for the rest of the season,"* Ferrari President Luca di Montezemolo was keen to remind us on Sunday. *"I don't think I was wrong. In Monaco we have lived through a perfect weekend. The strength of our team is its total understanding. You only had to look at how Schumacher and Irvine were with one another after the race."*

Villeneuve at home

It's lap 65 and the race is not yet over, but Jacques Villeneuve has already jumped on his Vespa and headed off through one of the tunnels under the rocks which leads to his home on the other side of the port. Once again, his race day ended ahead of schedule. It was the fourth time from four starts. The Canadian did his Mr. Sulky impersonation and could barely bring himself to exchange a few civil words with the small group of journalists from his native Quebec. *"We had gone for the extra soft tyres and it was the right choice,"* he said. *"I was actually lapping at the same pace as the leaders. Then, suddenly, as I came out of the tunnel, something broke. That was it. It's tough having to retire when you are pushing hard."*

Two Benettons in the points

This year, the Benettons appeared to be hurrying to go slowly. While both cars finished in the points in Monaco, it was thanks mainly to all the retirements further up the field.

Giancarlo Fisichella finished fifth, ahead of team mate Alexander Wurz, who thus scored his first point of the season. *"I had hoped to finish much better than fifth on this track,"* was Fisichella's less than delighted post race comment. *"This is my third points finish from four races, which proves we have reached a good level of reliability. And now we know what we must do to improve the car's performance. So I am quite optimistic for the rest of the season."* His optimism was to prove unfounded later in the year.

For Olivier Panis, no two Monaco Grands Prix are the same. In 1996, it was victory and glory. But in 1999, it was an anonymous retirement after a nondescript race. Yet another difficult year for the Prost team.

GRAND PRIX DE MONACO

Mika takes control again

The previous year, McLaren had swept all before it in the early part of the season, but this time they had been caught out by Ferrari who had won three out of four races.

In Barcelona, the silver arrows took control of the situation again with a one-two finish which relegated the red cars to the role of also-rans. In terms of outright speed, the Ferraris were not completely outclassed, but right from the start, the McLarens stamped their authority on the race. By the very first corner, Mika Hakkinen had already cleared off into the distance (photo.)

GRAN PREMIO MARLBORO DE ESPAÑA
BARCELONA

The German claims the McLarens start favourites

A 12 point lead but pessimistic

Michael Schumacher is well known for making pessimistic predictions before races he then goes on to win once Sunday comes. However, in Barcelona, the man who was happily leading the championship, did not seem to be crying wolf for once. He went as far as saying that the Montmelo track would be the most difficult of the season for Scuderia Ferrari. He did not know how prophetic were his words. *"It will be a tough weekend,"* was his prediction before first practice. *"Unfortunately, the new parts we should have had were not ready in time."*

According to the German, the characteristics of the circuit did not suit the F399. *"I could not tell you exactly what it is about this track which does not suit our car. It's probably a mixture of things. We are struggling on the aerodynamic front, and with a lack of mechanical grip and the engine is not right either. Add up all these little handicaps and you end up with a big one!"*

Hakkinen ahead of Irvine!?

Qualifying produced an unusual front row. With Eddie Irvine alongside Mika Hakkinen, the battle for the first corner promised to be hot. The Finn grabbed pole right at the last moment of the session, having been fifth for much of the hour. *"One quick lap at the end of the session is all it takes,"* quipped the Finn afterwards. *"In fact, it's thanks to David I'm here. This morning he did an incredible time and it was only thanks to his set-up that I was able to get pole this afternoon. The two of us work well together."*

Maybe David Coulthard should have kept his settings to himself, as he ended up down in third place. *"I tried to dial out the oversteer, but it didn't work and I ended up with more understeer."*

Sandwiched between the two McLarens was Eddie Irvine's Ferrari. *"It's great to be on the front row. It's fantastic and I hope to make the best start tomorrow and...win the race!"*

In the other Ferrari, Michael Schumacher was only fourth. *"My car was slower in qualifying than it had been in the morning session. We have to find out why."*

35 minutes of happiness

He was pumped up like in the old days was Jean Alesi. Hair a mess and dripping in sweat, on Saturday, the Frenchman was pleased with his work in qualifying. For a wonderful 35 minutes, his name stayed at the top of the time sheet and it was the best moment of his season so far. *"It was really fantastic,"* exclaimed back in the garage. *"My first lap was very good and it was a good feeling to see my name in first place. It is very easy to get the wrong set up on this circuit, but my car was perfectly balanced on the limit."*

With a quick lap in the bag, he savoured the moment from the pits. *"It was fun watching everyone trying to beat my time and missing out by a fraction. For a while I thought I could stay there, because the track was getting slower as time wore on."* In the end, Jean was fifth on the grid; his best performance of the season. *"Of course I'm happy. When the car is good, everything is great."*

STARTING GRID

		Mika HÄKKINEN 1'22"088
Eddie IRVINE 1'22"219	-1-	
		D. COULTHARD 1'22"244
M. SCHUMACHER 1'22"277	-2-	
		Jean ALESI 1'22"388
J. VILLENEUVE 1'22"703	-3-	
		R. BARRICHELLO 1'22"920
H.-H. FRENTZEN 1'22"938	-4-	
		Jarno TRULLI 1'23"194
R. SCHUMACHER 1'23"303	-5-	
		Damon HILL 1'23"317
Pedro DINIZ 1'23"331	-6-	
		G. FISICHELLA 1'23"333
J. HERBERT 1'23"505	-7-	
		Olivier PANIS 1'23"559
Mika SALO 1'23"683	-8-	
		A. ZANARDI 1'23"703
Alexander WURZ 1'23"824	-9-	
		P. de la ROSA 1'24"619
T. TAKAGI 1'25"280	-10-	
		Marc GENÉ 1'25"672
Luca BADOER 1'25"833	-11-	

The Finn chases the Reds

Mika halves the gap

McLaren-Mercedes team boss Ron Dennis was smiling again. In Barcelona, his drivers recorded their first one-two finish of the season, beating the Ferraris fair and square into the next two places.

Mika Hakkinen appeared to have had an easy time of it. Leading from the start, the Finn was never bothered, even though he finished only six seconds ahead of his team mate. *"That might have looked easy from the outside, but believe me it was not,"* said Hakkinen defensively in the post race press conference. *"It's true I had a big lead all race, but in these situations it is difficult to maintain concentration. You have to double your effort. But apart from that, the team did a really good job. The mechanics were perfect in the pit stops. I was able to pass the backmarkers quite easily because my car was faster in a straight line."* During the race, the speed trap at the end of the straight bore out that statement: Mika Hakkinen was credited with a top speed of 320.7 km/h while Michael Schumacher could "only" manage 307.4 km/h.

At the start of the race, the Ferrari driver found himself stuck behind Jacques Villeneuve. But, by lap 25, when he finally disposed of the Canadian, the German started to close on second placed Coulthard. In the space of 17 laps the Ferrari driver reduced the gap to the Scotsman from eighteen seconds to under one second! *"It was not a very comfortable time,"* admitted David Coulthard after the race.

"I realised right from the start that my car was not very well balanced and was oversteering. I told the team over the radio and the mechanics changed the tyre pressures on the set which they fitted at my first stop. But that made matters even worse as the car now started to understeer. I could not pull away from Michael and I lost at least a second each time we came up behind a group of backmarkers."

In the end, the McLarens managed to hang onto the first two places and that meant they now led Ferrari by nine points in the Constructors's championship. As for Hakkinen, he closed down the gap to Schumacher to just six points.

△ *Lightning pit stop for Mika Hakkinen. The Finn led from start to finish, apart from a handful of laps when he made his two pit stops.*

A doubtful Michael Schumacher (here with his engineer Ignazio Lunetta.) Nevertheless, his third place in Barcelona was not a bad sign.

▽

The McLaren was hard to drive

Despite winning in Barcelona, the McLaren team felt an unwelcome wind of change. It was clear that Michael Schumacher might well have won here, if he had not been delayed for a long time by Jacques Villeneuve. The German reinforced that impression by setting the race fastest lap.

The anxiety that was creeping into the McLaren camp could be detected in Mika Hakkinen's comments after the Spanish Grand Prix, as they did not sound like the words of a winner. *"The fact is that our car is very difficult to drive,"* confessed the Finn. *"It is still a long way off showing its true potential. We still have some work to do. Our engineers are working hard on this, spending a lot of time studying the telemetry data. Both the chassis and engine could be a lot better."*

Up until now, Mika Hakkinen had always said he was happy with his car. But now the Finn was even sounding doubtful about the team's ability to make the necessary step forward. *"I think we will manage to improve the car. Even if it takes time, we will do it. But we will have to wait and see when."*

Stunned by the unexpected competitiveness of the Ferrari, the McLaren clan's confidence had taken a battering, even though it had just recorded a one-two finish.

Mika comes out on top

Qualifying had not gone very well for him, as Michael Schumacher had taken pole for the first time this season.
But Mika Hakkinen made up for it in the race. While his rival crashed out, the Finn took a faultless victory, which put him back into the lead of the world championship.
Enough to put him in great good humour as he stepped out of the car (photo) after an action packed race.

GRAND PRIX AIR CANADA
MONTRÉAL

First pole of the season for the Ferrari driver

Michael's first

Less than three hundredths of a second. That was the whisper of a gap which separated Michael Schumacher from Mika Hakkinen at the end of the qualifying session for the Canadian Grand Prix. It was also a fair reflection of the parity of performance between the red racers and the silver arrows at this point in the season. The two rivals were pretty evenly matched. Michael Schumacher was happy to have recorded his first pole position of the season. *"Finally, our first pole. It is great for the whole team,"* he commented. *"I must admit, I hoped we might do it because the car has always gone well here. I must thank Eddie for having done a good development job last week when I was on holiday. It's a shame he couldn't do better today as it would have been nice to see two red cars on the front row."*

As for the race, the German felt he could contain the McLarens, but it had nothing to do with the new 048B engine which the Scuderia was using for the first time here. *"We will not use the new engine in the race,"* he confir-med. *"But anyway, it is only marginally better than the standard one. In fact, I am sure we could have done the same times with the normal 048."*

Eddie gets it wrong
Eddie Irvine had qualified third in the other Ferrari after being chased off the front row by Mika Hakkinen's McLaren in the last minutes of the session. *"Of course I am disappointed,"* admitted the Irishman. *"I made a mistake. I was keeping a little something back for my last lap but that's when my old friend Jean Alesi decided to stop. The yellow flags came out and I had to lift off. It's a shame, because it would have been great to keep Mika behind me."*

Naturally enough, Mika Hakkinen was happy to have got himself up between the two Ferraris. *"I am satisfied, because my car is now well set up for this circuit, which was not the case this morning. The hardest thing now, will be to finish the race. It is a very demanding track for engines and brakes."*

Jacques Villeneuve lowers his sights but is still wide of the mark

To many people Jacques Villeneuve seemed rather more subdued than usual. In a press conference held the Tuesday before the race, for the benefit of local media in downtown Montreal, the 1997 world champion no longer spoke of winning. This year he was under pressure simply to finish the Canadian Grand Prix. Up to this point in the 1999 season, he had started in five grands prix and failed to finish a single one. *"In 1997 and 1998 I failed to finish the Canadian Grand Prix. This year I want to do all I can not to disappoint anyone, because in my opinion this is a very important race. I would really like to score my first points here. The difference compared to previous years is that I have nothing to lose and that means I can attack to the maximum."* Unfortunately it all got off to a bad start and the qualifying session was a complete disaster for the BAR team. The man from Quebec could do no better than get himself onto the eighth row of the grid. Jacques was in the mire at home.

He complained that the car was not fast enough in a straight line and that it was badly balanced. For the BAR team, this awful qualifying performance, only just ahead of the Arrows and Minardis could not have come at a worse time. The team was looking for some extra funding and was canvassing several companies from North America. This was not the sort of qualifying which would get the cheque books out.

Having been replaced for three grands prix by Mika Salo, Ricardo Zonta was back at the wheel in Montreal. His enforced holiday did not result in miracles and he lined up 17th on the grid, just behind his Canadian team mate.

The circuit is located on the Ile Notre Dame, a man made island in the middle of a breathtaking waterway.

STARTING GRID

Mika HÄKKINEN 1'19"327	-1-	M. SCHUMACHER 1'19"298	
David COULTHARD 1'19"729	-2-	Eddie IRVINE 1'19"440	
Heinz-H. FRENTZEN 1'20"158	-3-	R. BARRICHELLO 1'19"930	
Jean ALESI 1'20"459	-4-	G. FISICHELLA 1'20"378	
Johnny HERBERT 1'20"829	-5-	Jarno TRULLI 1'20"557	
Alessandro ZANARDI 1'21"076	-6-	Alexander WURZ 1'21"000	
Damon HILL 1'21"094	-7-	Ralf SCHUMACHER 1'21"081	
Jacques VILLENEUVE 1'21"302	-8-	Olivier PANIS 1'21"252	
Pedro DINIZ 1'21"571	-9-	Ricardo ZONTA 1'21"467	
Pedro de la ROSA 1'22"613	-10-	Toranosuke TAKAGI 1'21"693	
Marc GENÉ 1'23"387	-11-	Luca BADOER 1'22"808	

Hakkinen avoids all the traps

Four times he was called out! Oliver Gavin the safety car driver was kept very busy during the Canadian Grand Prix. Once again, the unique layout of the Ile Notre Dame track provided a grand prix full of incident from start to finish.

When the red lights went out, it was ironic that the traditional first lap crash should yet again involve Jarno Trulli and Jean Alesi. Just as in 1998, the Italian's Prost harpooned the Frenchman's Sauber when the race was just 300 metres old (see below.)

At the head of the field, Michael Schumacher preceded Mika Hakkinen with their two respective team mates, Eddie Irvine and David Coulthard right behind. The race might have got a bit boring at this stage, except that Michael Schumacher crashed on lap 30.

For Mika Hakkinen, who was now left comfortably in the lead, the German's mistake was a gift from heaven. Never put under any pressure after this, he won the race as he pleased, thus regaining the lead of the championship. He was delighted. *"I am really very happy,"* he enthused as he came off the podium. *"It really was an excellent race."*

Excellent also for the Finn, was the way his competitor was eliminated, which was very similar to the accident that had accounted for Hakkinen in the San Marino Grand Prix, when he slammed into the wall while leading. *"It did remind me of my incident in Imola,"* he admitted. *"When I saw Michael in the wall, I thought ....mmm, that's racing,"* he laughed. *"In San*

Mika Hakkinen, Giancarlo Fisichella and Eddie Irvine made up an unusual threesome on the podium.

Marino our car was very difficult to drive. Here it went better and it now seems the Ferrari is trickier to drive."

Thanks to his win, Hakkinen was now leading the world championship again with a four point lead over Michael Schumacher. *"I did the right thing taking it easy in this race,"* concluded the Finn. *"There are always accidents on this track. I had decided not to take any risks and that was the right choice."*

Another coming together for Jean Alesi and Jarno Trulli

A case of Jean The Unlucky

Just before the start, Jean Alesi had told a reporter from the French TV station TF1 that he was worried about the first corner. Starting from the fourth row, he said he was most concerned about Jarno Trulli who was starting right behind him. He had even been over to warn the young Italian not to confuse the race with a qualifying session.

However, what will be will be: after 300 metres, Jarno Trulli's Prost tangled with Rubens Barrichello's Stewart and just as in 1997... Jean Alesi in the Sauber.

The Frenchman was forced to retire and got into a bit of a strop. *"What can I say?"* he barked before saying a lot: *"In the past there was no rule about this. Drivers could zig-zag as much as they liked and do anything. But today there is*

a commission set up to watch our behaviour. I don't know what happened with Trulli before he hit me and to be honest, I don't care. As far as I can see he does pretty much the same thing at every start and I think the time has come to heavily penalise drivers who behave like this."

Rubens Barrichello was equally forthright. *"What Jarno tried to do is terribly dangerous. When he hit my car, it was a big knock. It even took part of my helmet off!"*

In his defence, Trulli claimed the cause of the accident was none other than Heinz-Harald Frentzen. *"I had decided to take it easy at the start, but Heinz- Harald braked hard in front of me and I spun."*

Summoned before the stewards after the race, the Italian was actually absolved of all blame.

Eddie's mad afternoon

Eddie Irvine had a pretty crazy afternoon in Montreal. Overtaking moves, a spin, the odd trip onto the grass, a huge slide all eventually led to a third place finish. Despite his adventures he was still in the best of moods. *"To be honest, I think this was the best car I have ever driven in F1,"* he said.

Thanks to his on-form Ferrari he was able to pick off Johnny Herbert, Pedro Diniz and Ralf Schumacher one at a time in the closing stages of the race. *"Everything went well until David Coulthard hit me from behind. But its good to cause a bit of controversy in F1,"* was his ironic slant on the incident.

(left) *"I think I've got it a bit wrong!"* Jarno Trulli in trouble on the grass at the first corner. It is a classic accident scenario at this track that a driver who goes off on the grass inevitably runs back into the pack as it cuts across his trajectory.

Michael Schumacher in light and shade. The German's Canadian Grand Prix summed up in this half light photo. While he qualified on pole for the first time this season, the Ferrari driver ruined his chances with a rare error in the race. Mika Hakkinen did not have to be asked twice to make the most of it.

GRAND PRIX AIR CANADA

GRAND PRIX AIR CANADA

paddock

Three world champions went off at the same place

Johnny Herbert's drive to fifth place saw the Briton score points for the first time this season.

Heinz-Harald Frentzen should have finished second, but for a terrible accident three laps from the chequered flag.

Welcome to the wall

"Welcome to Quebec." The local tourist board's slogan was writ large on the concrete wall lining the outside of the final chicane on the track. Several drivers of note felt the urge to bury their cars and race hopes into the sign, giving the safety car plenty to do in the race. Jacques Villeneuve's team-mate Ricardo Zonta was the first to have a close look at the Fleur de Lys emblem on lap three. Twelve laps later, it was Damon Hill's turn, then it was Michael Schumacher who tried it while leading the race and finally local boy Jacques Villeneuve

completed the performance. *"It was my fault,"* he admitted unabashed. *"I just came into the corner too quickly. There was a lot of dust at that point and I went straight on."*
For Michael Schumacher, the incident had more serious consequences, as he had been leading the Canadian Grand Prix with panache up until that point. *"I was off line and my tyres picked up some dirt. It was entirely my fault,"* admitted the Ferrari driver. *"Usually, I make one mistake per season. Let's hope this is the last one of the year!"*

A hard knock for "HH"

Three laps from the end of the 1999 Canadian Grand Prix, Heinz-Harald Frentzen suffered the biggest accident of the race. The Montreal circuit is the toughest of the season on the brakes. The brake discs used are always the biggest allowed by the regulations, but even so they can become dangerously worn by the end of the event, although breakages are extremely rare. However, Heinz-Harald Frentzen did experience a failure as his right front brake disc exploded as he approached the first chicane, where the cars usually have to brake from over 250 km/h.
The lateral impact was very heavy. Stunned and with an injured left leg, he was transported by helicopter to the Sacre Coeur hospital in Montreal. FIA's chief medic, Professor Syd Watkins declared the German driver was okay. *"Heinz was conscious and he did not take long to get his sense of humour back,"* said Watkins when he returned to the track. *"He has some pain in his left leg and right shoulder, but there's nothing broken."* The German would be fit enough to race in France a fortnight later, but a more thorough examination later revealed he had cracked bones in both knees.

Yet another points finish for Ralf Schumacher. While his team-mate Alessandro Zanardi accumulated mechanical problems, the German was building a brilliant finishing record in the early part of the season.

Fisico is a fan of Montreal

He finished third in 1997, second in 1998 and second once again this year. The Montreal circuit certainly seemed to suit Giancarlo Fisichella.
"I am really very happy," enthused the Roman racer afterwards. *"Before the start, my aim was to score a few points. I did not expect to be on the podium."*
After an unremittingly unsuccessful start to the season, the Benettons finally seemed to have found a certain level of competitiveness. *"Our car has definitely been going better since the start of the weekend. I think we have come up with some good technical solutions,"* confirmed Fisichella. Sadly, these seemed to disappear as mysteriously as they arrived and the Benettons were never really on the pace for the rest of the season.
In the race, the Italian got delayed when trying to pass two backmarkers, Olivier Panis and Luca Badoer. In a mood, he made a mistake which allowed Frentzen to slip past. *"That made me mad,"* he recalled. *"On top of that, I lost concentration. Luckily for me, Heinz-Harald went off and I was back in second place again."*

An unexpected second place for Giancarlo Fisichella, who made the most of the retirements at the head of the field, to get onto the podium. The same would not happen again until the European Grand Prix, when the Italian was unable to capitalise on the opportunity presented.

results

PRACTICE TIMES

No	Driver	Car/Engine/Chassis	Practice Friday	Pos.	Practice Saturday	Pos.	Qualifying	Pos.	Warm-up	Pos.
1.	Mika Häkkinen	McLaren/Mercedes/MP4 -14/5	1'21"950	7°	1'19"568	3°	1'19"327	2°	1'21"244	4°
2.	David Coulthard	McLaren/Mercedes/MP4 -14/6	1'20"664	2°	0'19"543	2°	1'19"729	4°	1'20"614	1°
3.	Michael Schumacher	Ferrari/Ferrari/F399/194	1'21"276	3°	1'19"281	1°	1'19"298	1°	1'21"560	7°
4.	Eddie Irvine	Ferrari/Ferrari/F399/191	1'20"576	1°	1'19"631	4°	1'19"440	3°	1'21"534	6°
5.	Alessandro Zanardi	Williams/Supertec/FW21/05	1'23"824	18°	1'20"754	11°	1'21"076	12°	1'22"535	18°
6.	Ralf Schumacher	Williams/Supertec/FW21/04	1'22"506	12°	1'20"275	8°	1'21"081	13°	1'21"845	9°
7.	Damon Hill	Jordan/Mugen-Honda/199/4	1'22"734	14°	1'20"785	12°	1'21"094	14°	1'21"709	8°
8.	Heinz-Harald Frentzen	Jordan/Mugen-Honda/199/6	1'22"002	8°	1'19"940	5°	1'20"158	6°	1'22"156	13°
9.	Giancarlo Fisichella	Benetton/Playlife/B199/03	1'21"724	5°	1'20"162	6°	1'20"378	7°	1'21"530	5°
10.	Alexander Wurz	Benetton/Playlife/B199/05	1'22"646	13°	1'20"919	14°	1'21"000	11°	1'21"950	10°
11.	Jean Alesi	Sauber/Petronas/C18/03	1'21"510	4°	1'20"485	10°	1'20"459	8°	1'22"472	17°
12.	Pedro Diniz	Sauber/Petronas/C18/05	1'24"462	22°	1'21"022	17°	1'21"571	18°	1'21"984	11°
14.	Pedro de la Rosa	Arrows/Arrows/A20/04	1'23"996	20°	1'22"039	20°	1'22"613	20°	1'22"469	16°
15.	Toranosuke Takagi	Arrows/Arrows/A20/02	1'24"131	21°	1'21"810	19°	1'21"693	19°	1'22"323	15°
16.	Rubens Barrichello	Stewart/Ford/SF3/04	1'22"167	10°	1'20"261	7°	1'19"930	5°	1'21"012	2°
17.	Johnny Herbert	Stewart/Ford/SF3/05	1'23"177	16°	1'20"861	13°	1'20"829	10°	1'21"059	3°
18.	Olivier Panis	Prost/Peugeot/AP02/5	1'22"892	15°	1'20"935	16°	1'21"252	15°	1'22"027	12°
19.	Jarno Trulli	Prost/Peugeot/AP02/6	1'22"454	11°	1'20"396	9°	1'20"557	9°	1'22"228	14°
20.	Luca Badoer	Minardi/Ford/M01/01	1'23"778	17°	1'22"730	22°	1'22"808	21°	1'22"691	19°
21.	Marc Gené	Minardi/Ford/M01/04	1'23"826	19°	1'22"205	21°	1'23"387	22°	1'26"279	22°
22.	Jacques Villeneuve	BAR/Supertec/BAR01/03	1'22"021	9°	1'20"924	15°	1'21"302	16°	1'22"898	20°
23.	Ricardo Zonta	BAR/Supertec/BAR01/06	1'21"810	6°	1'21"235	18°	1'21"467	17°	1'23"256	21°

MAXIMUM SPEEDS

No	Driver	P1 Qualifs	Pos	P1 Race	Pos	P2 Qualifs	Pos	P2 Race	Pos	Finish Qualifs	Pos	Finish Race	Pos	Trap Qualifs	Pos	Trap Race	Pos
1.	M. Häkkinen	272,7	1°	261,1	2°	292,6	3°	282,7	3°	289,8	2°	287,3	4°	320,0	7°	321,7	9°
2.	D. Coulthard	268,1	4°	255,5	4°	285,4	11°	278,9	6°	290,9	1°	290,7	1°	324,7	1°	327,6	1°
3.	M. Schum.	268,3	3°	254,5	6°	294,0	2°	281,9	5°	286,9	9°	283,0	11°	320,9	3°	318,9	13°
4.	E. Irvine	266,8	5°	262,1	1°	296,1	1°	288,2	1°	285,7	10°	282,5	12°	319,4	11°	320,4	12°
5.	A. Zanardi	262,6	10°	247,4	14°	292,2	4°	270,0	13°	280,4	20°	281,4	14°	313,0	20°	316,6	14°
6.	R. Schumacher	262,7	8°	259,1	3°	287,3	9°	282,4	4°	277,9	22°	278,9	18°	307,6	21°	310,6	19°
7.	D. Hill	260,7	12°	241,3	17°	289,4	7°	258,0	18°	289,0	4°	283,1	10°	320,3	6°	322,5	8°
8.	H.-H. Frentzen	262,8	7°	250,2	12°	291,9	5°	276,2	9°	289,0	3°	288,5	3°	320,3	5°	326,0	3°
9.	G. Fisichella	258,8	16°	254,5	7°	284,1	13°	277,9	7°	282,3	18°	285,4	7°	314,0	17°	323,9	5°
10.	A. Wurz	257,3	19°	213,1	19°	280,9	17°	235,5	20°	283,9	16°	NQ	-	319,7	9°	124,1	20°
11.	J. Alesi	268,5	2°	NQ	-	290,4	6°	NQ	-	285,1	11°	NQ	-	315,1	16°	NQ	-
12.	P. Diniz	260,9	11°	253,0	8°	286,9	10°	282,8	2°	283,9	15°	280,5	16°	315,3	15°	316,2	15°
14.	P. de la Rosa	257,2	20°	248,1	13°	283,4	14°	261,0	17°	284,9	13°	284,5	9°	319,1	12°	321,0	10°
15.	T. Takagi	257,5	17°	251,9	9°	285,1	12°	273,9	12°	283,9	14°	285,3	8°	320,3	4°	322,7	7°
16.	R. Barrichello	262,7	9°	240,3	18°	288,2	8°	264,7	16°	288,3	7°	289,0	2°	319,6	10°	324,7	4°
17.	J. Herbert	264,9	6°	254,8	5°	278,4	19°	276,1	10°	288,9	5°	287,1	5°	319,9	8°	321,0	11°
18.	O. Panis	260,6	13°	251,8	10°	283,2	15°	274,0	11°	287,0	8°	287,0	6°	318,7	13°	326,9	2°
19.	J. Trulli	260,4	14°	NQ	-	277,2	20°	NQ	-	288,4	6°	NQ	-	321,4	2°	NQ	-
20.	L. Badoer	255,3	21°	247,3	15°	267,8	22°	277,3	8°	282,6	17°	281,1	15°	313,7	18°	322,7	6°
21.	M. Gené	244,5	22°	250,6	11°	272,5	21°	269,0	14°	280,9	19°	279,6	17°	313,3	19°	315,3	16°
22.	J. Villeneuve	257,4	18°	247,1	16°	278,9	18°	265,0	15°	279,9	21°	281,5	13°	307,0	22°	314,6	17°
23.	R. Zonta	259,4	15°	211,3	20°	281,0	16°	255,8	19°	285,1	12°	276,2	19°	316,1	14°	310,6	18°

CLASSIFICATION & RETIREMENTS

Pos	Drivers	Team	Time
1.	Häkkinen	McLaren Mercedes	in 1h41'35"727
2.	Fisichella	Benetton Playlife	at 0"781
3.	Irvine	Ferrari	at 1"796
4.	R. Schum.	Williams Supertec	at 2"391
5.	Herbert	Stewart Ford	at 2"804
6.	Diniz	Sauber Petronas	at 3"710
7.	Coulthard	McLaren Mercedes	at 5"003
8.	Gené	Minardi Ford	at 1 lap
9.	Panis	Prost Peugeot	at 1 lap
10.	Badoer	Minardi Ford	at 2 laps

Lap	Drivers	Team	Reason
1	Wurz	Benetton Playlife	accident
1	Trulli	Prost Peugeot	accident
1	Alesi	Sauber Petronas	accident
3	Zonta	BAR Supertec	accident
15	Barrichello	Stewart Ford	accident
15	Hill	Jordan Mugen Honda	accident
14	de la Rosa	Arrows	transmission
30	M. Schum.	Ferrari	accident
35	Villeneuve	BAR Supertec	accident
42	Takagi	Arrows	transmission
51	Zanardi	Williams Supertec	spin
66	Frentzen	Jordan Mugen Honda	off

FASTEST LAPS

	Drivers	Time	Lap
1.	Irvine	1'20"382	62
2.	M. Schum.	1'20"709	28
3.	Coulthard	1'20"961	35
4.	Häkkinen	1'21"047	28
5.	Frentzen	1'21"284	65
6.	Fisichella	1'21"345	65
7.	Diniz	1'21"864	63
8.	R. Schum.	1'22"002	28
9.	Herbert	1'22"078	64
10.	Panis	1'22"100	57
11.	Villeneuve	1'22"283	29
12.	Takagi	1'22"792	26
13.	Gené	1'22"888	60
14.	de la Rosa	1'23"280	19
15.	Badoer	1'23"394	32
16.	Zanardi	1'23"442	27
17.	Barrichello	1'23"785	11
18.	Hill	1'23"953	12
19.	Zonta	1'03"038	2

All results :
© 1999 Fédération International de l'Automobile, 2, Ch. Blandonnet, 1215 Genève 15, Suisse

LAP CHART

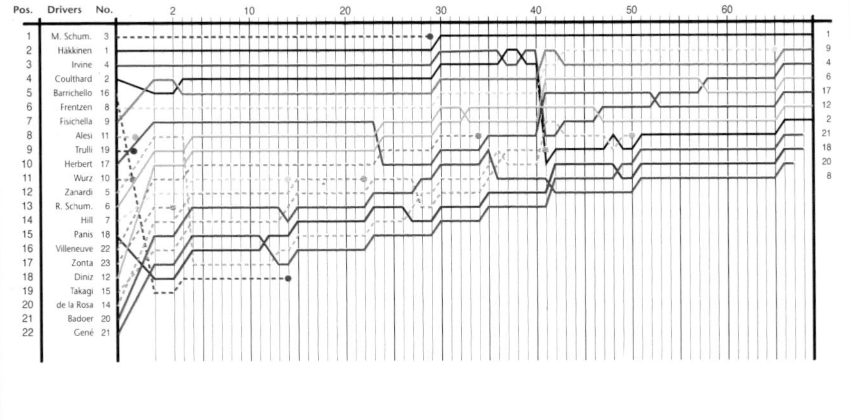

PIT STOPS

	Driver	Time	Lap	Stop n°
1.	Barrichello	2'58"079	1	1
2.	Herbert	26"526	24	1
3.	Takagi	26"514	28	1
4.	Fisichella	26"762	36	1
5.	Frentzen	25"746	36	1
6.	Diniz	28"924	36	1
7.	R. Schum.	28"450	36	1
8.	Herbert	32"728	36	2
9.	Häkkinen	26"079	37	1
10.	Badoer	29"452	36	1
11.	Irvine	29"317	37	1
12.	Panis	25"716	36	1
13.	Gené	39"525	36	1
14.	Zanardi	28"150	37	1
15.	Coulthard	27"916	38	1
16.	Coulthard	30"812	41	2
17.	Badoer	27"260	46	2
18.	Zanardi	26"890	48	2
19.	Coulthard	28"305	49	3
20.	Panis	27"530	49	2

THE CIRCUIT

SIXTH ROUND

AIR CANADA GRAND PRIX DU CANADA, MONTRÉAL

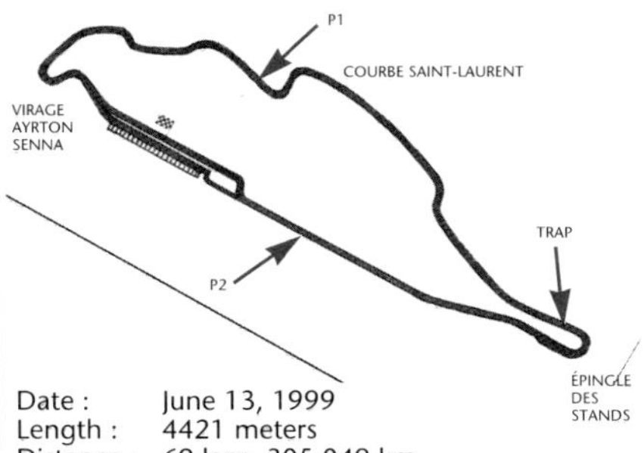

Date : June 13, 1999
Length : 4421 meters
Distance : 69 laps, 305.049 km
Weather : sunny, 30°

BRIDGESTONE

Quickest pit stop during the Canadian Grand Prix, taking on fuel and four new Bridgestone tyres:
Olivier Panis, Prost, 25"716

CHAMPIONSHIPS

(after six rounds)

Drivers :

1. M. Häkkinen 34
2. M. Schumacher 30
3. E. Irvine 25
4. H. Frentzen 13
   G. Fisichella 13
6. D. Coulthard 12
   R. Schumacher 12
8. R. Barrichello 6
9. D. Hill 3
10. J. Herbert 2
11. P. de la Rosa 1
    O. Panis 1
    J. Alesi 1
    A. Wurz 1
    J. Trulli 1
    P. Diniz 1

Constructors :

1. Ferrari 55
2. McLaren/Mercedes 46
3. Jordan/Mugen Honda 16
4. Benetton/Playlife 14
5. Williams/Supertec 12
6. Stewart/Ford 8
7. Prost/Peugeot 2
8. Sauber/Petronas 2
9. Arrows 1

RACE SUMMARY

- At the start, Michael Schumacher manages to keep the lead with some judicious swervery ahead of Mika Hakkinen. Further back, Jarno Trulli cuts across the grass, gets sideways and hits Rubens Barrichello's Stewart and Jean Alesi's Sauber as he rejoins the track.
- The Safety Car is called out while the Trulli and Alesi wrecks are pulled away: the same misfortune had befallen them the previous year.
- The Safety Car was only out for a lap, but no sooner back in pit lane, it was called out again when Ricardo Zonta crashed, staying out until lap 7.
- On lap 16, Damon Hill is the first to go off into what will become known as "The Wall Of Champions," (see opposite.)
- Michael Schumacher now tries to pull out a lead, but cannot shake off Mika Hakkinen. After 27 laps, the Finn is only 4.2s behind the German.
- Drama on lap 30. Michael Schumacher runs wide of the racing line by no more than a metre, gets on a dirty part of the track and hits the concrete barriers.
- 5 laps later and its Jacques Villeneuve's turn to crash at the very same spot, when he had been lying eighth.
- On lap 40, David Coulthard and Eddie Irvine have a coming together at the Senna corner, but carry on. Coulthard is given a ten second stop-go penalty for his behaviour..
- Lap 66 and second placed Heinz-Harald Frentzen has a huge shunt after a brake disc shatters. The race ends behind the Safety Car.

WEEKEND GOSSIP

- **Ford buys Stewart**

On Thursday, the American constructor, Ford Motor Company, announced it was buying the Stewart Grand Prix team. "Racing is a great way to reach our customers thanks to its exciting atmosphere and Formula 1 technology," explained the boss of the Detroit marque Jac Nasser. A great racing fan himself, he stressed the move would allow Ford to reinforce its image on a global scale.

- **Danni's turn**

The Canadian press, especially "le Journal de Montreal" was making a meal of the new love interest in Jacques Villeneuve's life. He was now romantically linked to the Australian soap star cum singer Danni Minogue. "If I had wanted to keep our relationship secret, I would not have gone out in Montreal with Danni," was all the young champ would say on the matter. Evidently his liaison with the singer Nathalie Imbruglia had lasted no longer than that with Vanessa Mae.

- **3000 dollars for a helmet**

On Saturday, Jean Alesi had to park his Sauber C18 at the hairpin at the end of the qualifying session. "The last time I'd had to park there was after I won the race in 1995. I felt I owed the crowd something, so I threw them my crash helmet." Patrick Vinet, a local photographer, witness the riot which followed before someone managed to grab the helmet. "A lady then offered 3000 dollars for it," recalled Vinet. "The man turned down the offer." Evidently a Jean Alesi helmet is priceless.

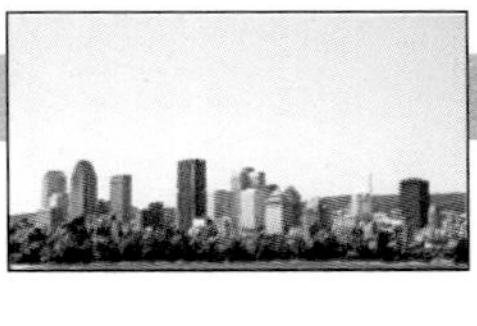

"HH" surfs the Magny-Cours wave

A dry start, a heavy downpour, crashes and overtaking moves by the bucketful, all made this a crazy French Grand Prix and Heinz-Harald Frentzen emerged as the surprise winner.

It was his one stop strategy which allowed the German to take the lead shortly before the chequered flag. He was a worthy winner, even if "HH" made the most of the mechanical misfortune of wet weather expert Michael Schumacher and his Ferrari.

Barrichello and Alesi on the front row: long odds on the top three at Magny-Cours

"We're the best!" Joy was unconfined in the Stewart camp, just after "Rubinho" obtained a very unexpected pole position.

▽

Getting the strategy right in qualifying was more important than ever at Magny-Cours. It rained non-stop throughout the hour, but as it got heavier after a few minutes, the very start of the session had been the best time to get out there and do the business. Prompt out of the pits, Rubens Barrichello and Jean Alesi managed to claim the two front row positions. It was the Brazilian's second pole of his career and this time, the circumstances were exactly the same as the first time when he took pole in Belgium in 1994 in changeable weather. *"A weather expert predicted the rain would get harder after the first quarter of an hour, so we decided to go out straight away,"* said an ecstatic "Rubinho." *"After my first lap, the team told me that Jean (Alesi) had gone a second and a half quicker. The rain was getting harder and I told myself it was now or never. I really drove on the limit and this is the result. Basically, it was all down to going out at the right time!"*

Two teams share the secret

A mutual friend of Peter Sauber and Jackie Stewart provided the correct weather forecast and theirs were the only two teams who shared the secret that the rain was due to get worse.

All the stars of the championship could have done with this advice, as Michael Schumacher was sixth and Mika Hakkinen could manage no better than fourteenth. *"I've got no excuses because the conditions were the same for everyone,"* confessed the Finn. *"I never felt comfortable in the car and that is why I am so far down the grid. But I am still optimistic, because after all, Sunday is the day you score points, not Saturday."* In the Ferrari camp, Michael Schumacher complained about the state of the track. *"It was a real nightmare. The track was very dangerous. There was a lot of aquaplaning and it was easy to spin even on the straights."*

Five pulled out of the 107% pool

Prost driver Olivier Panis made the most of the weather conditions to qualify third. Team-mate Jarno Trulli (photo) was eighth.

▷

It looked as though Mika Hakkinen was worried before going out on the track.

▷ ▽

Damon Hill had missed out on lapping in 1m 45.331s, the time which represented 107% of the pole position time, by just three thousandths of a second. Those three minuscule fractions of a second meant his uninspired performance put him out of the French Grand Prix. *"I think what has happened today is a perfect example of what is happening to me this season and why I have announced that I plan to retire soon,"* he announced. *"Usually, I like driving in the wet, but not today. I did not manage to get the most out of the car or out of myself, which is very frustrating. But today, I experienced worse conditions than I have ever encountered in qualifying. It was hell."* In the end though, because of the exceptional circumstances under which qualifying was run and using the get-out clause permitted under article 131 of F1's sporting code, the race director decided to reinstate the five drivers who were not originally qualified.

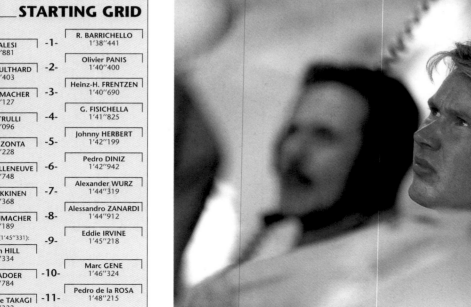

STARTING GRID

Jean ALESI 1'38"881	-1-	R. BARRICHELLO 1'38"441
David COULTHARD 1'40"403	-2-	Olivier PANIS 1'40"400
M. SCHUMACHER 1'41"127	-3-	Heinz-H. FRENTZEN 1'40"690
Jarno TRULLI 1'42"096	-4-	G. FISICHELLA 1'41"825
Ricardo ZONTA 1'42"228	-5-	Johnny HERBERT 1'42"199
Jacques VILLENEUVE 1'43"748	-6-	Pedro DINIZ 1'42"942
Mika HÄKKINEN 1'44"368	-7-	Alexander WURZ 1'44"319
Ralf SCHUMACHER 1'45"189	-8-	Alessandro ZANARDI 1'44"912
Over 107% (1'45"331):	-9-	Eddie IRVINE 1'45"218
Damon HILL 1'45"334		
Luca BADOER 1'46"784	-10-	Marc GENE 1'46"324
Toranosuke TAKAGI 1'48"322	-11-	Pedro de la ROSA 1'48"215

First win for the German since the 1997 San Marino Grand Prix

Heinz-Harald Frentzen splashes to victory

The man who crashed in Montreal was in fine form thanks very much. In Canada two weeks earlier, Heinz-Harald Frentzen had a huge shunt in the closing stages of the race, as he was heading for second place.

Having missed out on testing in between the races, as he recovered, he came back with a vengeance to win the French Grand Prix at Magny-Cours, from Mika Hakkinen and Rubens Barrichello. *"I still have some aches and pains after my Canadian accident, but when you are driving, you concentrate so much, that you don't feel anything. Also, luckily because of the rain, it was a not a very tiring race physically,"* explained the German.

The rain came quicker than expected

In fact, it was largely due to the Jordan team's daring strategy, opting for just a single pit stop, that the man from Monchengladbach was able to come out on top. *"At the start, we had no specific plan,"* he continued. *"We knew it was supposed to rain between forty five minutes and one hour after the start. But then it actually started to rain earlier than expected."*

As soon as the first drops began to fall, around 2.30 when the race was 19 laps old, Frentzen stopped to fit rain tyres, like all the other drivers. *"My stop lasted an eternity. I was getting very nervous and that was when I realised the team had changed the strategy and put the maximum amount of fuel in. At first, I was furious, because the car became very difficult to drive because of its weight and the aquaplaning. I had to work hard to keep it on the track."*

Eavesdropping

Throughout the weekend, radio communication between Heinz-Harald and his team on the pit wall, was being recorded by FIA

for testing purposes. *"I made the most of it to scream into the radio that the bloody Safety Car needed to be brought out, in the hope that the race director would hear me. The conditions were really terrible,"* continued the German.

Finally, they got the message, as the Safety Car did indeed come out for ten laps. While all the opposition had to make another pit stop, Heinz-Harald Frentzen had enough fuel on board to get to the finish, thus taking his first win in a Jordan and the second of his career.

Just as Barrichello had predicted

Rubens had said as much on Saturday afternoon after claiming pole position. He had every intention of finishing on the podium of the French Grand Prix.

Mission accomplished therefore, as the Brazilian finished third, after having led for 44 of the 72 laps. *"I've got mixed feelings,"* he declared after the race. *"On the one hand I am happy to be on the podium for the second time this season. But on the other hand, I think I could have won. When I saw David Coul-*

thard go out and then Michael Schumacher started to slow down, I thought my day had come."

Although he had been unable to hold off Mika Hakkinen and he had fallen victim to Heinz-Harald Frentzen's strategy, Rubens Barrichello was nevertheless happy with his race. *"I had good fun. We had a good clean fight without any bad moves. Unfortunately my car was not well balanced, especially through the last corner. I was losing a lot of time there."*

Mika's long haul

Mika Hakkinen went home after Magny-Cours having reduced his gap to Michael Schumacher in the points table by a further four points. It was a minor miracle considering that with around twenty laps to go, the Finn was paddling around in seventh place, while his German rival was loping along in the lead. Mika had an astonishing start to the race. Starting from 14th place on the grid, he dealt with his rivals one at a time to be second after just 19 laps. Then the rain came down and the Finn was caught out, spinning down to eighth place. He had to start all over again. Getting down to work once more, the world champion did it all over again and finished second. *"I did not win, because of my spin,"* he commented. *"But it's not that important because I really enjoyed driving in this race."*

"Heinz, you're the best!" Heinz-Harald is warmly congratulated by girlfriend Tania after the race.
◁▽

V for victory for Heinz-Harald Frentzen as Eddie Jordan joins him in parc ferme
▽

Mika Hakkinen ahead of Heinz-Harald Frentzen and Michael Schumacher: one of the many diverse phases of a completely crazy French Grand Prix. The Finn made no less than 35 passing moves in this race!

GRAND PRIX MOBIL 1 DE FRANCE

The accident which changed everything

The race had just been stopped and the red flags were being waved by the marshals. It was all too late for Michael Schumacher, who did not see them as he was busy attacking team mate Eddie Irvine. His brakes failed, he crashed into the barriers, he broke a leg in two places and the dream was over. The rest of the season would show that the 1999 championship had probably been his for the taking. Sadly for him, for Ferrari and for the tifosi, it all ended with this never ending braking (photo.)

RAC BRITISH GRAND PRIX
SILVERSTONE

Mika finally on form

▷

Mika Hakkinen and Michael Schumacher, side by side on the front row: a tempting prospect for a grand prix which would turn out to be the German's last race until Malaysia

Mika Hakkinen never varied his performance, topping the time sheet at the end of every single session from Friday morning through to Saturday qualifying for the British Grand Prix.

Judging by the way the qualifying session went, it even looked as though he had kept something in reserve. *"I gave up on completing my final quick lap,"* he commented. *"I went out behind Michael (Schumacher) and I saw how he was taking Becketts and Stowe. He was going very slowly and I thought there was no point continuing with my lap. I could see that Michael would never beat my time."*

In fact the wind had changed considerably during the session, while the temperature had gone up. These two factors combined to make the track slower towards the end of the session. *"You had to be out during the first twenty minutes to get a good time,"* confirmed Michael Schumacher. *"I did a very good lap at the start of the session so it wasn't worth going out again later in the same trim. We tried changing various settings but it didn't work. My very last lap wasn't bad but I went a bit over the limits of the car and I got into a slide."*

For his part, Mika Hakkinen had nothing but praise for his MP4/14. *"We tried several set-ups but I have to say the car was excellent whatever we did to it. My engineers have done a great job."*

To retire or not to retire? Damon Hill hams it up

The question seemed to have the whole of England in its thrall. On Thursday afternoon, it was certainly one of the main topics of conversation in the Silverstone paddock. Would the local hero Damon Hill retire from the sport on Sunday evening after his home grand prix?

The English driver had been playing the grand diva for much of the year. At the start of the season, Damon Hill had denied all rumours of impending retirement. At Magny-Cours, two weeks earlier, he said he wanted to retire but was sufficiently motivated to keep going until the end of the season (see page 146) Three days later, at the end of a disastrous French Grand Prix, he hinted he might hang up his helmet immediately.

Damon Hill seemed bored with it all during practice. Although he would not discuss the subject of his retirement, his mind seemed elsewhere at Silverstone
▷ ▽

Then, he came up with yet another "official" announcement that he would retire after the British Grand Prix, after a final farewell to his home crowd at Silverstone. On the Thursday, he was scheduled to hold a major press conference at two o'clock at the Jordan factory, just opposite the main gates of the circuit. Dozens of journalists turned up to pay homage to their hero one last time. But then, when everyone arrived at the track on Thursday morning, it was announced that the conference was cancelled and that Damon Hill was refusing to speak to anyone. Apparently, the 1996 world champion was having second thoughts about quitting. At this stage it was not so much indecision as a yo-yo show. The reason for this possible change of heart was the test he had carried out at Silverstone a week earlier. Damon had found that his Jordan 199 was "fantastic" and that was all it took to get him pumped up again. But while the Englishman was not sure what he wanted to do, his boss was thinking of making the decision for him. Disappointed with Hill's performances, Eddie Jordan was tempted to boot him out the door as soon as he could find a replacement.

A barrage of criticism

Damon Hill's hesitant attitude was niggling the paddock folk. Jackie Stewart was one of many who advised the Jordan driver to pack it in. *"Damon is 38 years old. That's an ideal age to start something new. In any case, all sportsmen have to stop one day."*

As far as Eddie Irvine was concerned, Hill was going about things the wrong way. *"Damon has no class,"* he said. *"Frankly, at Silverstone, he would do better to do a parade lap in a nice car to wave at the crowd. He would really look stupid if he raced anyway and then had an accident which could affect him for the rest of his life. You cannot decide to retire at the end of the year. The only way to do it in my opinion is Lauda-style and quit on the spot."*

STARTING GRID

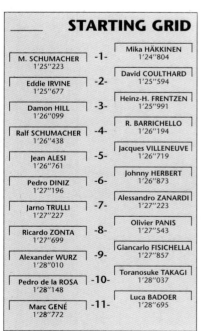

		Mika HÄKKINEN 1'24"804
M. SCHUMACHER 1'25"223	-1-	
		David COULTHARD 1'25"594
Eddie IRVINE 1'25"677	-2-	
		Heinz-H. FRENTZEN 1'25"991
Damon HILL 1'26"099	-3-	
		R. BARRICHELLO 1'26"194
Ralf SCHUMACHER 1'26"438	-4-	
		Jacques VILLENEUVE 1'26"719
Jean ALESI 1'26"761	-5-	
		Johnny HERBERT 1'26"873
Pedro DINIZ 1'27"196	-6-	
		Alessandro ZANARDI 1'27"223
Jarno TRULLI 1'27"227	-7-	
		Olivier PANIS 1'27"543
Ricardo ZONTA 1'27"699	-8-	
		Giancarlo FISICHELLA 1'27"857
Alexander WURZ 1'28"010	-9-	
		Toranosuke TAKAGI 1'28"037
Pedro de la ROSA 1'28"148	-10-	
		Luca BADOER 1'28"695
Marc GENÉ 1'28"772	-11-	

the race

Schumacher had a terrible accident at the first start

A big scare for Michael Schumacher

The race had been underway for less than a minute. On the grid, both Jacques Villeneuve and Alessandro Zanardi had not got away and the organisers decided to stop the race immediately.

The leading bunch was already on the straight leading to Stowe, when the track marshals, having been told by radio, got out the red flags. Michael Schumacher was fourth at the time and attacking his team-mate Eddie Irvine, going down the inside of the corner and he failed to see the flags indicating the race had been stopped. It was too late anyway: one of his rear brakes failed and his F399 ploughed straight on over the gravel trap, which hardly slowed it at all, before piling straight through a wall of tyres and burying its nose in the barrier.

It was a huge impact. Just before they reach the braking point for Stowe, the cars are timed at over 310 km/h. Michael Schumacher hit the barrier at very high speed, although later calculations produced a figure of 107 km/h. Conscious, but trapped in the cockpit, the German was prised out and taken to the circuit medical centre by ambulance.

He was then taken by helicopter to Northampton General Hospital, about twenty kilometres from the track. "*The tibia and fibula of his right leg are both broken, but it is a simple, clean fracture,*" explained the F1 doctor, Syd Watkins. A plaster would have been sufficient to fix this sort of break, but he was operated on to fit a metal plate which would speed up the healing process. The Ferrari people were feeling reassured. There had been talk of transferring Schumacher to Paris, to be treated by Professor Saillant, a personal friend of Jean Todt, the Scuderia's Sporting Director. Saillant had often treated injured top sports stars. But the idea was soon dropped. "*The operation Michael must undergo is really very straightforward,*" explained Ferrari's press officer Claudio Berro. "*It's the type of thing surgeons do hundreds of times. There is nothing to worry about. In any case, Professor Saillant has been in telephone contact with the Northampton hospital to supervise the operation if any difficulty arises.*"

The operation was carried out at around 4 pm and lasted two hours. Schumacher was back in Switzerland a day later, where he spent a few days in a private clinic before going back to his home in Vufflens-le-Chateau. He drove a car again one month later, but waited until Malaysia to make his return to competition. The German's championship challenge had ended that Sunday 11th July.

Mika loses a wheel

Having qualified brilliantly on pole position, Mika Hakkinen went home from Silverstone without a single point. He led the race comfortably for the first 24 laps, but his McLaren then developed a problem with its left rear wheel. Just after his first pit stop, feeling that something was wrong with the balance of the car, the Finn made a second stop to check the offending wheel. Once back on the track, it flew off in the middle of a corner. He managed to limp back to the pits on three wheels and got going yet again, but the team lost no time in calling him back, feeling that it was too big a risk to carry on. After his two stops, he was running in 16th place, one lap down and in any case, he had no chance of scoring any points.

Ralf third

Michael's little brother was naturally very worried about him on Sunday afternoon. It did not stop him from finishing on the third rung of the podium. "*Of course it was not very nice knowing Michael was in hospital. But my team kept me informed of his condition throughout the race. I knew he was alright and so I was not too worried. And after all, I am a professional. The team was counting on me, so I had to do my job and take part in this grand prix.*"

Victory for Coulthard ahead of Irvine

It took the emergency services several minutes to get Michael Schumacher out of his wrecked car.

The understudies' race

On Saturday, when he spoke about winning the British Grand Prix, his words had a ring of vain hope about them rather than a realistic hope. He had been conclusively outpaced by Mika Hakkinen in practice and was unhappy with his car. David Coulthard did not seem to have a hope of winning in front of his home crowd.

However, making the most of the absence of Michael Schumacher and Mika Hakkinen, it was indeed the Scotsman who went on to win the British Grand Prix, just ahead of Eddie Irvine. Fate had pushed the understudies to the front of stage. However, it was not an easy win for Coulthard. The Scotsman was under constant pressure from Irvine and he only won because the Irishman ran into bother during his first pit stop, which cost him a fatal three seconds. "*I am not really sure what happened, but that first pit stop really was the end of it. That was definitely the key moment in the race,*" regretted Eddie Irvine. Passed by David Coulthard, the Irishman was never able to worry him again.

For McLaren's Scottish driver, the ten points he scored allowed him to become a championship contender once again, although he was still 18 points behind Hakkinen and ten off Irvine. "*This win is a fantastic feeling,*" said the winner. "*But I must admit that all credit must go to the team who carried out two amazing pit stops.*"

Just as in practice, Coulthard complained his car was not perfect. "*I had to fight the car, because it was not well balanced.*" Irvine was now equal on points with Schumacher and was ready to pick up the baton.

"It has to be said you have more hair than me David!" Happy with the way the day went, Ron Dennis warmly congratulated David Coulthard as he stepped from the cockpit. Mika Hakkinen also came to congratulate his teammate.

 **RAC BRITISH GRAND PRIX**

Michael Schumacher before and after! At the first start, the German is certainly on the front row. At the second, his place is empty.

RAC BRITISH GRAND PRIX

Own goal for McLaren

The two silver arrows had certainly planned to make the most of Michael Schumacher's absence. Mika Hakkinen had said he hoped to notch up back to back wins in Austria and Germany, the races taking place just one week apart.

At Zeltweg, the campaign got off to a bad start. While everything went well in practice and at the start (photo,) David Coulthard threw it all away at the second corner, when he drove into his team mate. Eddie Irvine made the most of it to take his second win of the season.

GROSSER PREIS VON ÖSTERREICH
SPIELBERG

practice

McLarens in cruise mode

Mr. and Mrs. Hakkinen. With Michael Schumacher out of the way, Mika could afford to take life calmly. However, he still claimed pole position in qualifying.

Qualifying for the Austrian Grand Prix proved that nothing and no one was a match for the two McLaren-Mercedes this summer. With no Michael Schumacher, the quickest Ferrari was a full second off the pace of the silver arrows.

When it came to judging his performance, Eddie Irvine had, until now, always had Michael Schumacher as a benchmark but now there were no excuses. It was a new situation and it did not get off to the best of starts on Saturday as Irvine was a second behind Hakkinen's McLaren, which did not exactly lead one to expect a thrilling Austrian Grand Prix. Seeming as laid back as ever, the Irishman explained that the gap to the McLarens should have been half what it was, as he had been delayed with brake problems. *"In race trim, I reckon we will only be a couple of tenths off the McLarens. The car is well balanced and I am not too worried,"* he added. But a few tenths multiplied by 71 laps could soon add up.

Eddie Irvine had a lot to say

"When Michael comes back, he will be the Number 2 and have to help me win the title," the Irish driver had declared to some German journalists after the British Grand Prix. Unfortunately, Jean Todt does not appreciate other people making his decisions for him. On Thursday, he put Irvine in his place: *"If Mika (Salo) is ahead of Eddie in the race, we will look at all the options,"* said the Frenchman. Reading between the lines, it seemed the Scuderia was not necessarily putting its full weight behind Irvine.

Apparently, the Italian team's management did not believe Eddie Irvine was really capable of fighting Mika Hakkinen for the title. They

Seventh place on the grid for Mika Salo. It was not easy, learning to master a car like the F399 through Zeltweg's sweeping curves.

Too sure of himself?

were not alone. There were plenty in the Zeltweg paddock who felt the Irishman was incapable of winning the championship. *"Michael (Schumacher) was what made the difference,"* reckoned Gerhard Berger, former driver and now sporting director at BMW. *"Mika (Hakkinen) will have to keep his concentration and stay lucky, but he will be world champion. I can't see anyone beating him."*

At McLaren-Mercedes, it was the same story. *"Eddie would do better to concentrate on his work than make stupid remarks to the press,"* declared Ron Dennis. *"Anyway, we have definitely improved now. We will win the championship with or without Michael Schumacher."*

Mika Salo struggles

Michael Schumacher's replacement was having to come to terms with the enormity of the task facing him in practice. Not only did he have to adapt to the F399 and its complex systems - their were no less than 13 different functions on the steering wheel - but he also had to get used to the team and its work methods. On top of that there were all the little details, like the start of a grand prix, which was a tricky moment, even for Michael Schumacher. The Finn had yet to try it. *"I spoke to Michael to ask his advice on the start procedure,"* explained Salo. *"But I still have a lot to learn. Driving the car is not difficult; finding its limits is."* Having qualified seventh, he hoped to pick up at least a point.

STARTING GRID

David COULTHARD 1'11"153	-1-	Mika HÄKKINEN 1'10"954
Heinz-H. FRENTZEN 1'12"266	-2-	Eddie IRVINE 1'11"973
Johnny HERBERT 1'12"488	-3-	R. BARRICHELLO 1'12"342
Ralf SCHUMACHER 1'12"515	-4-	Mika SALO 1'12"514
Alexander WURZ 1'12"850	-5-	Jacques VILLENEUVE 1'12"833
Giancarlo FISICHELLA 1'12"924	-6-	Damon HILL 1'12"901
Alessandro ZANARDI 1'13"101	-7-	Jarno TRULLI 1'12"999
Pedro DINIZ 1'13"223	-8-	Ricardo ZONTA 1'13"172
Olivier PANIS 1'13"457	-9-	Jean ALESI 1'13"226
Toranosuke TAKAGI 1'13"641	-10-	Luca BADOER 1'13"606
Marc GENÉ 1'14"363	-11-	Pedro de la ROSA 1'14"139

"Don't sulk Helmut. It could be worse, it could be raining." The poor spectators who had opted to camp out suffered because of terrible storms which hit the region on the Thursday before the race. On that day, Formula 3000 qualifying had to be scrubbed because of the rivers running across the track!

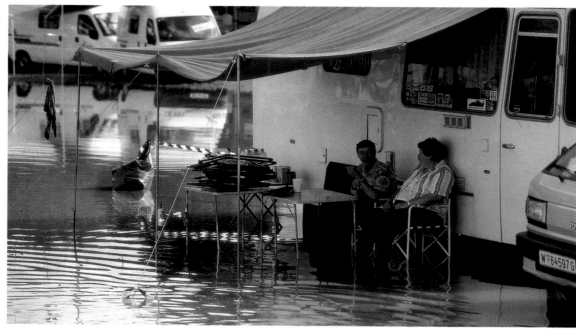

Eddie the Magnificent

Fantastic Eddie Irvine. The Irishman managed to stay cool under enormous pressure from David Coulthard to win the Austrian Grand Prix by 313 thousandths of a second. He was now just two points behind Mika Hakkinen in the championship.

It had thus taken but one grand prix for Irvine to silence his critics (see opposite). Those who thought him incapable of withstanding the pressure of being the number one driver at Ferrari had to eat their words.

In Austria, the Irishman put on a masterful performance. Third for much of the race, he bided his time before attacking. But above all, he managed to keep his lead, despite problems with the F399 and the fact that Coulthard was all over him. The Irishman finally crossed the line 313 thousandths of a second ahead of his Scottish rival. It was a victory snatched during the pit stops, which was just what was needed after David Coulthard had used the pits stops to beat Irvine two weeks earlier at Silverstone.

"So many things happened in this race that I have not got used to the idea that I have won," summarised Irvine as he stepped off the podium. *"The last few laps were terrible and I was just waiting for the chequered flag. I had brake problems; I was running out of fuel and the car had terrible understeer after the pit stop. I really had to fight to do competitive lap times and that was when David caught up with me. I still had brake trouble, but I had to ignore it and push hard."*

On several occasions, the Ferrari put out puffs of smoke. *"It was probably my brain boiling over,"* he joked. *"I was completely knackered with so many things to think about. In the*

first part of the race, when I was stuck behind Rubens Barrichello, everything was fine. I was driving steadily to save fuel and I only pushed just before the pit stops, as we had planned. I was praying the car would not break before then. The Italian press would never have believed I was taking it easy and they would have murdered me!"

This win meant Irvine was right on Hakkinen's tail in the championship. *"I am surprised I beat the McLarens, even though I knew we would be better in the race than in qualifying. It seems we can win even when we are not quickest,"* he added. Mind you, it needed the McLarens to trip over one another (see page 162.)

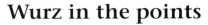

Wurz in the points

There was a slight improvement at Benetton. The anglo-italian team was going through one of the worst periods in its history. No one was too sure what would happen to the team, as it was rumoured the Benetton family was considering selling up and the B199 was such a dog, the drivers never had a good word to say about it.

In these difficult circumstances, fifth place at Zeltweg for local boy, Alex Wurz was greeted with great enthusiasm by the crowd as well as the team. *"I think I found the right rhythm at this circuit. Finishing fifth is cool,"* he said.

In the other Benetton, Giancarlo Fisichella was sixth for a long time before going off with brake problems. *"I managed to get back on the track, but my car was not handling as well as before."* He ended up twelfth at the flag.

◁
The Benetton mechanics celebrate Alexander Wurz's fifth place. The anglo-italian team were in such a sorry state that fifth was like a win to them.

"Not a bad shortcut." Heinz-Harald Frentzen finished fourth despite an off-track excursion.
▽

Zanardi and Alesi run out of fuel!

It always looks a bit stupid to run out of fuel on the motorway. But that's nothing compared with the shame when it happens to a Formula 1 driver who is paid a fortune and then forgets to stop at the fuel pumps!

At Zeltweg, this most stupid of situations happened to both Alex Zanardi and Jean Alesi, for whom this was a second offence after he did the same thing, driving for Benetton in the 1997 Australian Grand Prix. *"I feel a bit responsible for what happened,"* conceded Zanardi. *"My radio had stopped working and I was pushing*

Diniz so hard that I did not look at my pit board. I saw him third time round, but by then it was too late!"

Jean Alesi came up with the same excuse. *"What can I say? I was attacking like mad and I was using more fuel than I should have been. I was so close behind Hill that I didn't see the pit board and I could not hear anything on the radio. It's tough for me!"* And for the team then? After the race, Peter Sauber was not too hard on his driver: *"At least we scored a point with Diniz. It's not too bad."*

Jacques Villeneuve flies between the barriers on the Spielberg track. In Austria, the Canadian retired with transmission failure, which is what one had come to expect. The BAR team spent the summer tilting at the windmills of its own unreliability.

GROSSER PREIS VON ÖSTERREICH

Triumph at Hockenheim

A week after winning in Austria, Eddie Irvine did it again in Germany, where the Scuderia even treated itself to a sumptuous one-two finish thanks to Mika Salo's second place.
It was a lucky double nevertheless, as the Ferraris seemed powerless against the McLarens and they owed their success to the misfortune which yet again hit Mika Hakkinen.
The hero of the hour was without a doubt Mika Salo. The Finn led the race and would no doubt have won, but for the fact he very correctly let Eddie Irvine pass him.

GROSSER MOBIL 1 PREIS VON DEUTSCHLAND
HOCKENHEIM

Mika Hakkinen takes the Ostkurve absolutely flat out. In Hockenheim, the Finn recorded his eighth pole position in ten starts. And it was not over yet.

Mika Hakkinen takes the Ostkurve absolutely flat out. In Hockenheim, the Finn recorded his eighth pole position in ten starts. And it was not over yet.

By no stretch of the imagination could you describe the German Grand Prix as a traveller's delight, but at least the streets of Heidelberg are worth a brief detour .

Incredible Heinz-Harald Frentzen. Up until now, he had qualified on the third or fourth row, but here in Hockenheim, the German grabbed a place on the front row. For the home crowd, it was some consolation for the absence of Michael Schumacher.

"HH" is the big surprise

With no Michael Schumacher this year, the Hockenheim stadium was not as riotous as in previous years.

However, on Saturday, the fans all draped in red, forgot their passion for Ferrari and let themselves go for a brief moment to cheer Heinz-Harald Frentzen, "the other" German. For a few moments the Jordan driver actually topped the time sheet. In the end, Hakkinen took pole back by the tiny margin of five hundredths of a second. Everyone was surprised but nobody more so than Heinz-Harald himself.

"I expected the McLarens to be much stronger here at this track," remarked "HH," casting a sly grin at Mika Hakkinen and David Coulthard, sitting next to him in the press conference. *"We made some progress during testing in Monza and we also have a new engine, but all the same I'm surprised to be on the front row. When I did my time, the team did not have to tell me over the radio. I could tell from the reaction of the crowd that I was out in front. It was a great feeling."*

Although he had scored his eighth pole position from ten races, Mika Hakkinen was also surprised he had not been quicker. *"I expected a bigger gap to the Ferrari,"* commented the world champion. *"But I must say I could have done better if I had not lost some time because of gravel thrown onto the track."*

As Jean Todt pointed out, the German Grand Prix was going to be decided by a good strategy, partly due to the high ambient temperature. That did not worry the men from McLaren. *"Everybody goes on about Ferrari's tactical ability,"* retorted Ron Dennis. *"But we also have specialists who keep an eye on track traffic to help calculate the best moment to make a pit stop."*

Only fifth place for the Irishman

Eddie no better than row three

Eddie Irvine had certainly been hoping for more than a place on the third row before the qualifying session started. But an off-track excursion, errors in the set-up and traffic on the track accounted for his four attempts. He tried to make the best of it. *"Well, fifth is better than fourth on this track, because it is better to be on the outside line for the start. In fact, I think we are closer to the McLarens here* than in Austria, but we simply did not get the most out of the car."

For his part, Mika Salo qualified on the second row and the Finn was very happy with that.

"I made no mistakes and I got the result I was looking for. I am still not completely used to this car, but it's getting better. Its braking ability is mind-blowing."

STARTING GRID

Heinz-H. FRENTZEN 1'43"000	-1-	Mika HÄKKINEN 1'42"950
Mika SALO 1'43"577	-2-	David COULTHARD 1'43"288
R. BARRICHELLO 1'43"938	-3-	Eddie IRVINE 1'43"769
Damon HILL 1'44"001	-4-	Olivier PANIS 1'43"979
G. FISICHELLA 1'44"338	-5-	Jarno TRULLI 1'44"209
Jacques VILLENEUVE 1'44"508	-6-	Ralf SCHUMACHER 1'44"468
Alessandro ZANARDI 1'45"034	-7-	Alexander WURZ 1'44"522
Pedro DINIZ 1'45"335	-8-	Marc GENÉ 1'45"331
Ricardo ZONTA 1'45"460	-9-	Johnny HERBERT 1'45"454
Pedro de la ROSA 1'45"935	-10-	Luca BADOER 1'45"917
Toranosuke TAKAGI 1'46"209	-11-	Jean ALESI 1'45"962

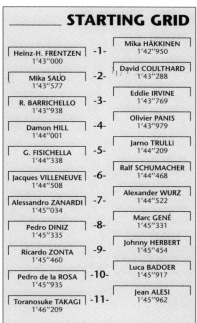

Ferrari's great good fortune

After a bad time in practice, the race did not exactly get off to a good start for Eddie Irvine. An average start had relegated him to sixth place at the end of the opening lap. When the Irishman realised he also had an oil temperature problem, he thought it was not his day. "At the start I had to lift off behind David Coulthard and I lost my momentum," he recalled. "Just after that, Rubens Barrichello passed me and I did not put up much of a fight as I reckoned he was on a two stop strategy. I quickly lost ground, but if I tried to go quicker, the oil temperature came up and I had to slow down. I thought it was better to wait and see how things developed."

Dropping like flies at the front

In the light of qualifying, Scuderia Ferrari did not start the grand prix with thoughts of winning, but rather they were looking for a few points in the championship. However, after Barrichello retired and after he got past Frentzen during the pit stops and then the two McLarens retired, Irvine found himself by some sort of miracle in the lead, or at least he did after his team mate had let him pass as per team orders.

The race was not yet won, as the Irishman's oil temperature problems prevented him from stepping up the pace while Heinz-Harald Frentzen was closing up. But the two Ferraris managed to hang on to the chequered flag. It was a totally unexpected win, which hoisted Irvine back into the lead of the world championship, with an eight point advantage over Mika Hakkinen. However, the Irishman was not prepared to think about the title: "I am too much of a realist to believe in it. Lots

of kids dream about this sort of thing, but I didn't. And I am not going to start today." Irvine added that he had no great desire to celebrate this win. "In fact the McLarens are much quicker than us. Under normal circumstances we would never have beaten them, so there is no point in getting too excited."

Luck was not the only deciding factor. One has to know how to seize the opportunity. At Hockenheim, the Ferraris had survived a race of terrible mechanical attrition.

The F399 seemed bulletproof as Eddie Irvine had scored points in all but one race up until this point in the season.

Super Salo

Mika Salo was the moral victor of the German Grand Prix. But for loyalty to the team, he could have won the race, as he was ahead of Eddie Irvine in a car that was running perfectly. "Mika is the real winner today," claimed Eddie Irvine. "I think I'll give him the trophy."
For his part, the Finn was modest about his achievement. "I don't want to think about winning," he affirmed. "We had decided on the strategy, Eddie and me and I stuck to it, that's all. But in the end it was not so easy. Eddie was crui-

sing and I had Frentzen all over me. I had to call the pits and ask them to tell Eddie to speed up!"
At Hockenheim, the Finn admitted that he felt more comfortable in the Ferrari, even though there was still room for improvement. "I've still got a lot to learn. For example, I am not yet using the brake balance control and other adjustments like this. I had spoken to Michael (Schumacher) by phone before the race. He told me 'just drive and the team will do the rest.' He was right."

"HH" on the podium once again

Sunday after Sunday, Frentzen was confirming his great talent and his rediscovered form since joining the Jordan team.
After winning in Magny-Cours, here he was on the podium again, with a third place just four seconds behind the winner. "It's true that I am quite close to the winner, but I got it all wrong at the start," he explained. "I was looking at the red lights and suddenly my water temperature warning light came on and it distracted me. I got too much wheelspin and Salo and Coulthard managed to get past me."
The Jordan driver was then passed by Eddie Irvine during the pit stops. "We refuelled as quickly as possible without any problem," he went on. "So I don't know how Ferrari managed to get ahead of us."
He was now third in the world championship, 19 points down on Irvine, but the German said he did not rate his chances for the title. "To become world champion, you have to start by winning races, a lot of races. Even though our car is very good this year, sometimes we lose a bit of our potential. We have to analyse why this happens and rectify the situation for 2000."

△
Lap 25. Mika Salo leads briefly from Eddie Irvine (in the background.) The Finn did not hesitate in letting his team leader pass.

Incredible double for the Ferraris and a great atmosphere on the podium.
▽

Schumacher live

Michael Schumacher was able to speak to his army of fans in the Motodrom stadium section of the Hockenheim circuit. Sitting at home in Vufflens-le-Chateau in Switzerland, the German was beamed in by satellite to the giant screens around the track. He explained that he was recovering quicker than expected from his accident, but that it would be several weeks before he was fully fit. The link-up met with mixed reaction as some fans reckoned he should have made the trip by helicopter.

◁
The two Minardis in action. At Hockenheim, Marc Gene and Luca Badoer finished the grand prix in 9th and 10th places respectively.

GROSSER MOBIL 1 PREIS VON DEUTSCHLAND

And another point for Olivier Panis, who finishes sixth in a hectic German Grand Prix. At a time when scoring points in Formula 1 is increasingly difficult, a sixth place is as good as a win for the small teams.

GROSSER MOBIL 1 PREIS VON DEUTSCHLAND

Mika takes his revenge

After drawing a blank in the last four grands prix, Mika Hakkinen took his revenge in Budapest.
On a track which should have favoured the Ferraris, the Finn scored a very convincing win, which also saw his rival Eddie Irvine relegated to third place.
With David Coulthard second, McLaren's triumph was complete. Watching the way he punched the air on the podium it was easy to understand the frustration Mika had felt in England, Austria and Germany.

MARLBORO MAGYAR NAGYDÍJ
BUDAPEST

practice

Hakkinen and Irvine on the front row

Jean Alesi, David Coulthard and Toranosuke Takagi in action. The three men would qualify on the 11th, 3rd and 21st rows respectively, thus representing three different performance levels on the starting grid. For Jean Alesi, a relatively poor performance would come to a sticky end this weekend. After the race, the Frenchman announced he would be leaving the Sauber team at the end of the season.

▽

Nine drivers covered by a handkerchief

While Mika Hakkinen notched up his ninth pole position in Budapest, Eddie Irvine only gave away one tenth of a second. All in all, nine drivers qualified in the same second! Narrow and twisty, the Hungaroring layout appeared to have been designed to induce a Sunday siesta in the spectators. Overtaking was a virtual impossibility and races often became processional, interrupted only by the need to refuel.

In this context, securing pole position takes on a similar importance to Monaco. In obtaining his ninth pole of the season, Mika Hakkinen had laid the groundwork for victory. He

was very aware of that fact. *"It's a shame for Eddie (Irvine,) but I am very confident about my chances of winning here. That would help me forget the bad memories of the last three grands prix."* His pole position was given a joyous reception by the thousands of Finns who had made the journey to Budapest and had swamped the circuit's grandstands. *"I don't know why so many of my fellow countrymen are here,"* puzzled Hakkinen. *"It might be that the Hungarian mentality is similar to that of the Finns. Maybe it has something to do with the fact there are now two Finns with a chance of winning, with Mika Salo at Ferrari. All I know is that 23 extra flights were*

organised from Helsinki to Budapest this weekend." Eddie Irvine, sitting next to Mika in the press conference, suggested that must correspond to the entire population of Finland.

Irvine was rather disappointed to have missed out on pole position by just one tenth of a second, especially as he felt his F399 was capable of doing better. *"I had thought that if there was anywhere I could get pole, it would have been here,"* he said with regret in his voice. *"Unfortunately we were giving away too much to the McLarens in a straight line. On top of that, I was held up by a Stewart on my final lap. Otherwise, I think I could have done a time in the 1m 17s."*

STARTING GRID

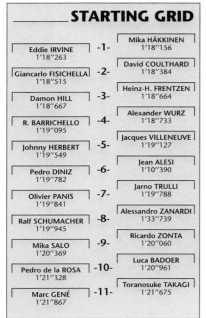

	Mika HÄKKINEN 1'18"156	
Eddie IRVINE 1'18"263	**-1-**	
	David COULTHARD 1'18"384	
Giancarlo FISICHELLA 1'18"515	**-2-**	
	Heinz-H. FRENTZEN 1'18"664	
Damon HILL 1'18"667	**-3-**	
	Alexander WURZ 1'18"733	
R. BARRICHELLO 1'19"095	**-4-**	
	Jacques VILLENEUVE 1'19"127	
Johnny HERBERT 1'19"549	**-5-**	
	Jean ALESI 1'10"390	
Pedro DINIZ 1'19"782	**-6-**	
	Jarno TRULLI 1'19"788	
Olivier PANIS 1'19"841	**-7-**	
	Alessandro ZANARDI 1'33"739	
Ralf SCHUMACHER 1'19"945	**-8-**	
	Ricardo ZONTA 1'20"060	
Mika SALO 1'20"369	**-9-**	
	Luca BADOER 1'20"961	
Pedro de la ROSA 1'21"328	**-10-**	
	Toranosuke TAKAGI 1'21"675	
Marc GENÉ 1'21"867	**-11-**	

△ *A helicopter shot of the Hungaroring circuit. Hungary has staged a grand prix every year since 1986. Since then, the circuit facilities have been gradually improved and this year, the number of spectators had again gone up when compared to the drop in numbers recorded in 1997.*

Return to the summit

Finally! Having lost a wheel at Silverstone, after being hit by David Coulthard at Zeltweg and then enduring a tyre problem at Hockenheim, Mika Hakkinen finally got it all right in Budapest. Starting from pole position, the Finn did not entrust the task of leading the race to anyone else from start to finish.

This time there were no disasters waiting on the way. *"It's really great,"* rejoiced the Finn. *"With ten laps to go, I said to myself, if anything has to go wrong then it's now or never. But everything went well. The car was really fantastic today."*

One only had to look at the tyres that came off both McLarens after the race to see they were on another planet. They were still perfect, while those off the Ferraris and Jordans were down to the canvas. Yet more proof of how well balanced was the MP4/14 chassis.

The car was good enough to give Hakkinen a thirty second lead over the field within a matter of a few laps. *"30 seconds in Formula 1 is huge,"* he said. *"It really was a fantastic feeling to have such a big lead. It meant I could choose my line carefully and slow down a bit, even though you cannot really drop the pace too much because then the tyre pressures go down and the car's balance is altered."*

Unfortunately, Hakkinen's return to the winner's enclosure also signalled the return of soporific racing. The only exciting moment in Budapest took place when Eddie Irvine and David Coulthard decided to refuel at the same time on lap 58. The Scotsman was hoping this would be his chance to take second place off the Irishman. But the Ferrari mechanics were as quick as the McLaren crew and it did not work out. *"Actually I wanted to stop one lap ahead of Eddie to get at least one clear lap,"* explained Coulthard. *"But it was fun stopping at the same time. After that, I was stuck behind Eddie, hoping he would make a mistake and that is exactly what happened."*

Mika Hakkinen's ten points were all the more valuable as Eddie Irvine, his main rival in the race for the title, only finished third (see below.)

Three more points for Heinz-Harald

By finishing fourth in the Hungarian Grand Prix, Heinz-Harald Frentzen had scored points for the fifth time in a row. It showed great consistency and was rewarded with third place in the championship, equal with David Coulthard. *"Everything went well. The car was consistent and reliable, which is why I could score points for the eighth time this year,"* was "HH's" straightforward comment. In fact, the German could have done better, but the team got his refuelling strategy wrong. Coming into the pits too soon enabled David Coulthard to pass him.

In the other Jordan, Damon Hill finished sixth. Towards the end of the race, the Englishman had to slow down because of an engine air pressure problem.

△
They're off! Mika Hakkinen makes a perfect start and takes the lead from Eddie Irvine

"I know you are looking for stars for your next film, my dear Sly. Did you know I'm a great actor? Sometimes I can even manage a smile when Eddie wins a grand prix."
◁▽

Mika Hakkinen at work. Victory awaits at the end of the day
▽

Eddie could do no better

Third place and a paltry four points was all Scuderia Ferrari could take home from the Hungarian Grand Prix: not a lot when closest rivals McLaren picked up 16 points for a one-two finish.

From all accounts, something had gone seriously wrong this weekend in the Ferrari camp. *"Yes, we had problems,"* admitted Eddie Irvine. *"I made quite a good start but my tyres went off after only two or three laps and there was nothing I could do. I had problems with the front and the back of the car. It was all over the road. We made a lot of mistakes this weekend. Now we have to study everything and try and solve the problems."*

Irvine could have finished second ahead of Coulthard, if he had not gone slightly wide at Turn 5. *"I knew David was quicker than me and I was pushing as hard as I could to stay ahead. But I overdid it and went off. By the time I was back on the track there was nothing I could do about him."*

Those four points for third place were just enough to keep him in the lead of the championship, two points ahead of Hakkinen. *"It was a disappointing race of course,"* he concluded. *"But we had two good weekends in a row, so its normal to have a bad one now and again. I did manage to score four points. It could have been worse."*

Having started from 18th place on the grid, Mika Salo finished 12th. It was a minor catastrophe for the man who had been capable of winning the previous race at Hockenheim two weeks earlier. *"I had a terrible race,"* he admitted. *"I was stuck behind slower cars that I just couldn't pass."* The car was awful and was all over the place. To make matters worse for the Finn, the loose end of his safety harness got stuck behind his right shoulder and he was in great pain, which affected his concentration. *"I feel I have let the team down. It's very embarrassing,"* he continued. *"I am keen to start testing again next week, so that I can understand what happened with my car today."*

 **MARLBORO MAGYAR NAGYDÍJ**

Alexander Wurz was almost in front of his home crowd in Hungary, which borders Austria. Unfortunately, the Benetton driver was unable to make anything of it as he could manage no better than seventh place, a little over five seconds behind Damon Hill in sixth spot. In Budapest he suffered because there were few retirements at the front and because it was impossible to overtake. Mika Salo in 12th place, knew all about that.

MARLBORO MAGYAR NAGYDÍJ

Two weeks is a long time in F1. Having been the star of Hockenheim, Mika Salo was lost in Budapest.

"I would rather block my ears than listen to this incessant criticism!" Jacques Villeneuve posted yet another retirement in Budapest; this time with a clutch problem.

"Luckily there are no breathalysers on the track!" Stewart had organised a whisky tasting one afternoon. It was a Scottish thing.

The splendour of Budapest. Inexorably, year after year, western culture slowly seeps into the former communist capital. Today, it is rare to come across a Trabant, while one can find McDonalds everywhere.

Alesi splits with Swiss

It was a tough weekend for the Saubers. Jean Alesi was forced to retire with a fuel feed problem, which occurred no less than three times during the race before finally stopping the engine.

It was the final straw for the Frenchman. Back in the garage he eventually let rip. *"I don't know what I will do next year. Maybe I'll go cycling, or drive in F1 or try karting, or I might become a fireman. But one thing's for certain, I will not be driving for Sauber!"* Peter Sauber's only regret was that Alesi had made his feelings known in public. *"It's a shame, Jean did not keep silent,"* commented the man from Zurich. *"We had decided it was in the best interest of all concerned not to say anything until the Belgian or Italian Grands Prix."* Now, the only question related to the Frenchman's future. In Budapest, he spent part of Sunday at the Prost motorhome; the Guyancourt-based team being one of his options for 2000. *"But I have also got options in the States and Japan,"* added Alesi. *"I would like to thank the Sauber team, which gave me the chance to pursue my career after two years with Benetton. But now, I've had enough."*

Pedro Diniz was also angry with Peter Sauber, but for other reasons: the Brazilian spent the first 19 laps of the race behind Alesi, until his boss got on the radio and ordered him to let the Frenchman pass. While the Brazilian's engineer was telling him to push to close up on Alexander Wurz, Peter Sauber was insisting he slow down to let Alesi through. *"I did it, but I was furious,"* ranted Diniz after the race. *"I lost concentration then and I spun. Anyway, the car had too much oversteer."*

Michael Schumacher hesitates then gives up

In July, Michael Schumacher's entourage insisted that their driver would not be back behind the wheel for several months; probably in time for the Malaysian Grand Prix in mid-October.

It was a big surprise therefore, when on 3rd August, Schumacher's manager Willi Weber announced that his charge intended testing his Ferrari the following Saturday at the team's private Fiorano test track. *"If Michael can drive without any problems, we will think about him taking part in the Hungarian Grand Prix,"* concluded Willi Weber.

Heiner Buchinger, Schumacher's personal press officer, was not singing off the same hymn sheet. *"It is very unlikely that Michael will be able to test on Saturday,"* he said. *"On Friday, he must undergo a medical examination in Switzerland and his doctor will then decide if he is up to trying to drive. Michael will follow his advice come what may."*

Even though the double fracture of his right leg was healing normally, Schumacher could not yet put any weight on his foot. It seemed unlikely therefore that the doctor would let him drive. *"Michael can only walk with two sticks,"* continued Buchinger. *"And even if his doctor lets him drive, it is quite possible that Syd Watkins, the F1 doctor, will not pass him fit for Budapest."*

Finally, Michael Schumacher underwent the examination in a Geneva clinic on Friday 6th August and the doctors advised him to delay his comeback. *"He has been advised not to try driving a Formula 1 car just yet,"* said Buchinger. *"There is too great a risk of aggravating his injuries. Not so much because of the risk of another accident, but mainly because of the vibrations a driver is subjected to in a grand prix car. These vibrations could loosen the screws in the bone. The doctors have not forbidden him from driving, but they reckon it is pointless taking the risk of aggravating his injuries, thus further delaying his return to the cockpit. It is essential that Michael does some testing before tackling a grand prix, to see how much pain it causes him."* Nevertheless, Michael Schumacher was getting better quickly. The week before the Hungarian Grand Prix, he underwent another operation to remove the screws from his right leg, to speed up his recovery.

results

PRACTICE TIMES

No	Driver	Car/Engine/Chassis	Practice Friday	Pos.	Practice Saturday	Pos.	Qualifying	Pos.	Warm-up	Pos.
1.	Mika Häkkinen	McLaren/Mercedes/MP4 -14/4	1'19"722	2°	1'18'219	1°	1'18"156	1°	1'20"435	2°
2.	David Coulthard	McLaren/Mercedes/MP4 -14/6	1'20"117	3°	1'18'890	2°	1'18"384	3°	1'20"420	1°
3.	Mika Salo	Ferrari/Ferrari/F399/195	1'20"989	5°	1'20'139	15°	1'20"369	18°	1'22"226	14°
4.	Eddie Irvine	Ferrari/Ferrari/F399/191	1'19"476	1°	1'19'817	11°	1'18"263	2°	1'21"083	5°
5.	Alessandro Zanardi	Williams/Supertec/FW21/05	1'21"251	7°	1'19'926	14°	1'19"924	15°	1'22"530	16°
6.	Ralf Schumacher	Williams/Supertec/FW21/06	1'21"481	9°	1'19'825	12°	1'19"945	16°	-	-
7.	Damon Hill	Jordan/Mugen-Honda/199/4	1'22"182	16°	1'19'356	7°	1'18"667	6°	1'22"321	15°
8.	Heinz-Harald Frentzen	Jordan/Mugen-Honda/199/5	1'21"185	6°	1'19'012	3°	1'18"664	5°	1'20"454	3°
9.	Giancarlo Fisichella	Benetton/Playlife/B199/07	1'21"673	14°	1'19'641	9°	1'18"515	4°	1'20"704	4°
10.	Alexander Wurz	Benetton/Playlife/B199/05	1'21"456	8°	1'19'715	10°	1'18"733	7°	1'21"154	7°
11.	Jean Alesi	Sauber/Petronas/C18/06	1'22"009	15°	1'20'323	17°	1'19"390	11°	1'21"083	6°
12.	Pedro Diniz	Sauber/Petronas/C18/07	1'23"096	20°	1'20'342	18°	1'19"782	12°	1'21"853	13°
14.	Pedro de la Rosa	Arrows/Arrows/A20/04	1'24"064	22°	1'21'398	19°	1'21"328	20°	1'23"812	20°
15.	Toranosuke Takagi	Arrows/Arrows/A20/02	1'23"216	21°	1'22'213	22°	1'21"675	21°	1'23"364	19°
16.	Rubens Barrichello	Stewart/Ford/SF3/04	1'20"547	4°	1'19'186	5°	1'19"095	8°	1'21"671	12°
17.	Johnny Herbert	Stewart/Ford/SF3/05	1'21"486	10°	1'19'164	4°	1'19"389	10°	1'21"549	10°
18.	Olivier Panis	Prost/Peugeot/AP02/5	1'21"525	12°	1'19'920	13°	1'19"841	14°	1'21"561	11°
19.	Jarno Trulli	Prost/Peugeot/AP02/7	1'22"360	18°	1'19'518	8°	1'19"788	13°	1'21"364	9°
20.	Luca Badoer	Minardi/Ford/M01/01	1'21"635	13°	1'21'523	20°	1'20"961	19°	1'22"849	17°
21.	Marc Gené	Minardi/Ford/M01/04	1'22"380	19°	1'21'568	21°	1'21"867	22°	1'24"065	21°
22.	Jacques Villeneuve	BAR/Supertec/BAR01/08	1'21"504	11°	1'19'332	6°	1'19"127	9°	1'21"211	8°
23.	Ricardo Zonta	BAR/Supertec/BAR01/05	1'22"290	17°	1'20'152	16°	1'20"060	17°	1'22"889	18°

MAXIMUM SPEEDS

No	Driver	P1 Qualifs	Pos	P1 Race	Pos	P2 Qualifs	Pos	P2 Race	Pos	Finish Qualifs	Pos	Finish Race	Pos	Trap Qualifs	Pos	Trap Race	Pos
1.	M. Häkkinen	286,7	1°	281,4	2°	231,8	5°	225,7	5°	259,0	1°	252,6	4°	290,0	1°	287,9	5°
2.	D. Coulthard	285,7	2°	287,5	1°	231,4	6°	227,6	1°	257,8	2°	255,0	1°	286,4	2°	292,7	1°
3.	M. Salo	278,2	18°	276,5	13°	226,0	17°	219,4	16°	248,9	18°	249,3	13°	276,4	17°	286,3	10°
4.	E. Irvine	278,9	13°	280,3	4°	229,3	11°	222,8	10°	251,7	9°	250,8	8°	279,0	14°	286,5	8°
5.	A. Zanardi	283,4	3°	273,0	18°	226,8	15°	215,9	20°	252,5	7°	245,7	18°	-	-	285,9	14°
6.	R. Schumacher	282,0	4°	280,0	5°	227,8	14°	221,9	12°	252,5	6°	250,2	11°	282,5	3°	289,9	2°
7.	D. Hill	279,3	12°	278,9	8°	233,0	2°	226,7	3°	251,2	11°	252,4	5°	278,9	15°	286,4	9°
8.	H.-H. Frentzen	279,4	10°	275,2	14°	230,3	9°	227,4	2°	253,8	3°	252,9	3°	280,1	6°	286,2	11°
9.	G. Fisichella	279,6	7°	277,9	10°	230,3	10°	223,1	9°	250,8	12°	250,5	10°	279,7	11°	287,6	6°
10.	A. Wurz	279,5	9°	276,8	12°	228,3	12°	221,0	14°	251,2	10°	250,8	9°	280,0	9°	288,0	4°
11.	J. Alesi	279,5	8°	279,5	6°	230,6	8°	225,6	7°	250,5	14°	252,4	6°	-	-	286,1	12°
12.	P. Diniz	278,4	16°	275,2	15°	230,8	7°	221,3	13°	249,4	16°	248,4	15°	280,0	7°	285,4	15°
14.	P. de la Rosa	273,0	20°	272,9	19°	223,0	21°	217,2	19°	245,3	21°	245,3	19°	271,2	19°	281,9	18°
15.	T. Takagi	271,3	22°	271,2	22°	221,8	22°	211,0	22°	244,6	22°	244,2	21°	270,1	20°	281,4	21°
16.	R. Barrichello	278,2	17°	279,1	7°	235,0	1°	226,3	4°	252,5	5°	253,3	2°	279,0	13°	287,3	7°
17.	J. Herbert	279,3	11°	277,5	11°	231,8	4°	225,7	6°	252,6	4°	249,9	12°	280,0	8°	284,5	16°
18.	O. Panis	278,9	15°	273,1	17°	225,4	18°	218,7	18°	249,4	17°	246,4	17°	279,7	12°	280,3	22°
19.	J. Trulli	279,9	6°	275,1	16°	226,7	16°	220,5	15°	250,8	13°	246,6	16°	281,9	4°	283,0	17°
20.	L. Badoer	274,6	19°	272,3	21°	225,0	19°	219,2	17°	247,7	19°	244,8	20°	277,5	16°	281,7	19°
21.	M. Gené	271,8	21°	272,6	20°	223,4	20°	215,3	21°	245,6	20°	244,0	22°	273,2	18°	281,7	20°
22.	J. Villeneuve	280,7	5°	281,1	3°	232,1	3°	222,0	11°	252,0	8°	251,5	7°	280,9	5°	289,5	3°
23.	R. Zonta	278,9	14°	278,0	9°	228,0	13°	225,2	8°	250,3	15°	248,6	14°	279,7	10°	286,1	13°

CLASSIFICATION & RETIREMENTS

Pos	Drivers	Team	Time
1.	Häkkinen	McLaren Mercedes	in 1h45'523"536
2.	Coulthard	McLaren Mercedes	at 9"706
3.	Irvine	Ferrari	at 27"228
4.	Frentzen	Jordan Mugen Honda	at 31"815
5.	Barrichellol	Stewart Ford	at 43"808
6.	Hill	Jordan Mugen Honda	at 55"726
7.	Wurz	Benetton Playlife	at 61"012
8.	Trulli	Prost Peugeut	at 1 tour
9.	R. Schum.	Williams Supertec	at 1 tour
10.	Panis	Prost Peugeot	at 1 tour
11.	Herbert	Stewart Ford	at 1 tour
12.	Salo	Ferrari	at 2 tours
13.	Zonta	BAR Supertec	at 2 tours
14.	Badoer	Minardi Ford	à 2 tours
15.	de la Rosa	Arrows	at 2 tours
16.	Gené	Minardi Ford	at 3 tours

Lap	Drivers	Team	Reason
75	Alesi	Sauber Petronas	fuel pressure
11	Zanardi	Williams Supertec	broken différential
20	Diniz	Sauber Petronas	off
27	Takagi	Arrows	transmission
53	Fisichella	Benetton Playlife	engine
61	Villeneuve	BAR Supertec	transmission

FASTEST LAPS

	Drivers	Time	Lap
1.	Coulthard	1'20"699	69
2.	Häkkinen	1'20"710	44
3.	Alesi	1'20"830	45
4.	Frentzen	1'20"991	71
5.	Irvine	1'21"010	62
6.	Hill	1'21"180	31
7.	Zonta	1'21"343	32
8.	Fisichella	1'21"469	51
9.	Wurz	1'21"539	71
10.	Barrichello	1'21"707	38
11.	R. Schum.	1'21"745	48
12.	Trulli	1'21"936	45
13.	Villeneuve	1'21"975	49
14.	Diniz	1'22"452	19
15.	Herbert	1'22"455	70
16.	Panis	1'22"587	59
17.	Salo	1'22"684	49
18.	Badoer	1'23"456	45
19.	de la Rosa	1'23"520	47
20.	Zanardi	1'24"297	7
21.	Gené	1'24"807	28
22.	Takagi	1'25"483	11

LAP CHART

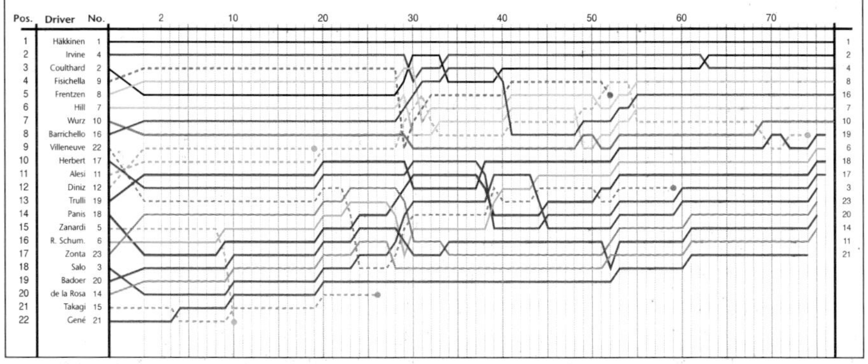

All results :

© 1999 Fédération Internationale de l'Automobile, 2, Ch. Blandonnet, 1215 Genève 15, Suisse

PIT STOPS

	Driver	Time	Lap	Stop n°
1.	Villeneuve	31"005	23	1
2.	Takagi	30"757	25	1
3.	Fisichella	30"796	28	1
4.	R. Schum.	32"494	28	1
5.	de la Rosa	31"412	28	1
6.	Irvine	30"782	29	1
7.	Hill	33"109	29	1
8.	Wurz	30"132	29	1
9.	Trulli	29"468	29	1
10.	Zonta	32"999	29	1
11.	Badoer	30"310	29	1
12.	Frentzen	29"146	30	1
13.	Häkkinen	30"002	31	1
14.	Alesi	29"850	32	1
15.	Coulthard	29"284	33	1
16.	Zonta	31"816	33	2
17.	Gené	35"960	33	1
18.	Herbert	34"625	38	1
19.	Panis	32"556	38	1
20.	Barrichello	33"654	40	1
21.	Salo	31"394	44	1
22.	Hill	31"063	48	2
23.	Frentzen	30"213	50	2
24.	Trulli	29"957	50	2
25.	Villeneuve	32"393	50	2
26.	Wurz	30"613	51	2
27.	R. Schum.	29"889	51	2
28.	Badoer	30"681	51	2
29.	de la Rosa	31"660	52	2
30.	Alesi	46"069	54	2
31.	Häkkinen	30"692	55	2
32.	Irvine	28"868	58	2
33.	Coulthard	28"593	58	2
34.	Zonta	31"554	60	3
35.	Alesi	33"622	69	3

BRIDGESTONE

Quickest pit stop during the Hongarian Grand Prix, taking on fuel and four new Bridgestone tyres:

David Coulthard, McLaren, 28"593

CHAMPIONSHIP

(after eleven rounds)

Drivers :

	Driver	Points
1.	Eddie IRVINE	56
2.	Mika HÄKKINEN	54
3.	David COULTHARD	36
	Heinz-Harald FRENTZEN	36
5.	M. SCHUMACHER	32
6.	R. SCHUMACHER	22
7.	Giancarlo FISICHELLA	13
8.	Rubens BARRICHELLO	12
9.	Mika SALO	6
	Damon HILL	6
11.	Alexander WURZ	3
	Pedro DINIZ	3
13.	Johnny HERBERT	2
	Olivier PANIS	2
15.	Pedro de la ROSA	1
	Jean ALESI	1
	Jarno TRULLI	1

Constructors :

	Constructor	Points
1.	Ferrari	94
2.	McLaren Mercedes	90
3.	Jordan Mugen Honda	42
4.	Williams	22
5.	Benetton Playlife	16
6.	Stewart Ford	14
7.	Sauber Petronas	4
8.	Prost Peugeot	3
6.	Arrows	1

THE CIRCUIT

ELEVENTH ROUND

MARLBORO MAGYAR NAGYDÍJ, BUDAPEST

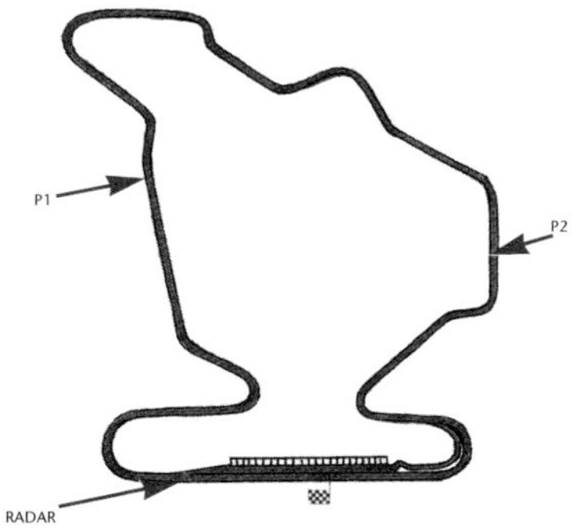

Date : August 15, 1999
Lenght : 3972 meters
Distance : 77 laps, 305.921 km
Weather : cloudy, 26°

RACE SUMMARY

- Mika Hakkinen doesn't allow anyone any hope and charges off into the lead and rapidly pulls away.
- Behind him, Eddie Irvine has to wait until lap 16 before he is able to put in a quicker lap than the Finn, by just two hundredths of a second.
- Eddie Irvine is the first to refuel on lap 30. One lap later and its Mika Hakkinen's turn.
- David Coulthard stops on lap 32 and gets out ahead of Giancarlo Fisichella and Heinz-Harald Frentzen.
- At the front, the gap between Hakkinen and Eddie Irvine increases again. From 20.1s on lap 36, it reaches 29.0s on lap 53.
- Irvine has Coulthard on his tail. After the second pit stops, the Irishman runs wide and the Scot makes the most of it to pass him.

WEEKEND GOSSIP

• Mika is spoiled for choice

After his great race in Hockenheim, Michael Schumacher's replacement Mika Salo had received no less than six job offers for the 2000 season, or at least that is what he said.

• The sun has an appointment with the moon

Everyone was talking about the total eclipse of the sun which occurred on 11thAugust. This event apparently inspired Jean Alesi to go all poetic on us in Budapest: "Eddie Irvine can say what he likes, but he is nothing without Michael Schumacher, who developed the car. Irvine is the moon and Schumacher the sun. Sometimes the moon can hide the sun, but not for long."

• Trulli to Jordan

The transfer market is in full swing. On Friday, Jarno Trulli signed a contract to drive for Eddie Jordan in 2000. The Italian had a get out clause in his contract with the Prost team, which said he could leave if the team had not scored a certain number of points.

• An extra wing

The Jordan team re-introduced the fashion for mid-mounted wings, fitted above the engine cover and supposed to provide extra aerodynamic downforce on slow circuits like the one in Budapest. "Up until now, this solution is working well, as the wing has gone the whole day without breaking," was Eddie Jordan's ironic remark on Friday.

• An enquiry with no results

The enquiry into Mika Hakkinen's tyre failure in the German Grand Prix came up with no conclusive answers. The Bridgestone engineers decided there was nothing wrong with their tyre, while McLaren said the fault was not caused by any element of the chassis.

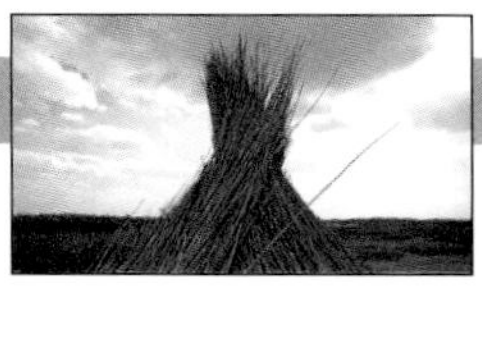

David defies Mika

Of course, Mika Hakkinen was on pole position. But it was David Coulthard who made the best start. In what looked like a replay of their collision in Austria, the two McLarens had a coming together at the Source hairpin. Coulthard came off best and stole the lead (photo.)

The rest of the race was tediously processional with Hakkinen showing no appetite for attacking the other Silver Arrow. With no team orders being in place at McLaren, David stayed ahead of Mika to finish in the wrong order and in turmoil.

**FOSTER'S BELGIAN GRAND PRIX
SPA FRANCORCHAMPS**

Major moments at the Raidillon

The section from Eau Rouge to Raidillon, with its long descent followed by an uphill chicane constitutes without a doubt the most challenging corner in the whole championship. Seen from the side of the track, the cars seem to be glued to the track as they face a wall of tarmac at crazy speeds. No other corner creates such an impression of speed.

In a Formula 1 car, the challenge comes from trying to tackle this section absolutely flat out. Only the very best drivers in the best cars can pull off this stunt.

On Saturday, the corner claimed the two British American Racing cars of Jacques Villeneuve and Ricardo Zonta, within minutes of one another. They both lost the back end before hitting the tyres with a huge whack.

In both cases, the cars were completely destroyed. Seeing both drivers step out unharmed was like watching a miracle take place. Not only did Jacques Villeneuve get out of the wreck with barely a shrug of the shoulders, he then proceeded to jog back to the pits while waving at the crowd. *"Ricardo's and my accident were not caused by any failure on the cars. The BAR01 is hard to master. It is a bit light at the back end, making the car unstable and we just tried a bit too hard. I wanted to take Raidillon flat but I clipped a kerb and that was that. I think taking it flat was on the cards. On the previous lap, I had just feathered the throttle and everything seemed alright."*

Everyone fears the Raidillon a little bit. Third in practice, Heinz-Harald Frentzen admitted that he also had a struggle getting through the corner. *"At Spa, your set-up is a compromise between Raidillon and the rest of the circuit. Before the climb, the suspension is compressed then bounces up in one go. The telemetry shows that it generates a force of 5 G at the bottom of the compression. You don't get that anywhere else as the cars usually run on tracks that are more or less flat."*

Mika yet again

On Saturday, Mika Hakkinen secured his tenth pole position of the season from twelve grands prix. As usual, the Finn managed to lap the track just fractions of a second quicker than his team-mate David Coulthard. *"I cannot really explain why I am always quicker than David,"* admitted Hakkinen. *"It probably comes from the fact I am more experienced and from the confidence I have in my car. It is not just down to set-up and technique. It also depends on concentration."*

But what the Finn was particularly happy about was seeing how far back the Ferraris were. *"Oh, I am really pleased with that,"* he added with a laugh.

Ferrari left for dead

In stark contrast to the satisfaction in the McLaren camp, the Reds were bitterly disappointed. At Spa, the Ferraris could no better than sixth (Eddie Irvine) and ninth place (Mika Salo.) To make their gloom complete, they were over a second and a half down on the McLarens and so there was a lot of work to do. *"Of course we are very disappointed,"* confessed the team's sporting director Jean Todt. *"It will not be an easy race for us. But we have to try and be positive."*

STARTING GRID

David COULTHARD 1'50"484	-1-	Mika HÄKKINEN 1'50"329		
Damon HILL 1'51"372	-2-	Heinz-H. FRENTZEN 1'51"332		
Eddie IRVINE 1'51"895	-3-	Ralf SCHUMACHER 1'51"414		
Alessandro ZANARDI 1'52"014	-4-	R. BARRICHELLO 1'51"974		
Johnny HERBERT 1'52"164	-5-	Mika SALO 1'52"124		
Jarno TRULLI 1'52"644	-6-	Jacques VILLENEUVE 1'52"235		
Ricardo ZONTA 1'52"840	-7-	Giancarlo FISICHELLA 1'52"762		
Jean ALESI 1'52"921	-8-	Alexander WURZ 1'52"847		
Pedro DINIZ 1'53"778	-9-	Olivier PANIS 1'53"148		
Luca BADOER 1'54"197	-10-	Toranosuke TAKAGI 1'54"099		
Pedro de la ROSA 1'54"579	-11-	Marc GENÉ 1'54"557		

the race

David Coulthard refuses to let Mika Hakkinen pass, much to the fury of the Finn

It seemed that David Coulthard was prepared to do almost anything to further his own cause. Even if this policy meant eliminating his team mate Mika Hakkinen, who was way ahead on points in the race for the world championship. Five weeks earlier, at the start of the Austrian grand prix, the Scotsman had made a hash of trying to get ahead of Hakkinen, relegating Hakkinen to the back of the field. However, under pressure from the British press who kept speculating about his abilities as a driver, Coulthard took another huge risk at Spa-Francorchamps.

He got off the line better than Hakkinen and then shut the door at the first corner. The two McLarens touched. *"I had no intention of being aggressive,"* said Coulthard in his own defence after the race. *"I was in front and it was not easy to see exactly where Mika was. When I felt the knock, I thought I better move over in the corner to leave him some room, then I accelerated, that's all."*

Ferrari lose their heads

It was a bad day for the Reds. Until now, the absence of Michael Schumacher had not prevented the Scuderia from putting on some spectacular displays, but the German's brio was sadly lacking in Belgium.

On the roller-coaster Spa circuit, Eddie Irvine never managed to record any competitive lap times. The Irishman accused his car of being all over the road, while team-mate Mika Salo was in even worse shape.

A few weeks earlier at Hockenheim the Finn had claimed that anyone incapable of getting the Ferrari F399 into the top four was a useless tugger. He should have kept his mouth shut. At Spa, he had to settle for ninth place in qualifying.

In the race, Eddie Irvine was incapable of worrying Frentzen, who was ahead of him in the Jordan, let alone the McLarens. Finishing fourth, the Irishman was now second in the championship, one point behind Hakkinen.

It was indeed all for the rest of the race. Knowing who he had to deal with, Hakkinen decided to settle calmly for second place for the rest of the race. Neither McLaren was damaged in the collision, but the Finn didn't even bother to stay withing striking distance of his team-mate. *"There was no point in trying to pass David,"* said the world champion to justify his actions, or lack of them. *"Driving the same cars, there would have been little I could do. When I saw he did the quickest lap early on in the race, I realised it would be better to concentrate on making sure of second place rather than try to keep up with him, push hard*

Ralf Schumacher finished fifth behind Eddie Irvine's Ferrari. A good result in itself, but it left the German driver and the entire Williams team in a state of high dudgeon. It had gone for a one stop strategy and under

McLaren out of order

and risk breaking the car or crashing. I settled for maintaining my advantage over Heinz-Harald Frentzen."

From that moment on, Coulthard was never bothered on the way to his second win of the season. It was a major blow for Hakkinen, who had hoped his team would intervene and ask the Scotsman to move over. When he was asked after the race, if he expected team orders to be issued, he smiled, took a deep breath and... refused to answer. On the podium, he refused to shake the winner's hand and studiously avoided him during the champagne spraying ritual.

Patrick Head furious

normal circumstances, that should have seen Ralf Schumacher finish ahead of Irvine. They had not counted on the blocking tactics of Mika Salo in the second Ferrari, who did everything he could to let Eddie pull away. Patrick Head, the Williams technical director was furious at these tactics. *"Ralf was a victim of Ferrari's cynical tactics,"* he bellowed. *"I am surprised Mika Salo went along with this sort of thing. Ferrari has been doing it for years and I must say, I prefer McLaren's more sporting approach. They definitely deserve to win the world championship and I sincerely hope they do."*

David Coulthard was pleased with himself. This win brought him to within 14 points of Mika Hakkinen in the championship, with four grands prix to go to the end of the season. It was an incentive to fight his own corner even more than before.

Yet another podium for Heinz-Harald Frentzen. Spa marked the sixth consecutive points finish for the German.

Ralf Schumacher was badly held up by Mika Salo, who was protecting Eddie Irvine. The Williams team was furious.

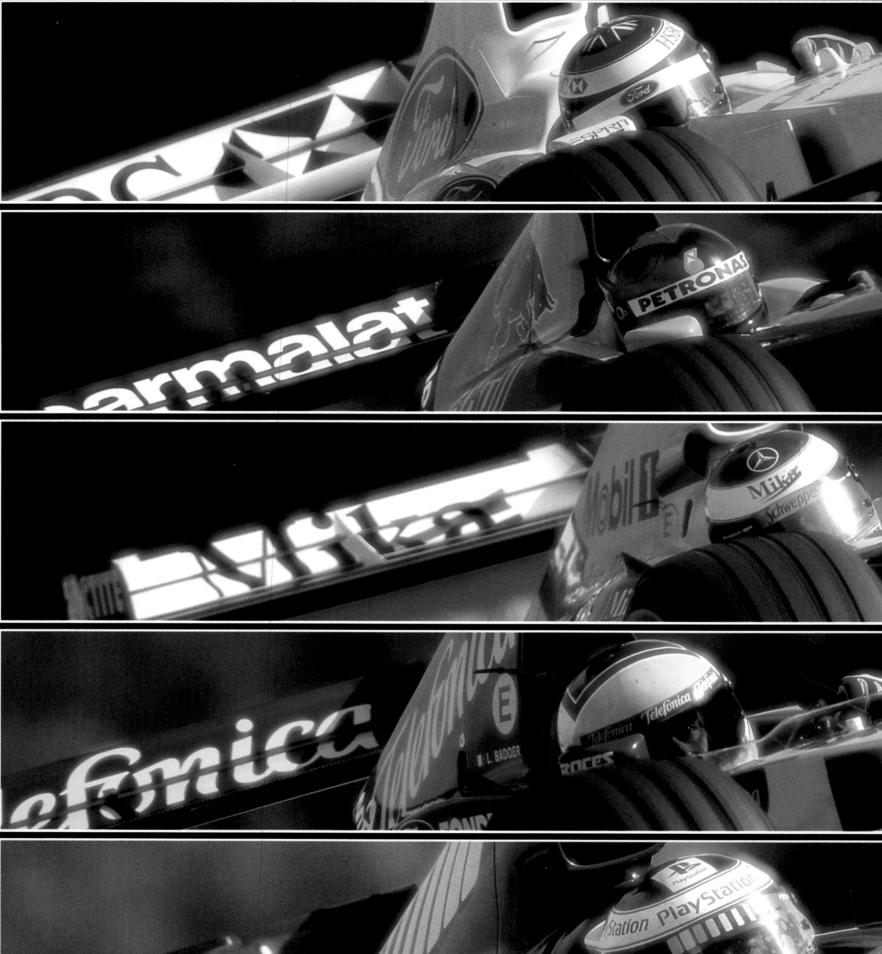

FOSTER'S BELGIAN GRAND PRIX

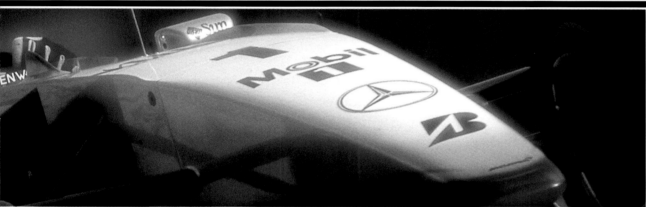

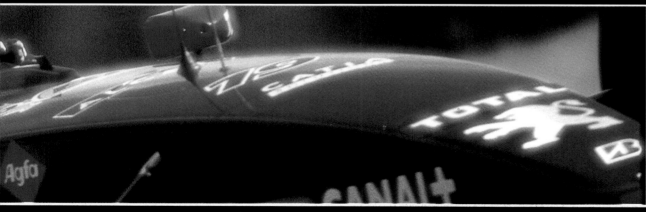

Early morning light at Francorchamps. A dream circuit for the drivers and also for the photographers, who can mess around with the spectacular scenery of the Belgian Ardennes. Except of course when it's raining!

FOSTER'S BELGIAN GRAND PRIX

Toranosuke Takagi was definitely out of luck this season. In Spa he qualified 19th, but did not complete a single lap of the race after an electrical problem on his Arrows.

Olivier Panis was stunned in Spa, after discovering that Jean Alesi and Nick Heidfeld had been employed by Prost. Until then, the man from Grenoble had thought his seat was safe for 2000.
▽▷

Chocolate and Formula 1 go well together. In Brussels, the famous Wittamer shop window had grasped the grand prix theme in spectacular fashion. Yum- yum!
▽

Alain Prost chooses Jean Alesi and Nick Heidfeld

There had not been so many people under the awning of the Prost Grand Prix team motorhome for a long time. On Friday, at half past five in the afternoon, it was packed, as everyone wanted to hear the name of the team's second driver for 2000. Even Alain Prost himself was surprised at the size of his audience. Alongside him, Nick Heidfeld was all smiles. Fifteen days earlier in Budapest, the German had clinched the Formula 3000 championship. It did not take him long to turn the title into an F1 drive, with help from Mercedes and McLaren, Heidfeld having a contract with them as a test driver. *"I am very happy to be driving for Alain Prost,"* remarked the young German. *"I think it is an excellent team with which to learn about F1 and I am counting on Alain's experience to help me a lot."* Heidfeld's contract was only for one year, with an option for 2001. *"I think that the pairing of Jean Alesi and Nick Heidfeld constitutes the perfect marriage between experience on the one hand and youth on the other,"* was Alain Prost's analysis of his choice. *"With these two drivers, we will have two completely different styles and two different working practices."*

In passing, Alain Prost made a point of thanking Olivier Panis for all his help since the creation of the team. *"Olivier brought a lot to the team. Of course, it is sad that we cannot continue, but Formula 1 is a complex alchemy. I could not take the risk of having two drivers of the same nationality, when there was a good chance they would not get on well together."*

With uncertainty looming over the future of Peugeot in Formula 1, it seemed as though the appointment of Heidfeld might be connected to the French team creating a link to Mercedes, who could be persuaded to supply Prost Grand Prix with engines in 2001. Alain Prost was quick to deny such a suggestion. *"Employing Nick is not linked to any other possible contract. However, F1 is not just a sport, it's a business as well. The German market is very important for our partners, which certainly influenced our decision in employing Nick."*

Chewing over the tobacco issue

It was a complicated tale, like all the best Belgian stories. A few months before the Belgian Grand Prix, the federal parliament in Brussels voted in a law, banning all tobacco advertising in Belgium. The French-speaking Walloons voted with their eyes tight shut, without realising this move could put the grand prix, where the cars had always carried their tobacco advertising, in jeopardy. Finally waking up to what they had done and the fact it could cost the region millions of francs, the Walloons quickly voted in a local decree, which over-ruled the federal law.

Or at least that was the theory. Because, in practice, this very "Belgian" arrangement forced the Brussels government to threaten the teams with heavy fines and imprisonment. Right from the start of the weekend, government agents were present at the circuit to check that all tobacco advertising had indeed been covered up on the cars.

This irritated the teams, as the ruling was only made public days before the event. If things did not change for 2000, then this act could signal the death of the Belgian Grand Prix.

results

PRACTICE TIMES

No	Driver	Car/Engine/Chassis	Practice Friday	Pos.	Practice Saturday	Pos.	Qualifying	Pos.	Warm-up	Pos.
1.	Mika Häkkinen	McLaren/Mercedes/MP4-14/04	1'54"021	2°	1'52"259	7°	1'50"329	1°	1'54"019	1°
2.	David Coulthard	McLaren/Mercedes/MP4-14/06	1'53"577	1°	1'51"729	3°	1'50"484	2°	1'54"923	7°
3.	Mika Salo	Ferrari/Ferrari/F399/195	1'55"032	8°	1'52"528	8°	1'52"124	9°	1'55"434	13°
4.	Eddie Irvine	Ferrari/Ferrari/F399/191	1'55"242	9°	1'52"160	6°	1'51"895	6°	1'54"906	6°
5.	Alessandro Zanardi	Williams/Supertec/FW21/02	1'55"743	14°	1'53"301	12°	1'52"014	8°	1'55"366	10°
6.	Ralf Schumacher	Williams/Supertec/FW21/06	1'54"899	6°	1'51"417	2°	1'51"414	5°	1'54"255	2°
7.	Damon Hill	Jordan/Mugen-Honda/199/4	1'54"892	5°	1'51"833	4°	1'51"372	4°	1'54"888	5°
8.	Heinz-Harald Frentzen	Jordan/Mugen-Honda/199/5	1'54"678	4°	1'51"047	1°	1'51"332	3°	1'55"409	12°
9.	Giancarlo Fisichella	Benetton/Playlife/B199/07	1'54"066	3°	1'53"463	15°	1'52"762	13°	1'55"886	17°
10.	Alexander Wurz	Benetton/Playlife/B199/04	1'55"486	12°	1'53"325	14°	1'52"847	15°	1'55"363	9°
11.	Jean Alesi	Sauber/Petronas/C18/04	1'55"271	10°	1'53"317	13°	1'52"921	16°	1'54"799	4°
12.	Pedro Diniz	Sauber/Petronas/C18/07	1'56"310	17°	1'54"112	18°	1'53"778	18°	1'56"990	18°
14.	Pedro de la Rosa	Arrows/Arrows/A20/07	1'56"749	19°	1'54"592	20°	1'54"579	22°	1'57"873	20°
15.	Toranosuke Takagi	Arrows/Arrows/A20/05	1'56"263	16°	1'54"258	19°	1'54"099	19°	1'57"555	19°
16.	Rubens Barrichello	Stewart/Ford/SF3/04	1'55"484	11°	1'52"769	9°	1'51"974	7°	1'55"485	14°
17.	Johnny Herbert	Stewart/Ford/SF3/05	1'54"975	7°	1'52"849	10°	1'52"164	10°	1'55"329	8°
18.	Olivier Panis	Prost/Peugeot/AP02/5	1'55"541	13°	1'53"595	16°	1'53"148	17°	1'54"757	3°
19.	Jarno Trulli	Prost/Peugeot/AP02/7	1'56"765	20°	1'53"061	11°	1'52"644	12°	1'55"394	11°
20.	Luca Badoer	Minardi/Ford/M01/01	1'56"090	15°	1'54"768	21°	1'54"197	20°	1'58"213	21°
21.	Marc Gené	Minardi/Ford/M01/04	1'56"855	21°	1'54"860	22°	1'54"557	21°	1'55"843	16°
22.	Jacques Villeneuve	BAR/Supertec/BAR01/03	1'56"429	18°	1'52"111	5°	1'52"235	11°	1'55"738	15°
23.	Ricardo Zonta	BAR/Supertec/BAR01/01	1'57"717	22°	1'53"926	17°	1'52"840	14°	1'58"442	22°

MAXIMUM SPEEDS

No	Pilote	P1 Qualifs	Pos	P1 Race	Pos	P2 Qualifs	Pos	P2 Race	Pos	Finish Qualifs	Pos	Finish Race	Pos	Trap Qualifs	Pos	Trap Race	Pos
1.	M. Häkkinen	330,1	3°	329,2	4°	191,4	1°	181,5	4°	271,1	2°	266,5	2°	297,9	1°	291,8	1°
2.	D. Coulthard	331,6	1°	327,4	10°	186,8	8°	181,2	6°	271,8	1°	267,3	1°	290,8	6°	285,8	3°
3.	M. Salo	323,9	16°	326,8	11°	187,6	6°	182,0	3°	265,5	9°	264,2	5°	282,7	15°	282,6	7°
4.	E. Irvine	325,9	8°	331,6	1°	183,0	17°	177,2	15°	266,5	5°	263,4	9°	285,3	11°	276,2	15°
5.	A. Zanardi	325,6	11°	327,7	7°	185,5	11°	180,8	9°	264,9	12°	263,5	8°	290,4	7°	287,5	2°
6.	R. Schumacher	327,8	5°	325,6	12°	184,5	14°	177,3	14°	265,8	7°	262,6	11°	293,2	4°	285,7	4°
7.	D. Hill	325,5	13°	329,7	2°	183,5	16°	181,0	8°	267,5	4°	264,9	3°	296,2	2°	281,2	10°
8.	H.-H. Frentzen	330,9	2°	328,6	5°	187,0	7°	180,4	10°	270,0	3°	264,3	4°	289,0	9°	278,2	12°
9.	G. Fisichella	327,0	6°	322,9	15°	185,4	12°	178,7	13°	263,2	17°	259,5	15°	285,2	13°	282,1	8°
10.	A. Wurz	329,7	4°	325,5	13°	184,7	13°	175,3	20°	265,4	10°	260,8	13°	285,1	14°	277,9	13°
11.	J. Alesi	325,5	12°	327,5	8°	188,0	5°	180,1	11°	264,3	14°	261,9	12°	282,5	16°	274,8	16°
12.	P. Diniz	325,1	14°	324,8	14°	182,3	21°	174,2	21°	264,9	13°	258,3	18°	272,9	20°	256,4	20°
14.	P. de la Rosa	324,1	15°	316,8	21°	182,9	19°	176,5	17°	260,3	21°	257,0	20°	286,4	10°	279,5	11°
15.	T. Takagi	322,8	18°	NQ	- -	181,3	22°	NQ	-	260,6	20°	NQ	-	293,2	5°	NQ	--
16.	R. Barrichello	325,9	9°	329,5	3°	188,7	3°	183,2	1°	265,6	8°	263,9	6°	285,2	12°	281,9	9°
17.	J. Herbert	322,9	17°	327,5	9°	189,5	2°	181,0	7°	266,4	6°	263,8	7°	289,0	8°	283,3	5°
18.	O. Panis	326,3	7°	321,9	16°	188,4	4°	182,6	2°	261,5	18°	258,8	17°	278,9	18°	274,8	17°
19.	J. Trulli	325,7	10°	328,5	6°	185,5	10°	179,9	12°	264,1	16°	263,0	10°	271,9	21°	270,0	18°
20.	L. Badoer	322,4	19°	319,7	19°	184,3	15°	176,0	18°	261,1	19°	256,3	21°	275,5	19°	276,4	14°
21.	M. Gené	320,2	21°	320,9	18°	182,9	18°	175,8	19°	258,6	22°	257,6	19°	280,8	17°	282,7	6°
22.	J. Villeneuve	321,2	20°	321,1	17°	185,8	9°	176,5	16°	264,1	15°	260,6	14°	293,3	3°	269,6	19°
23.	R. Zonta	319,0	22°	319,0	20°	182,6	20°	181,5	5°	265,0	11°	259,0	16°	270,4	22°	252,7	21°

CLASSIFICATION & RETIREMENTS

Pos	Drivers	Team	Time
1.	Coulthard	McLaren Mercedes	in 1h25'43"057
2.	Häkkinen	McLaren Mercedes	at 10"469
3.	Frentzen	Jordan Mugen Honda	at 33"433
4.	Irvine	Ferrari	at 44"948
5.	R. Schum.	Williams Supertec	at 48"067
6.	Hill	Jordan Mugen Honda	at 54"916
7.	Salo	Ferrari	at 56"249
8.	Zanardi	Williams Supertec	at 67"022
9.	Alesi	Sauber Petronas	at 73"848
10.	Barrichellol	Stewart Ford	at 80"742
11.	Fisichella	Benetton Playlife	at 92"195
12.	Trulli	Prost Peugeot	at 96"154
13.	Panis	Prost Peugeut	at 1'01"543
14.	Wurz	Benetton Playlife	at 1'17"745
15.	Villeneuve	BAR Supertec	at 1 lap
16.	Gené	Minardi Ford	at 1 lap

Lap	Drivers	Team	Reason
1	Takagi	Arrows	clutch
20	Diniz	Sauber Petronas	off
28	Herbert	Stewart Ford	brakes
34	Zonta	BAR Supertec	gearbox
34	Badoer	Minardi Ford	suspension
36	de la Rosa	Arrows	transmission

FASTEST LAPS

	Driver	Time	Lap
1.	Häkkinen	1'53"955	23
2.	Coulthard	1'54"088	28
3.	Hill	1'54"954	25
4.	Salo	1'55"299	43
5.	Frentzen	1'55"412	24
6.	Irvine	1'55"582	27
7.	Zanardi	1'55"786	33
8.	R. Schum.	1'55"964	27
9.	Alesi	1'56"016	31
10.	Barrichello	1'56"131	34
11.	Trulli	1'56"367	28
12.	Panis	1'56"681	24
13.	Gené	1'56"789	27
14.	Fisichella	1'57"037	27
15.	Herbert	1'57"094	18
16.	Wurz	1'57"526	27
17.	Villeneuve	1'57"619	23
18.	Badoer	1'57"929	31
19.	Diniz	1'58"179	12
20.	de la Rosa	1'58"480	16
21.	Zonta	1'58"918	25

LAP CHART

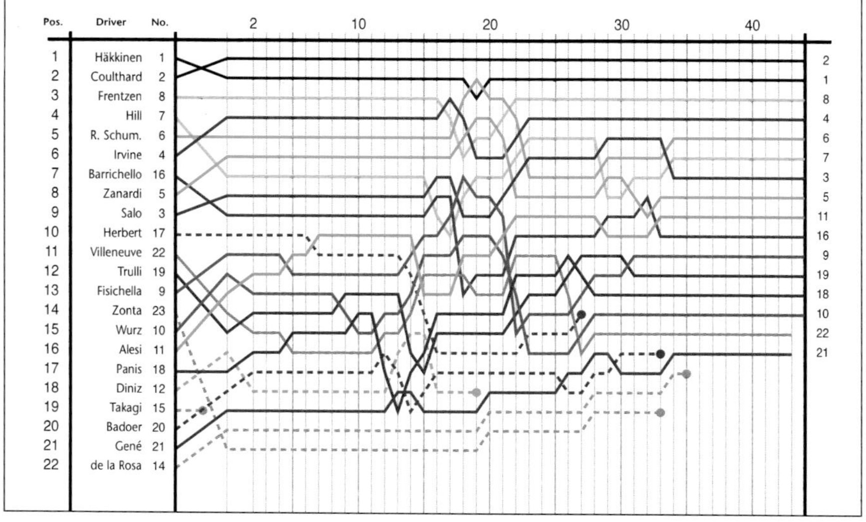

PIT STOPS

	Driver	Time	Lap	Stop n°
1.	Panis	30"260	12	1
2.	Badoer	32"123	13	1
3.	Alesi	32"343	14	1
4.	Trulli	29"281	14	1
5.	Gené	30"399	14	1
6.	de la Rosa	30"309	14	1
7.	Herbert	32"282	15	1
8.	Diniz	31"008	15	1
9.	Hill	28"743	16	1
10.	Frentzen	29"533	17	1
11.	Salo	29"990	17	1
12.	Barrichello	33"038	17	1
13.	Häkkinen	29"917	18	1
14.	Irvine	28"824	18	1
15.	Coulthard	29"025	19	1
16.	Zanardi	30"818	21	1
17.	Fisichella	32"824	21	1
18.	R. Schum.	33"944	22	1
19.	Wurz	32"561	22	1
20.	Zonta	33"351	21	1
21.	Villeneuve	31"944	26	1
22.	Badoer	31"758	26	1
23.	Panis	29"909	27	2
24.	Hill	29"480	28	2
25.	Alesi	29"849	29	2
26.	Gené	31"109	29	2
27.	de la Rosa	31"700	29	2
28.	Trulli	28"683	30	2
29.	Häkkinen	31"749	31	2
30.	Zanardi	28"711	31	2
31.	Coulthard	28"784	32	2
32.	Frentzen	28"275	32	2
33.	Irvine	29"522	32	2
34.	Barrichello	29"874	32	2
35.	Salo	28"379	34	2

BRIDGESTONE

Quickest pit stop during the Belgian Grand Prix, taking on fuel and four new Bridgestone tyres:

H.-H. Frentzen, Jordan, 28"275

CHAMPIONSHIP

(after eight rounds)

Drivers :

1. Mika HÄKKINEN 60
2. Eddie IRVINE 59
3. David COULTHARD 46
4. Heinz-Harald FRENTZEN 40
5. M. SCHUMACHER 32
6. R. SCHUMACHER 24
7. Giancarlo FISICHELLA 13
8. Rubens BARRICHELLO 12
9. Damon HILL 7
10. Mika SALO 6
11. Alexander WURZ 3
    Pedro DINIZ 3
13. Johnny HERBERT 2
    Olivier PANIS 2
15. Pedro de la ROSA 1
    Jean ALESI 1
    Jarno TRULLI 1

Constructors :

1. McLaren Mercedes 106
2. Ferrari 97
3. Jordan Mugen Honda 47
4. Williams 24
5. Benetton Playlife 16
6. Stewart Ford 14
7. Sauber Petronas 4
8. Prost Peugeot 3
6. Arrows 1

THE CIRCUIT

TWELTH ROUND

FOSTER'S BELGIAN GRAND PRIX, SPA-FRANCORCHAMPS

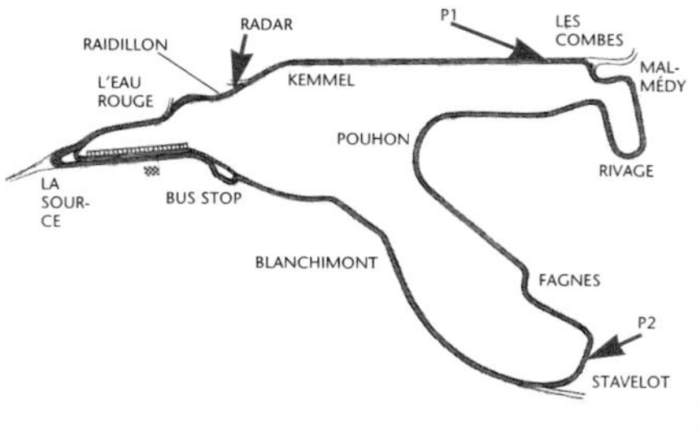

Date : August 29, 1999
Length : 6968 meters
Distance : 44 laps, 306.592 km
Weather : sunny, 27°

RACE SUMMARY

- At the start, David Coulthard is the first away as Mika Hakkinen almost jumps the start. The Scot goes through La Source in front, while the Finn tries to come up the inside and the two McLarens touch.
- Coulthard soon builds up a lead over his team mate. After five laps, he leads by 3 seconds. After 17 laps the gap is 10.2s.
- Behind the McLarens, Heinz-Harald Frentzen drops further back but not enough for Eddie Irvine to pass him.
- The first pit stops come on lap 19. Once out of the way, the race continues in somewhat monotonous fashion.
- The order remains the same to the chequered flag. McLaren made no attempt to impose team orders on its drivers.

WEEKEND GOSSIP

- **Villeneuve at last!**

  It was a moral victory for the British American Racing team. At Spa, Jacques Villeneuve finished a grand prix for the first time this season. Even though it was only in 15th place, it showed the team was making some slight progress. *"It is difficult to be happy with 15th place, but at least it's better than retiring,"* admitted the Canadian.

- **Mika Salo to Sauber**

  It did not take Peter Sauber long to find a replacement for Jean Alesi. At Spa, the Hinwil-based team announced it had signed Finland's Mika Salo to drive in 2000 and 2001. Sauber declared he was delighted with his choice: *"Mika has often shown his true potential against more famous team-mates,"* commented the Swiss team owner. *"He has also shown the ability to stand up to great pressure and I am convinced he will help the team move forward."* Two weeks earlier in Hungary, the Finn claimed he had received six different offers to drive in 2000. It was therefore surprising to say the least that he had taken up Peter Sauber's, given that his cars had not exactly set the world alight over the past few years. It seemed that Mika Salo's disappointing performance in Budapest, where he finished twelfth, seriously reduced the number of offers still on the table. Particularly annoying was the disappearance of an offer from the Stewart team.

- **Schumi tests at Mugello**

  On 20th August, Michael Schumacher drove a Ferrari for the first time since his Silverstone accident. He reeled off 65 laps of Mugello and was quicker than Eddie Irvine! *"It's like coming back to work after being on holiday for too long,"* observed Schumacher.

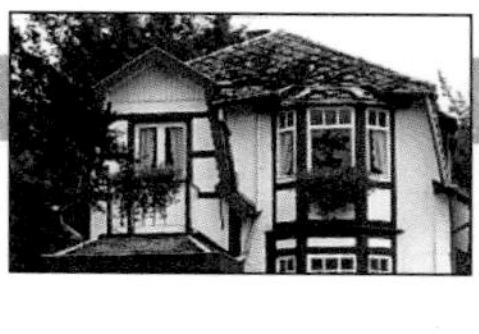

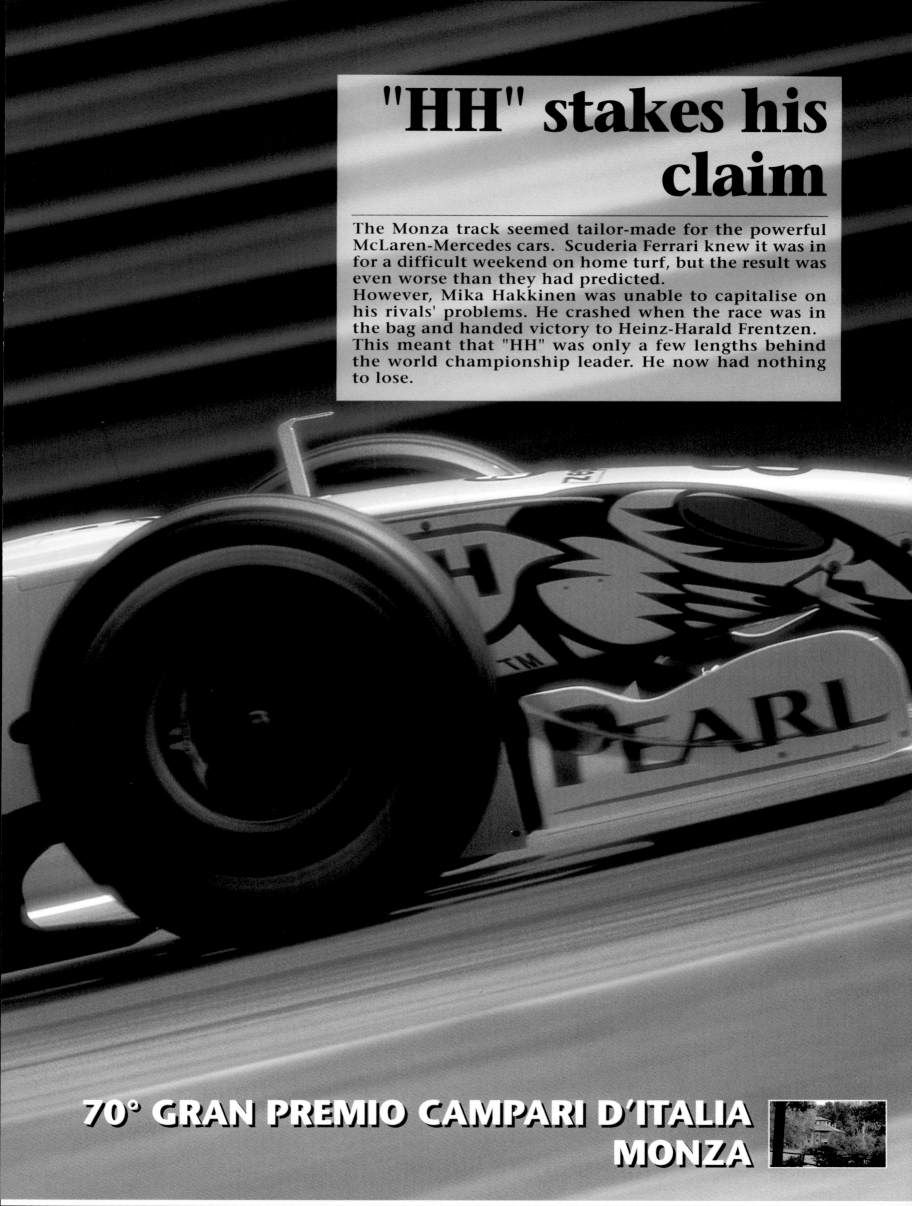

"HH" stakes his claim

The Monza track seemed tailor-made for the powerful McLaren-Mercedes cars. Scuderia Ferrari knew it was in for a difficult weekend on home turf, but the result was even worse than they had predicted.
However, Mika Hakkinen was unable to capitalise on his rivals' problems. He crashed when the race was in the bag and handed victory to Heinz-Harald Frentzen. This meant that "HH" was only a few lengths behind the world championship leader. He now had nothing to lose.

70° GRAN PREMIO CAMPARI D'ITALIA
MONZA

 **70° GRAN PREMIO CAMPARI D'ITALIA**

Replacing Michael Schumacher is pretty much an impossible task. Mika Salo tried and produced some erratic results. Having shone at Hockenheim, he was nowhere in Budapest and at Spa. In Monza, he finished third on a circuit where it is easier to find the limits of the than the previous two tracks.

70° GRAN PREMIO CAMPARI D'ITALIA

The Italian Grand Prix was the best race of the season to date for the Williams team. Alessandro Zanardi eventually finished out of the points in seventh place, but the Italian drove a respectable race which saw him in third place for much of the time behind Mika Hakkinen and Heinz-Harald Frentzen. He could no doubt have finished second, but for a mechanical problem - after the race, his mechanics discovered that the flat bottom had become detached from the chassis. These problems allowed his team mate, Ralf Schumacher to take second place. Pleased with his car, Schumacher was just three seconds behind Heinz-Harald Frentzen. "But I knew I couldn't pass him, so I just tried to put him under pressure," explained the Williams driver.

Eddie Irvine was only sixth

Ferrari off the pace at home

Mika Hakkinen's mistake should have been the opportunity for the win that Scuderia Ferrari had dreamed of. But it came to nought as Mika Salo finished third and Eddie Irvine could do no better than sixth.

It was a minor catastrophe as Mika Salo admitted when he stepped off the podium: *"Last week's testing here on this track had gone well,"* he claimed. *"But nothing went right this weekend. Since Friday, we have been in trouble and actually we were very lucky to qualify in the top ten. We managed to improve the car since then, but we are still way off the pace."*

Eddie Irvine's sixth place was enough to put him back in the joint lead of the championship with Mika Hakkinen, but he was not optimistic about the future. *"I was very careful at the start, because I wanted to make sure I did not get involved in an accident,"* declared the Irishman. *"We made changes to the set up which made the car quicker in a straight line, but it was terrible over the kerbs. We knew this would*

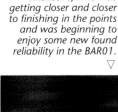

Eighth place for Jacques Villeneuve, who was getting closer and closer to finishing in the points and was beginning to enjoy some new found reliability in the BAR01.

be a difficult grand prix here and I am looking forward to the circuits we will be racing on from now on. They should suit our car a lot better." Several new aerodynamic developments were due to be fitted to the F399 for the next race, the European Grand Prix, to be held in two weeks time at the Nurburgring. These modifications were due to be tested at Mugello in the week after the Italian Grand Prix.

Barrichello signs for Ferrari and has no regrets

It was without a doubt the worst kept secret in the paddock, but it was only on the 4th September that Scuderia Ferrari officially confirmed that it had engaged the young Brazilian, Rubens Barrichello to partner Michael Schumacher in 2000 and 2001.

The Brazilian would thus replace Eddie Irvine, in what was apparently a straight swop as Eddie was rumoured to be moving to Stewart-Ford.

In Monza, Barrichello admitted that he could have driven for Ferrari four years ago at the end of 1995, instead of Eddie Irvine. At the time,

"Rubinho" had chosen to stay at Jordan. *"Ferrari were not in a position to confirm it until it was too late. I had to sign with Jordan by then and I ran the risk of finding myself without a drive. But I have no regrets. At the time, I was still too inexperienced to get the most out of Ferrari. However, today I feel ready for it."*

At least the Brazilian did not seem bothered about squaring up to Michael Schumacher. *"Michael is the best and I am sure I will learn a lot being alongside him. Ferrari is the opportunity of a lifetime. It is a very important step for me. It's unique."*

PRACTICE TIMES

No	Driver	Car/Engine/Chassis	Practice Friday	Pos.	Practice Saturday	Pos.	Qualifying	Pos.	Warm-up	Pos.
1.	Mika Häkkinen	McLaren/Mercedes/MP4-4/05	1'25"103	5°	1'23"482	3°	1'22"432	1°	1'25"854	3°
2.	David Coulthard	McLaren/Mercedes/MP4-4/07	1'25"347	8°	1'23"412	2°	1'23"177	3°	1'25"667	2°
3.	Mika Salo	Ferrari/Ferrari/F399/196	1'25"931	17°	1'24"091	10°	1'23"657	6°	1'27"685	18°
4.	Eddie Irvine	Ferrari/Ferrari/F399/191	1'25"897	16°	1'24"330	12°	1'23"765	8°	1'27"096	14°
5.	Alessandro Zanardi	Williams/Supertec/FW21/05	1'24"823	3°	1'23"721	4°	1'23"432	4°	1'26"712	13°
6.	Ralf Schumacher	Williams/Supertec/FW21/06	1'24"507	1°	1'23"663	7°	1'23"636	5°	1'26"166	7°
7.	Damon Hill	Jordan/Mugen-Honda/199/4	1'25"397	10°	1'23"921	6°	1'23"979	9°	1'27"131	15°
8.	Heinz-Harald Frentzen	Jordan/Mugen-Honda/199/5	1'25"577	13°	1'23"142	1°	1'22"926	2°	1'26"446	10°
9.	Giancarlo Fisichella	Benetton/Playlife/B199/07	1'25"701	14°	1'24"995	17°	1'24"862	17°	1'26"404	9°
10.	Alexander Wurz	Benetton/Playlife/B199/04	1'25"742	15°	1'24"576	14°	1'24"593	14°	1'27"425	17°
11.	Jean Alesi	Sauber/Petronas/C18/04	1'25"030	4°	1'24"770	16°	1'24"591	13°	1'27"226	16°
12.	Pedro Diniz	Sauber/Petronas/C18/07	1'25"388	9°	1'24"739	15°	1'24"596	16°	1'26"119	4°
14.	Pedro de la Rosa	Arrows/Arrows/A20/07	1'27"542	21°	1'26"617	21°	1'26"383	21°	1'28"488	22°
15.	Toranosuke Takagi	Arrows/Arrows/A20/05	1'27"931	22°	1'26"631	22°	1'26"509	22°	1'27"973	20°
16.	Rubens Barrichello	Stewart/Ford/SF3/04	1'25"499	11°	1'23"837	6°	1'23"739	7°	1'25"397	1°
17.	Johnny Herbert	Stewart/Ford/SF3/05	1'25"551	12°	1'23"971	9°	1'24"594	15°	1'26"126	5°
18.	Olivier Panis	Prost/Peugeot/AP02/5	1'25"138	6°	1'24"240	11°	1'24"016	10°	1'26"310	8°
19.	Jarno Trulli	Prost/Peugeot/AP02/2	1'24"692	2°	1'23"833	5°	1'24"293	12°	1'26"603	11°
20.	Luca Badoer	Minardi/Ford/M01/01	1'26"633	20°	1'25"605	19°	1'25"348	19°	1'28"185	21°
21.	Marc Gene	Minardi/Ford/M01/04	1'26"069	18°	1'25"595	18°	1'25"695	20°	1'27"825	19°
22.	Jacques Villeneuve	BAR/Supertec/BAR01/06	1'25"307	7°	1'24"412	13°	1'24"188	11°	1'26"137	6°
23.	Ricardo Zonta	BAR/Supertec/BAR01/07	1'26"181	19°	1'25"761	20°	1'25"114	18°	1'26"704	17°

MAXIMUM SPEEDS

No	Driver	P1 Qualifs	Pos	P1 Race	Pos	P2 Qualifs	Pos	P2 Race	Pos	Finish Qualifs	Pos	Finish Race	Pos	Trap Qualifs	Pos	Trap Course	Pos
1.	M. Häkkinen	333,1	2°	303,7	12°	338,9	2°	335,4	6°	325,3	1°	319,3	5°	355,3	1°	351,1	6°
2.	D. Coulthard	330,3	3°	306,1	11°	339,8	1°	342,5	1°	324,8	2°	323,7	1°	352,9	3°	361,8	1°
3.	M. Salo	326,1	9°	296,8	15°	334,3	9°	332,2	10°	320,6	9°	317,5	10°	348,4	10°	347,6	12°
4.	E. Irvine	*	22°	309,3	9°	*	17°	331,8	12°	*		314,2	15°	*	22°	345,6	15°
5.	A. Zanardi	327,3	6°	311,1	7°	327,7	21°	323,2	21°	316,4	18°	310,1	18°	340,1	21°	336,2	21°
6.	R. Schumacher	329,3	4°	324,6	1°	331,0	15°	325,8	19°	316,9	17°	309,1	20°	342,3	19°	338,8	19°
7.	D. Hill	314,5	17°	298,6	14°	334,5	7°	334,4	7°	323,6	3°	318,0	8°	348,7	7°	349,4	8°
8.	H.-H. Frentzen	334,5	1°	311,2	6°	335,1	6°	334,0	8°	323,0	4°	317,6	9°	348,7	8°	345,9	14°
9.	G. Fisichella	315,0	16°	270,8	20°	328,9	20°	326,6	16°	317,0	15°	311,8	16°	349,0	6°	349,0	9°
10.	A. Wurz	313,8	19°	290,1	19°	334,5	8°	329,2	15°	319,5	11°	314,6	14°	353,5	2°	350,1	7°
11.	J. Alesi	327,5	5°	311,8	5°	336,5	3°	339,0	3°	322,7	5°	319,3	6°	349,4	5°	351,6	4°
12.	P. Diniz	326,0	10°	240,5	21°	332,5	12°	331,2	13°	320,7	8°	314,7	13°	347,0	13°	337,7	20°
14.	P. de la Rosa	314,5	18°	314,1	3°	331,5	14°	324,0	20°	317,2	14°	309,9	19°	341,8	20°	342,4	17°
15.	T. Takagi	312,2	20°	295,4	16°	326,3	22°	326,4	18°	314,8	21°	311,5	17°	342,7	17°	341,9	18°
16.	R. Barrichello	325,4	11°	312,8	4°	335,9	4°	337,8	5°	322,3	6°	321,8	2°	351,4	4°	351,5	5°
17.	J. Herbert	320,5	12°	292,6	18°	335,2	5°	339,9	2°	321,5	7°	321,4	4°	348,6	9°	355,0	2°
18.	O. Panis	326,1	8°	316,6	2°	333,0	11°	333,7	9°	319,8	10°	321,8	3°	348,4	11°	348,6	10°
19.	J. Trulli	320,3	13°	309,8	8°	333,4	10°	337,8	4°	318,6	12°	318,3	7°	347,3	12°	354,3	3°
20.	L. Badoer	316,9	14°	293,7	17°	328,9	19°	326,5	17°	315,1	20°	309,0	21°	345,8	14°	345,3	16°
21.	M. Gené	301,1	21°	233,8	22°	329,1	18°			316,1	19°			344,6	15°	248,9	22°
22.	J. Villeneuve	316,1	15°	298,8	13°	330,0	16°	331,8	11°	317,0	16°	315,6	11°	342,5	18°	348,4	11°
23.	R. Zonta	326,9	7°	308,8	10°	332,3	13°	330,3	14°	317,6	13°	315,5	12°	344,6	16°	347,2	13°

* technical problems

CLASSIFICATION & RETIREMENTS

Pos	Drivers	Team	Time
1.	Frentzen	Jordan Mugen Honda	in 1h17'02"923
2.	R. Schum.	Williams Supertec	à 3"272
3.	Salo	Ferrari	à 11"932
4.	Barrichello	Stewart Ford	à 17"630
5.	Coulthard	McLaren Mercedes	à 18"142
6.	Irvine	Ferrari	à 27"402
7.	Zanardi	Williams Supertec	à 28"047
8.	Villeneuve	BAR Supertec	à 41"797
9.	Alesi	Sauber Petronas	à 42"198
10.	Hill	Jordan Mugen Honda	à 56"259
11.	Panis	Prost Peugeot	DNF

Lap	Drivers	Team	Reason
1	Gené	Minardi Ford	accident/de la Rosa
2	Fisichella	Benetton Playlife	off
2	Diniz	Sauber Petronas	off
12	Wurz	Benetton Playlife	gearbox
24	Badoer	Minardi Ford	accident/Takagi
25	Zonta	BAR Supertec	brakes
30	Trulli	Prost Peugeot	gearbox
30	Häkkinen	McLaren Mercedes	off
36	de la Rosa	Arrows	suspension
36	Takagi	Arrows	off
41	Herbert	Stewart Ford	clutch

FASTEST LAPS

	Driver	Time	Lap
1.	R. Schum.	1'25"579	48
2.	Salo	1'25"630	44
3.	Barrichello	1'25"825	51
4.	Coulthard	1'25"832	32
5.	Alesi	1'25"911	52
6.	Frentzen	1'25"917	32
7.	Panis	1'25"953	31
8.	Zanardi	1'26"047	51
9.	Häkkinen	1'26"060	24
10.	Herbert	1'26"253	18
11.	Villeneuve	1'26"338	48
12.	Hill	1'26"342	41
13.	Irvine	1'26"387	48
14.	Trulli	1'26"493	23
15.	Zonta	1'26"945	24
16.	Wurz	1'28"338	6
17.	dela Rosa	1'28"516	15
18.	Badoer	1'28"914	10
19.	Takagi	1'29"216	12

LAP CHART

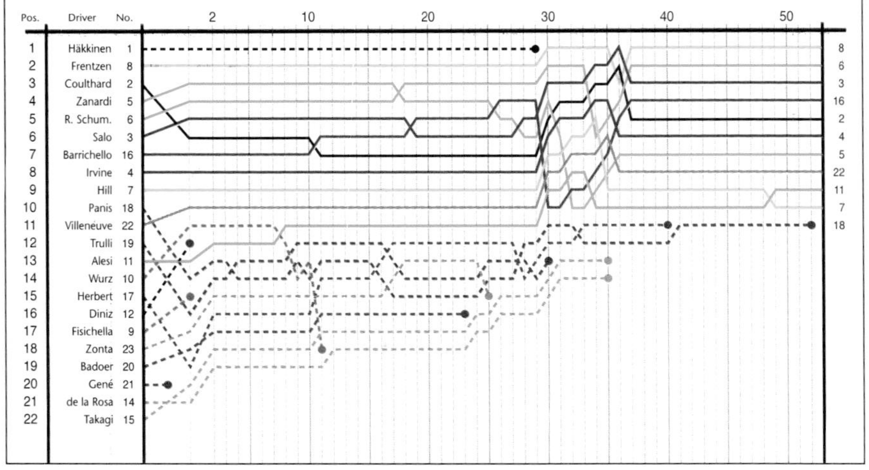

Pos.
Driver
No.
2
10
20
30
40
50
Häkkinen 1
Frentzen 8
Coulthard 2
Zanardi 5
R. Schum. 6
Salo 3
Barrichello 16
Irvine 4
Hill 7
Panis 18
Villeneuve 22
Trulli 19
Alesi 11
Wurz 10
Herbert 17
Diniz 12
Fisichella 9
Zonta 23
Badoer 20
Gené 21
de la Rosa 14
Takagi 15
8
6
3
16
2
4
5
22
11
7
18

PIT STOPS

	Driver	Time	Lap	Stop n°
1.	de la Rosa	2'48"645	1	1
2.	Panis	19"569	16	1
3.	Trulli	19"446	17	1
4.	Takagi	38"995	24	1
5.	Zonta	29"057	25	1
6.	Herbert	25"360	27	1
7.	Barrichello	23"128	29	1
8.	Panis	20"722	32	2
9.	R.Schumacher	21"102	33	1
10.	Alesi	20"781	33	1
11.	Hill	22"442	34	1
12.	de la Rosa	21"741	31	2
13.	Frentzen	19"299	35	1
14.	Irvine	18"961	35	1
15.	Villeneuve	20"931	35	1
16.	Salo	19"301	36	1
17.	Coulthard	20"137	36	1

BRIDGESTONE

Quickest pit stop during the Italian Grand Prix, taking on fuel and four new Bridgestone tyres:

Eddie Irvine, Ferrari, 18"961

THE CIRCUIT

THIRTEENTH ROUND

GRAN PREMIO CAMPARI D'ITALIA, MONZA

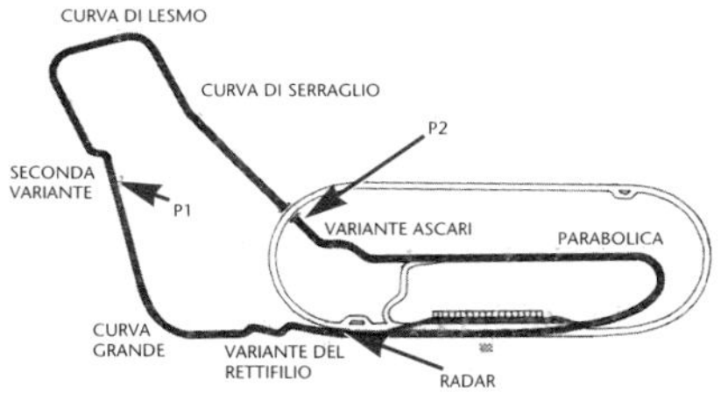

CURVA DI LESMO
CURVA DI SERRAGLIO
P2
SECONDA VARIANTE
P1
VARIANTE ASCARI
PARABOLICA
CURVA GRANDE
VARIANTE DEL RETTIFILIO
RADAR

Date : September 12, 1999
Length : 5765 meters
Distance : 53 laps, 305.548 km
Weather : sunny, 23°

All results :
© 1999 Fédération Internationale de l'Automobile, 2, Ch. Blandonnet, 1215 Genève 15, Suisse

CHAMPIONSHIP

(after thirteen rounds)

Drivers :

1. M. HÄKKINEN 60
2. E. IRVINE 60
3. H.-H. FRENTZEN.............................50
4. D. COULTHARD...............................48
5. M. SCHUMACHER 32
6. R. SCHUMACHER.............................30
7. R. BARRICHELLO.............................15
8. G. FISICHELLA 13
9. M. SALO...10
10. D. HILL..7
11. A. WURZ...3
    P. DINIZ...3
13. J. HERBERT.......................................2
    Olivier PANIS 2
15. Pedro de la ROSA 1
    Jean ALESI..1
    Jarno TRULLI.....................................1

Constructors :

1. McLaren Mercedes 108
2. Ferrari..102
3. Jordan Mugen Honda 57
4. Williams..30
5. Stewart Ford 17
6. Benetton Playlife............................16
7. Sauber Petronas...............................4
8. Prost Peugeot 3
6. Arrows...1

RACE SUMMARY

- Mika Hakkinen is first away. At the first chicane, he is followed by a surprising Alessandro Zanardi, who is immediately passed by Heinz-Harald Frentzen at the Seconda Variante.
- Under braking for the Ascari chicane, Mika Salo attacks and passes David Coulthard.
- At the end of the first lap, Hakkinen leads Frentzen by 1.2s. By lap 5, the gap has grown to 3.0s and then 5.0s on lap 10.
- Lap 11 and Rubens Barrichello passes David Coulthard, who is finding it hard to tame a recalcitrant McLaren.
- Lap 18 and Alex Zanardi lets team-mate Ralf Schumacher past.
- Lap 25 and Toranosuke Takagi's Arrows piles into Luca Badoer's Minardi. At the same time, Zanardi slows and is passed first by Barrichello and then Salo.
- Rubens Barrichello finds himself third before the pit stops, 17.2 seconds down on Hakkinen.
- Lap 30 sees Mika Hakkinen crash out of the race, when he had a solid lead over Heinz-Harald Frentzen. The Finn bursts into tears in the Monza woods.
- Lap 34 and the pit stops begin. Frentzen keeps the lead, ahead of Ralf Schumacher and Salo.
- Frentzen appears to lose ground to Ralf Schumacher. From 5.4 seconds on lap 38, the gap drops to 3.2 on lap 52. However, Ralf is incapable of threatening Heinz-Harald is just making sure he gets to the flag.
- The order remains unchanged to the end of the race.
- Eddie Irvine finishes sixth to score one point at the wheel of an uncooperative car.

WEEKEND GOSSIP

• Renault returns...

Christian Contzen, the managing director of Renault Sport was in the Monza paddock, thus adding substance to the rumour that the French company was preparing to come back into Formula 1, possibly in association with Arrows and maybe under the name of Nissan, as Renault had recently forged links with the Japanese company.

• ...and Michelin also

The French tyre manufacturer Michelin appeared to have decided on an F1 comeback after an absence of over ten years. Teams rumoured to be already thinking of signing up with the French company were Benetton and Williams, the latter because of their future tie-up with BMW, which has close links to the tyre maker. Michelin had until 31st December 1999 to confirm its participation commencing 2001 to FIA.

• All bright and shiny

The British American Racing cars were due to have an all-new chrome coloured livery for 2000, a colour never yet seen in Formula 1. One thing was certain, the team did not want to keep its current look, with the cars bisected longitudinally to publicise two different cigarette brands. The colours of the BAR02 were accidentally revealed by Bernie Ecclestone, who was holding the relevant piece of artwork behind his back, while walking through the paddock. Several photographers went to work with their long lenses.

• Jean Alesi ninth

Jean Alesi did not seem very motivated by his Sauber team, four events from the end of the season. *"It's a real shame, but it's down to the aerodynamic faults on the car. The race was difficult, especially because I love Monza so much."*

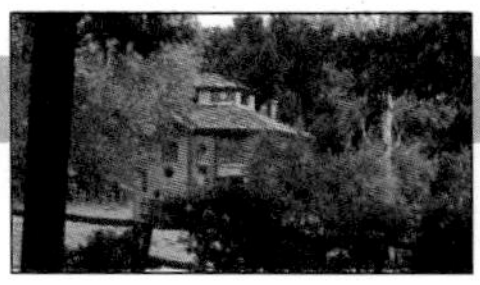

The craziest one of the year

What a race! The European Grand Prix, run at the Nurburgring, was the most chaotic race we have seen for a good many years. With weather conditions alternating between wet and dry, cars were crashing off the track all over the place. After several changes of fortune, it was Johnny Herbert who eventually took the top honours for Stewart. The grand prix could just as easily have been won by David Coulthard, Heinz- Harald Frentzen, Giancarlo Fisichella or Ralf Schumacher, if they had not all been victims of misfortune in some form or other. Neither of the title contenders, Eddie Irvine or Mika Hakkinen were in the running, as they made strategic errors.

WARSTEINER GRAND PRIX OF EUROPE
NÜRBURGRING

Confusion in Kuala Lumpur

The Ferraris had been astounding on the track. Back to business after an enforced three month lay-off, Michael Schumacher had driven a fantastic race, possibly the best of his career, even if he had to hand over the victor's laurels to his team-mate and settle for second.

Then suddenly, two hours after the race, his performance lay in ruins. The F399s were deemed illegal and were disqualified. Mika Hakkinen, who had finished third, was declared the winner and thus world champion as well. Ferrari appealed and one week later its two cars were reinstated.

PETRONAS MALAYSIAN GRAND PRIX
KUALA LUMPUR

With the Thursday acclimatisation sessions for new tracks no longer in operation, all the drivers discovered the delights of the Sepang track on Friday morning. As it rained that morning, their task was complicated by running in the wet, which made the process rather delicate. It came as no surprise that those wet weather wizards Michael Schumacher and Jean Alesi came out best. However, came the end of the day and Jacques Villeneuve was the biggest surprise, setting the quickest time.

Malaysia might be a beautiful country and Sepang is a great circuit, but the heat and especially the humidity are unbearable. On Sunday, some photographers had to head for the pits to cool off.

"The hard or the soft? The soft or the hard?" With a few minutes to go before the start of qualifying, Ron Dennis and the McLaren team were still not decided as to which tyre compound they should use for the rest of the weekend.

The German celebrated his return with pole position.

Schumacher proves he is still the best

Grands prix do not always follow the laws of science. Mechanical problems, unforseen weather conditions and accidents, make race results something of a lottery and the best laid plans can come to nothing when faced with the roll of a dice. That is what makes F1 an exciting spectacle.

Qualifying however, provides a more accurate barometer of the true state of play and the hierarchy of the sport. It is a purist pursuit with less unknown parameters. Therefore, for Michael Schumacher, qualifying in Sepang was the perfect opportunity to show what he could do after his three month lay-off following his accident in the British Grand Prix. He more than proved his point by the end of the session. He took just eight laps to set a time which guaranteed him pole position and was a whopping second ahead of the rest. *"I am surprised the gap is so big, but not that I am in front,"* he commented after the session. *"The car is definitely better than it was three months ago, both aerodynamically and mechanically."*

Whatever, the German was in very confident mood. *"I decided not to do too many laps, so as to save as many tyres as possible for the race. My plan is to go flat out from start to finish. But of course I will let Eddie pass if he is behind me."*

The opinion of those who know him well was that Schumacher had never appeared so calm and collected in his career. Under no pressure, the German seemed ready to give the best of himself for the last of the two grands prix of the season to help Ferrari to the Constructors' Championship.

The German was all smile after the session. Shaking hands with all his mechanics, he was evidently pleased with his work and the way he had turned over his old rival Mika Hakkinen. Because, by setting a time over one second quicker than the Finn, the German had made the point that, but for his accident at Silverstone, he would no doubt have won the 1999 Drivers' title. *"If"* does not count for much in Formula 1, but the future champion could see his title devalued by the German's performance.

Hakkinen feels uncomfortable

With two minutes to go before the start of qualifying, Mika Hakkinen still did not know what tyres to choose. The rules demand that a driver chooses one type of tyre before qualifying begins and then he can only use that type for the rest of the weekend.

At the Bridgestone enclosure - the Japanese company supplying all the teams - the two McLaren tyre men were on standby with radios, waiting for the last minute choice from the Finn. He was still hesitating between the super-softs which would be quickest for qualifying and the softs, which would be slower but might improve the balance of the car in the race.

Finally, at the very last moment, the Finn opted for the harder of the two compounds, which would give him more confidence in his car.

Having gone for the softer option, David Coulthard out-qualified his team-mate for the very first time this year, apart from the French GP when the rain turned the session on its head. *"I will not make life difficult for Mika. He is fighting for the championship and I'm not,"* Coulthard was quick to point out.

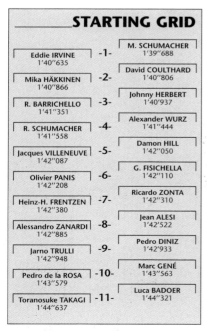

STARTING GRID

		M. SCHUMACHER 1'39"688
Eddie IRVINE 1'40"635	-1-	
		David COULTHARD 1'40"806
Mika HÄKKINEN 1'40"866	-2-	
		Johnny HERBERT 1'40"937
R. BARRICHELLO 1'41"351	-3-	
		Alexander WURZ 1'41"444
R. SCHUMACHER 1'41"558	-4-	
		Damon HILL 1'42"050
Jacques VILLENEUVE 1'42"087	-5-	
		G. FISICHELLA 1'42"110
Olivier PANIS 1'42"208	-6-	
		Ricardo ZONTA 1'42"310
Heinz-H. FRENTZEN 1'42"380	-7-	
		Jean ALESI 1'42'522
Alessandro ZANARDI 1'42"885	-8-	
		Pedro DINIZ 1'42'933
Jarno TRULLI 1'42"948	-9-	
		Marc GENÉ 1'43'563
Pedro de la ROSA 1'43"579	-10-	
		Luca BADOER 1'44"321
Toranosuke TAKAGI 1'44"637	-11-	

It's Super Schumi

Scuderia Ferrari had a dream race in the Malaysian Grand Prix. By scoring a one-two finish, Eddie Irvine moved back into the lead of the championship, with one race to go. It was all thanks to the incredible talent of Michael Schumacher, who played with the opposition, doing what he pleased throughout the race.

After a lean period since its last win in the German Grand Prix, the Scuderia was back on form at Sepang. Having monopolised the front row of the grid, it went on to score a one-two finish. But life was not that simple and they would have to fight twice for their victory (see next page.)

Having decided on a one stop strategy, despite having opted for the super-soft tyres, Schumacher had to fight off the attentions of Mika Hakkinen and on completely worn tyres he had to try and slow him down. The tyres were blistered and had lost all their tread. *"Looking at the state of my tyres, I must admit, I don't know how I managed to stay on the track,"* admitted the German after the race. *"We started with the option of one or two pit stops. After a few laps, we realised it should be possible on just the one. We spoke a lot on the radio during this grand prix."* Michael Schumacher looked as fresh as

a daisy during the post race press conference. The same could not be said of Mika Hakkinen, who almost collapsed on the podium. *"I'm better now,"* insisted the Finn. *"But it was definitely the toughest race of my career. I was flat out from start to finish, but these two guys* (he said pointing at Schumacher and Irvine) *did a good job. I tried to pass Michael, but he changed his tactics every lap, sometimes slowing down at one point and then slowing down somewhere else. It was very hard on the nerves, especially as the car was sliding everywhere. It was hell."*

The best number 2

To see Michael Schumacher meekly slowing down to let his team-mate through was an unbelievable sight. Never in his entire Formula 1 career had the German voluntarily moved over for another driver.

At Sepang, he was Mr. Perfect from every point of view and Eddie Irvine most definitely owed him his win, the second one he was gifted that season, after Mika Salo let him pass in Hockenheim. *"Michael did it all,"* the Irishman willingly conceded. *"What can you say* about him. We knew he was the best Number One and now he is the best Number Two as well!"* Once he had taken the chequered flag, the Scuderia got on the radio to thank its favourite son. *"I replied that I owed them,"* recounted Schumacher. *"For three and half years, Ferrari has done everything for me. It's more than right for me to pay them back today,. Of course I would have preferred to win the race, but it would not have made any sense in terms of the championship."*

An audacious manoeuvre

After he let Eddie Irvine pass on lap 4, Michael Schumacher's aim was to slow the two McLarens of David Coulthard and Mika Hakkinen. It was a mission only half accomplished as the Scotsman went down the inside at the second corner, surprising the German as he took a place off him. *"I was being careful to look after my tyres and I was not expecting this move. I suppose I am out of practice after three months off. I'm lacking experience,"* he joked after the race.

"David forced me out a bit and we touched. My front wing was damaged and it caused me a bit of a problem in the second part of the race."

In the end, Coulthard did not constitute a real threat to Irvine as the Scotsman's McLaren-Mercedes expired on lap 15 with an electrical problem. *"It was a really frustrating day for me,"* revealed Coulthard later. *"I think I could have caught up to Eddie, but my fuel pump suddenly stopped working."*

Winner on the track, then disqualified and reinstated: Eddie Irvine will long remember the Malaysian Grand Prix.

The circuit had been designed with spectators in mind. This is the Petronas grandstand and its buffet.

Sepang sets a new standard

Even before the cars had turned a wheel on the new Sepang circuit, many drivers had already declared it a complete success. With two long straights and several quick corners it seemed far more interesting than many of the recently build circuits. The track was also very wide, up to 22 metres in parts and this should ease overtaking. *"As far as I can see, it is a fabulous circuit,"* commented Mika Hakkinen. *"They have done a fantastic job."*
Malaysia was definitely proud of its new

toy. Built with government money, the circuit had cost 120 million dollars. The mechanics had huge garages to work in, fitted out with air-conditioned offices. This was no luxury with temperatures reaching 34 degrees and humidity of around 100 percent making working conditions unpleasant without it.

Everyone likes the track

Over the past ten years, the new circuits which have appeared on the calendar have been rather flat, dull and aseptic from the driving point of view. For safety reasons, fast corners have all but disappeared, replaced by tight corners and those dreaded chicanes.
Sepang appeared to be the exception to this sad rule. At the end of the first day's practice, all the drivers seemed to be in agree-

ment that driving it was just as good as walking it had been on the Thursday,. *"It's a very nice circuit,"* said Jacques Villeneuve. *"It is great to drive, even though it is hard to find the braking point in some corners."*
The Williams duo felt the layout was both superb and difficult. *"It's a real challenge,"* was Ralf Schumacher's view. *If you turn in too early or too late, you get it wrong; its as simple as that. With fast and slow sections, it is hard to set up the car."* His brother Michael confirmed that the track had several interesting corners, *"which is unusual for a new circuit."* Eddie Irvine's view was that its interest lay in its difficulty.
The Malaysian government had to sign a huge cheque to build the Sepang complex, in order to show the world what its country could do. As far as the drivers were concerned they had succeeded.

Crowned champion thanks to a mistake from Johnny

Johnny Herbert was an unintentional key figure in the 1999 championship. At Sepang, towards the end of the race, the Englishman was running third, just ahead of Mika Hakkinen. If he managed to finish on the podium, then the Finn would only be fourth and score just three championship points. That would have meant Eddie Irvine could have been champion in Japan if he finished second, a position which Michael Schumacher would have handed him, Mika Hakkinen was thus crowned

thanks to an error from Johnny Herbert. The Stewart was fending off the attentions of the McLaren, but in the end Johnny made a slight slip which allowed Hakkinen to squeeze through. *"He went wide into Turn 9 and that's how I passed him,"* explained the Finn. Herbert was disappointed to have missed out on yet another podium finish, three weeks after winning in Nurburgring. *"It was a very hard and physical race. I only made one mistake all weekend, and it cost me a place on the podium,"* he regretted.

results

PRACTICE TIMES

No	Driver	Car/Engine/Chassis	Practice Friday	Pos.	Practice Saturday	Pos.	Qualifying	Pos.	Warm-up	Pos.
1.	Mika Häkkinen	McLaren/Mercedes/MP4 -14/4	1'43"153	8°	1'41"107	3°	1'40"866	4°	1'41"818	3°
2.	David Coulthard	McLaren/Mercedes/MP4 -14/6	1'42"519	2°	1'41"269	5°	1'40"806	3°	1'41"765	2°
3.	Michael Schumacher	Ferrari/Ferrari/F399/195	1'42"875	5°	1'40"424	1°	1'39"688	1°	1'42"563	5°
4.	Eddie Irvine	Ferrari/Ferrari/F399/196	1'42"725	4°	1'40"506	2°	1'40"365	2°	1'42"243	4°
5.	Alessandro Zanardi	Williams/Supertec/FW21/05	1'45"833	20°	1'43"108	17°	1'42"885	16°	1'44"347	17°
6.	Ralf Schumacher	Williams/Supertec/FW21/06	1'45"164	18°	1'42"153	9°	1'41"558	8°	1'43"835	12°
7.	Damon Hill	Jordan/Mugen-Honda/199/4	1'43"417	12°	1'42"861	15°	1'42"050	9°	1'44"663	18°
8.	Heinz-Harald Frentzen	Jordan/Mugen-Honda/199/5	1'43"677	14°	1'42"282	10°	1'42"380	14°	1'43"950	14°
9.	Giancarlo Fisichella	Benetton/Playlife/B199/07	1'43"403	11°	1'42"292	11°	1'42"110	11°	1'43"725	11°
10.	Alexander Wurz	Benetton/Playlife/B199/04	1'43"311	9°	1'42"755	14°	1'41"444	7°	1'42"745	7°
11.	Jean Alesi	Sauber/Petronas/C18/04	1'42"701	3°	1'42"042	8°	1'42"522	15°	1'43"686	10°
12.	Pedro Diniz	Sauber/Petronas/C18/05	1'43"006	6°	1'42"473	12°	1'42"933	17°	1'42"846	8°
14.	Pedro de la Rosa	Arrows/Arrows/A20/07	1'45"397	19°	1'43"729	18°	1'43"579	20°	1'44"941	20°
15.	Toranosuke Takagi	Arrows/Arrows/A20/05	1'46"690	21°	1'44"978	22°	1'44"637	22°	1'45"288	21°
16.	Rubens Barrichello	Stewart/Ford/SF3/04	1'43"042	7°	1'41"608	7°	1'41"351	6°	1'41"679	1°
17.	Johnny Herbert	Stewart/Ford/SF3/05	1'43"349	10°	1'41"111	4°	1'40"937	5°	1'42"681	6°
18.	Olivier Panis	Prost/Peugeot/AP02/5	1'43"500	13°	1'44"032	20°	1'42"208	12°	1'43"540	9°
19.	Jarno Trulli	Prost/Peugeot/AP02/7	1'43"793	15°	1'42"946	16°	1'42"948	18°	1'44"032	15°
20.	Luca Badoer	Minardi/Ford/M01/01	1'44"818	16°	1'43"981	19°	1'44"321	21°	1'44"677	19°
21.	Marc Gené	Minardi/Ford/M01/04	1'49"451	22°	1'44"937	21°	1'43"563	19°	1'45"341	22°
22.	Jacques Villeneuve	BAR/Supertec/BAR01/06	1'42"407	1°	1'41"560	6°	1'42"087	10°	1'44"079	16°
23.	Ricardo Zonta	BAR/Supertec/BAR01/07	1'44"968	17°	1'42"578	13°	1'42"310	13°	1'43"894	13°

MAXIMUM SPEEDS

No	Driver	P1 Qualifs	Pos	P1 Race	Pos	P2 Qualifs	Pos	P2 Race	Pos	Finish Qualifs	Pos	Finish Race	Pos	Trap Qualifs	Pos	Trap Race	Pos
1.	M. Häkkinen	290,0	2°	292,4	1°	223,4	4°	227,9	1°	267,5	1°	267,8	1°	299,1	2°	304,2	1°
2.	D. Coulthard	291,4	1°	290,3	2°	224,2	1°	219,8	12°	266,4	2°	264,5	5°	299,7	1°	299,0	5°
3.	M. Schum.	288,8	3°	288,8	3°	221,6	5°	223,6	5°	264,3	5°	264,9	4°	297,6	4°	300,7	2°
4.	E. Irvine	287,0	7°	287,7	6°	220,9	6°	225,0	4°	265,2	3°	263,4	8°	298,8	3°	298,2	6°
5.	A. Zanardi	285,4	12°	285,1	10°	213,1	22°	215,9	15°	259,0	18°	258,9	15°	295,0	13°	295,1	11°
6.	R. Schum.	284,9	14°	278,9	19°	217,7	14°	209,1	19°	259,9	15°	254,3	20°	294,4	14°	289,3	17°
7.	D. Hill	287,4	5°	DNF	-	219,3	8°	DNF	-	263,0	9°	DNF	-	295,7	10°	DNF	-
8.	H.-H. Frentzen	284,1	15°	284,8	11°	217,5	15°	221,8	9°	264,1	6°	264,3	7°	294,0	15°	296,1	8°
9.	G. Fisichella	285,1	13°	285,8	8°	215,7	18°	221,3	10°	261,3	13°	260,3	11°	296,3	8°	295,5	9°
10.	A. Wurz	283,1	17°	281,4	15°	216,9	17°	218,9	14°	260,3	14°	258,5	16°	292,5	16°	292,7	12°
11.	J. Alesi	282,1	18°	288,6	4°	219,6	7°	223,5	6°	259,6	16°	263,4	9°	290,4	20°	299,0	4°
12.	P. Diniz	283,7	16°	285,7	9°	219,2	9°	222,4	7°	258,2	19°	261,9	10°	290,0	22°	295,4	10°
14.	P. de la Rosa	279,4	22°	280,7	16°	217,3	16°	220,3	11°	257,3	21°	257,7	17°	291,1	19°	292,6	13°
15.	T. Takagi	281,7	19°	279,5	17°	214,9	21°	210,6	18°	257,4	20°	260,1	12°	292,3	17°	291,6	14°
16.	R. Barrichello	287,1	6°	287,4	7°	223,6	2°	225,7	2°	263,4	7°	265,3	3°	297,5	5°	300,2	3°
17.	J. Herbert	287,5	4°	288,6	5°	223,5	3°	225,2	3°	264,3	4°	265,6	2°	296,1	9°	83,4	20°
18.	O. Panis	285,7	11°	279,5	18°	219,1	11°	213,3	16°	263,3	8°	258,9	14°	295,2	12°	287,9	19°
19.	J. Trulli	285,9	10°	DNF	-	219,2	10°	DNF	-	262,5	10°	DNF	-	297,2	7°	DNF	-
20.	L. Badoer	279,7	21°	277,0	20°	215,1	20°	207,8	20°	257,0	22°	254,8	19°	290,3	21°	288,4	18°
21.	M. Gené	281,6	20°	281,7	14°	215,3	19°	219,6	13°	259,0	17°	259,5	13°	291,2	18°	290,1	16°
22.	J. Villeneuve	286,4	8°	284,1	12°	218,0	13°	222,3	8°	262,5	11°	264,5	6°	295,2	11°	298,1	7°
23.	R. Zonta	286,2	9°	282,7	13°	218,9	12°	211,6	17°	261,5	12°	257,3	18°	297,4	6°	291,5	15°

CLASSIFICATION & RETIREMENTS

Pos	Drivers	Team	Time
1.	Irvine	Ferrari	en 1h38"494
2.	M. Schum.	Ferrari	à 1"040
3.	Häkkinen	McLaren Mercedes	à 9"743
4.	Herbert	Stewart Ford	à 17"538
5.	Barrichello	Stewart Ford	à 32"296
6.	Frentzen	Jordan Mugen Honda	à 34"884
7.	Alesi	Sauber Petronas	à 54"408
8.	Wurz	Benetton Playlife	à 60"934
9.	Gené	Minardi Ford	à 1 tour
10.	Zanardi	Williams Supertec	à 1 tour
11.	Fisichella	Benetton Playlife	à 4 tours

Lap	Drivers	Team	Reason
1	Trulli	Prost Peugeot	moteur
1	Hill	Jordan M. Honda	accident
6	Panis	Prost Peugeot	moteur
7	Zonta	BAR Supertec	fuite d'eau
8	Takagi	Arrows	problème d'axe
8	R. Schum.	Williams Supertec	sortie de route
15	Coulthard	McLaren Mercedes	pompe à essence
16	Badoer	Minardi Ford	accrochage/Diniz
31	de la Rosa	Arrows	moteur
45	Diniz	Sauber Petronas	sortie de route
49	Villeneuve	BAR Supertec	problème hydraulique

FASTEST LAPS

	Drivers	Time	Lap
1.	M. Schum.	1'40"267	25
2.	Frentzen	1'40"631	53
3.	Barrichello	1'40"810	55
4.	Fisichella	1'40"960	36
5.	Häkkinen	1'41"103	49
6.	Irvine	1'41"254	38
7.	Alesi	1'41"328	56
8.	Herbert	1'41"383	50
9.	Diniz	1'41"639	20
10.	Villeneuve	1'41"769	35
11.	Wurz	1'41"950	36
12.	Zanardi	1'42"056	27
13.	Gené	1'42"490	54
14.	Coulthard	1'42"940	11
15.	de la Rosa	1'43"885	22
16.	Badoer	1'46"367	9
17.	R.Schum.	1'46"418	5
18.	Takagi	1'46"441	4
19.	Zonta	1'46"444	2
20.	Panis	1'46"874	4

All results :
© 1999 Fédération Internationale de l'Automobile, 2, Ch. Blandonnet, 1215 Genève 15, Suisse

LAP CHART

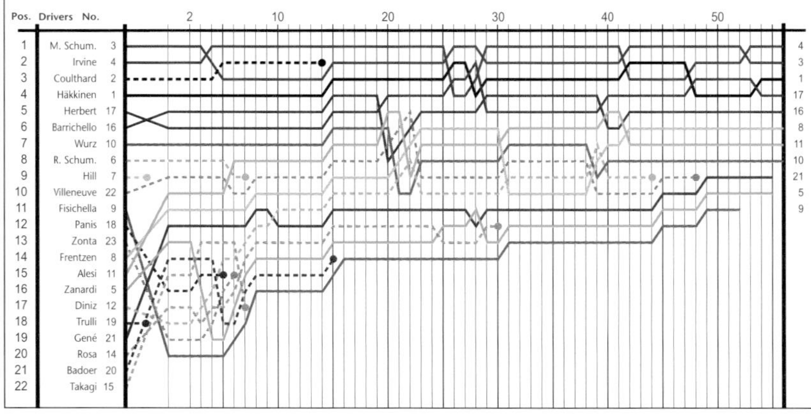

PIT STOPS

	Driver	Time	Lap	Stop n°
1.	Fisichella	6'50"649	1	1
2.	Zanardi	29"094	3	1
3.	Badoer	35"435	12	1
4.	Barrichello	30"266	19	1
5.	Wurz	30"530	20	1
6.	Alesi	30"425	21	1
7.	Villeneuve	30"515	22	1
8.	Diniz	29"695	22	1
9.	Fisichella	29"839	20	2
10.	de la Rosa	32"443	24	1
11.	Irvine	28"899	25	1
12.	Häkkinen	29"149	27	1
13.	Gené	32"624	27	1
14.	M.Schum.	32"523	28	1
15.	Herbert	35"081	28	1
16.	Zanardi	32"546	28	2
17.	Frentzen	30"607	30	1
18.	Wurz	28"755	38	2
19.	Villeneuve	30"817	38	2
20.	Barrichello	29"983	39	2
21.	Diniz	28"975	39	2
22.	Irvine	28"224	41	2
23.	Alesi	29"338	41	2
24.	Fisichella	29"249	37	3
25.	Häkkinen	28"388	47	2
26.	Zanardi	27"435	48	3

THE CIRCUIT

FIFTEENTH ROUND

PETRONAS MALAYSIAN GRAND PRIX, KUALA LUMPUR

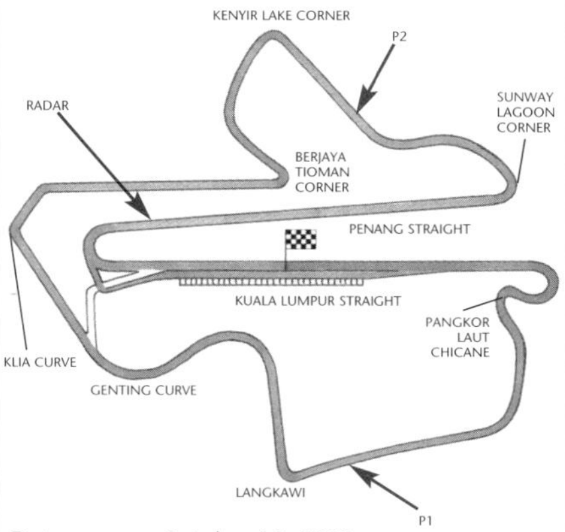

Date : October 17, 1999
Longueur : 5542 meters
Distance : 56 laps, 310.352 km
Weather : sunny, 31°

BRIDGESTONE

Quickest pit stop during the Malaysian Grand Prix, taking on fuel and four new Bridgestone tyres:

Alessandro Zanardi, Williams, 27"435

CHAMPIONSHIPS

(after fifteen rounds)

Drivers

1. E. Irvine 70
2. M. Häkkinen 66
3. H.-H. Frentzen 51
4. D. Coulthard 48
5. M. Schumacher 38
6. R. Schumacher 33
7. R. Barrichello 21
8. J. Herbert 15
9. G. Fisichella 13
10. M. Salo 10
11. J. Trulli 7
    D. Hill 7
13. A. Wurz 3
    P. Diniz 3
15. O. Panis 2
16. P. de la Rosa 1
    J. Alesi 1
    M. Gené 1

Constructors :

1. Ferrari 118
2. McLaren/Mercedes 114
3. Jordan/Mugen Honda 58
4. Stewart/Ford 36
5. Williams/Supertec 33
6. Benetton/Playlife 16
7. Prost/Peugeot 9
8. Sauber/Petronas 4
9. Arrows 1
   Minardi/Ford 1

RACE SUMMARY

- Michael Schumacher was first away and by the second lap, he was already 3.1 seconds ahead of Eddie Irvine, but slowed to let the Irishman past on lap 4. Schumacher then tried to hold up David Coulthard, but the Scotsman forced his way through one lap later and closed on the leader, catching up to him on lap 11.
- On lap 15, David Coulthard retired. Irvine had a 4.5 second lead over Michael Schumacher and was 5.3 s ahead of Mika Hakkinen.
- After the first run of pit stops, the German used all his skill to slow the Finn, who was 6.6 s down on Irvine on lap 30. By lap 38, the gap had stretched to 17.2s.
- Eddie Irvine and Mika Hakkinen made their second pit stop, but not Michael Schumacher, who again let his team-mate pass him on lap 53.
- After his pit stop, Mika Hakkinen found himself behind Johnny Herbert, but he got past on lap 54.

WEEKEND GOSSIP

• Jean Todt takes all the blame

After the European Grand Prix and the saga of the missing wheel, Jean Todt decided he should be the scapegoat for everything. *"The engineers for each of the two cars are responsible for warning the mechanics when their car is coming in for a pit stop,"* he explained. *"But at the end of the day, I am in charge. If anyone is responsible for what happened at the Nürburgring, then it is me."*

• The Black Prince has disappeared

There was no trace of Prince Malik, who had bought into Tom Walkinshaw's Arrows team. Now, he was described by several team members as a crook and the Nigerian had disappeared along with his "T-minus" brand. The money he had promised was never seen and the budget had hit rock bottom, which was why the team had hardly done any testing since July.

• Panis at McLaren

Unable to find a drive for 2000, Olivier Panis signed a contract to drive in the German DTM Touring Car Championship for Mercedes. He would also do some testing for McLaren, his first run in their car taking place after the Malaysian Grand Prix.

• Jean Todt backs Eddie

Ever since Eddie Irvine signed a contract to drive for Jaguar Racing in 2000, rumour had it that the Scuderia might not be that motivated when it came to trying to win a championship with a driver who was leaving the team, taking the coveted Number 1 with him to an opposing team. In Sepang, Jean Todt decided to put everyone's mind at rest. *"I can assure you, that from my point of view, Eddie would be an ideal champion. I would be happy to personally go and stick the Number 1 on his new car. It would be a pleasure."*

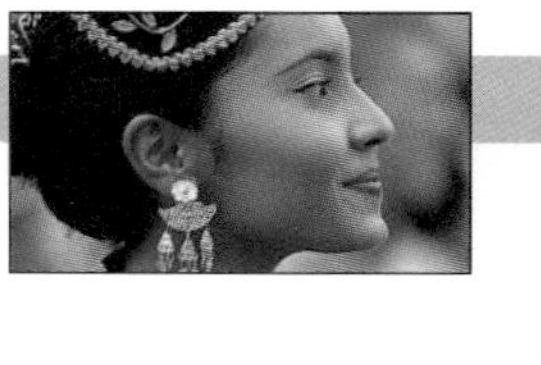

Mika does it

Mika Hakkinen arrived in Suzuka trailing Eddie Irvine by four points in the championship. To take the title, he only had one option; he had to win the Japanese Grand Prix.

The Finn was therefore under enormous pressure as he lined up on the grid in the land of the rising sun. He coped with that pressure in admirable fashion, driving what was probably the best race of his career. Leading almost the entire event, he was chased at a devilish pace by Michael Schumacher, but never put a foot or a wheel wrong. The brilliant drive wiped out any lingering memories of previous errors this season and was well worth a world championship on its own.

FUJI TELEVISION JAPANESE GRAND PRIX
SUZUKA

One final effort and the final pole for Michael

Michael Schumacher added to his comeback pole position in the Malaysian Grand Prix, by taking his second consecutive pole. "We have made a lot of progress with the car since yesterday and it was handling really well. I am pleased, because this shows people that this performance has nothing to do with the old barge boards. It will silence the critics who tend to always exaggerate the importance of some things."

Eddie Irvine was not in the same festive mood. He was over a second and a half down on Schumacher, way back on the third row having had a big shunt. All weekend long, he had failed to find the right set up for Suzuka circuit. "I don't know what happened to Eddie," said Michael with a hint of irony. "He is finding it hard to get into a rhythm, maybe because he is fighting for the championship for the first time in his life. But he has had the opportunity to do well because he has got the best equipment this weekend. I don't know what happened. Whatever happens, my tactic for the race will be to try and win. That's the best thing I can do to help him become champion." Victory for the German would also give Ferrari the Constructors' crown.

For his part, Eddie Irvine made light of the situation, affirming he had finally found the right settings at the end of the session. "We had just made a major modification to the front of the car which was a big improvement," claimed the Irishman. "But it made the rear of the car nervous and that's why I lost it. My neck hurts a bit, but it shouldn't be a problem for the race. Of course, starting from the third row is not ideal, but at least I'm starting from the clean side of the track."

STARTING GRID

Mika HÄKKINEN 1'37"820	-1-	M. SCHUMACHER 1'37"470
Heinz-H. FRENTZEN 1'38"696	-2-	David COULTHARD 1'38"239
Olivier PANIS 1'39"623	-3-	Eddie IRVINE 1'38"975
Johnny HERBERT 1'39"706	-4-	Jarno TRULLI 1'39"644
Jean ALESI 1'39"721	-5-	R. SCHUMACHER 1'39"717
Damon HILL 1'40"140	-6-	Jacques VILLENEUVE 1'39"732
G. FISICHELLA 1'40"261	-7-	R. BARRICHELLO 1'40"140
A. ZANARDI 1'40"403	-8-	Alexander WURZ 1'40"303
Ricardo ZONTA 1'40"861	-9-	Pedro DINIZ 1'40"740
Marc GENÉ 1'41"529	-10-	Toranosuke TAKAGI 1'41"067
Luca BADOER 1'42"515	-11-	Pedro de la ROSA 1'41"708

Jean Alesi: close encounter of the third kind

Mika Hakkinen was second in his McLaren, frustrated at not having been able to improve his time at the end of the session. Just as he was about to start his flying lap, he saw Jean Alesi's Sauber cut the chicane and overtake him going backwards. "Jean was on a quick lap and I wasn't," explained the Finn. "Difficult to blame him, but let's just say this sort of thing is not what one expects from such an experienced driver."

For his part, Alesi was furious: "Mika was not on a quick lap, but he had been slowing me down since the hairpin. At the chicane he slowed down and I had to go straight on to avoid him. FIA should take a closer look at what happens on the track."

△ *No last minute revival for Benetton in Nippon. Giancarlo Fisichella qualified down in 14th place, just ahead of team mate Alexander Wurz. Both cars suffered from a lack of grip which the engineers could not cure.*

Game, set and match to Mika. The title is won in the first second.

It was a more than convincing demonstration. Mika Hakkinen had to win at all costs in Suzuka to assure himself of the world championship. Despite the pressure engendered by this sort of situation, the Finn acquitted himself admirably, taking the lead at the start and only giving it up briefly, during the pit stops. However, the race was by no means a Sunday afternoon drive. He had Michael Schumacher on his tail and the German's task was to wrest the lead, thus handing the world championship to Eddie Irvine. At the end of the day, Hakkinen won the race when the lights went out. *"The start is not easy here, because it is downhill and you must not let the car run away from you,"* he explained as he got down from the podium. *"But I knew it would be the key to the race and that it had to go well. As soon as I selected second gear, I knew I was ahead. Then I told myself I had to stay there until the end of the race!"* At the wheel of a car which was set up perfectly, the Finn controlled the entire race. *"I had no difficulty in pulling out a gap to Michael, which surprised me a bit. The car was really good."* At the end of a race which turned into an extended sprint, Mika Hakkinen richly deserved a world title which brought a difficult season to a happy end. *"This year was very tough,"*

he admitted. *"I expected it to be harder to win a second title than it was first time round, but not as hard as this."* it was very hard psychologically and I will need some time for it to sink in. Luckily the team was fantastic with me and I was able to get away from Formula 1 between the last couple of races and relax mentally. When it goes down to the last race, it is very hard on the nerves. I do not recommend it to anyone! I have done it for two years now and I think that's more than enough." Now, he was off for a well-deserved holiday.

Ferrari settles for the constructors

With Michael Schumacher and Eddie Irvine finishing second and third respectively, Ferrari's dreams of winning the 1999 Drivers' Championship were over.
However, on the pit wall, the mechanics were hugging one another and jumping for joy as the chequered flag fell. Even Jean Todt was all smiles, shaking hands with everyone around him. It looked as though the Scuderia staff did not consider themselves among the day's losers.
"Before this race, we had two objectives; to win the drivers' and constructors' championships," explained Jean Todt. *"Today, we have taken the constructors's title for the first time in 16 years, despite Michael Schumacher being absent for seven races. I am proud to have led this team and the title proves we are the best team in F1."*

Ferrari President Luca di Montezemolo was not in Japan. So, just after the race, he telephoned Jean Todt to express his happiness with the result. It was perhaps a somewhat hollow sentiment, because in the eyes of the public, it is the drivers' championship which carries the most weight. Yet again, the Scuderia had missed out on the ultimate prize at the final round, for the third year in succession. At any rate, Michael Schumacher was unable to do anything about Mika Hakkinen in the race, as he made a poor start. *"I am still not sure what happened,"* said the German. *"I had the same problem at the start of the formation lap and I knew the start would be difficult. We will have to look at this over the winter."*
From that point onwards, the Ferrari chased round after the McLaren, but to no avail.

△
At Suzuka it was the best of all possible worlds. With the two world championships split between McLaren and Ferrari, everyone had something to cheer about. Even Adrian Newey and Mario Illien (above) were spotted celebrating. A rare sight indeed.
▽

Coulthard-Schumacher open up old wounds

Olivier Panis made a great start in Suzuka. He went off like a rocket, moving from sixth to third at the first corner. He kept that place until his pit stop, which was followed shortly after by retirement.

Michael Schumacher did not hold back on the subject of David Coulthard after the race. *"David was a lap down when I caught him. He obviously had problems with his car. He was very slow and he started zig-zagging in front of me to slow me down. It was very dangerous and I was very disappointed to see a driver like him behave in this way. When you are fighting for a place, okay, but when you are a lap down you must move over. He was shown the blue flags all around the circuit, but he ignored them. It cost me at least ten seconds. Without that, the race might have ended differently. I don't know why McLaren would do this sort of thing. Last year, I believed David when he said the accident at Spa was a mistake. Now I am not so sure."* (in driving rain, the Scotsman slowed down in front of the German who rammed him.)

This was British American Racing's last chance to score a point. While it was the first time that both Jacques Villeneuve and Ricardo Zonta made it to the chequered flag, they were well out of the points in 9th and 12th places.

David Coulthard was not impressed with these remarks. *"Michael has slandered my image in public. He must apologise,"* declared the Scotsman in front of the McLaren office. *"Maybe he thinks he is on a different level to the other drivers, but he should watch what he says. This could end badly for him. I will seek legal advice if necessary."*

A few moments later, Schumacher, wearing a white T-shirt went into the office and spent ten minutes with Coulthard. It was a failed attempt at a reconciliation. *"We each explained our point of view and I do not agree with Michael,"* reported David. *"I did nothing dangerous and I only held him up for four seconds at the most, not ten. He should never have complained in public. While I still respect Michael as a driver, I no longer respect him as a man."*

The last goodbye for Damon Hill during the drivers' parade.

Damon's farewell

116 grands prix, 22 wins, 20 pole positions and a world championship title in 1996: that's the curriculum vitae pinned to Damon Hill's record sheet in the sport's history books.

The Englishman said farewell to Formula 1 in Suzuka, driving in his last ever grand prix at the wheel of a Jordan. The race did not go too well, as he retired in dismal circumstances after 22 laps. He had gone off the road shortly before his first pit stop and the team had to change his front wing. *"I lost so much time in the pits that in the end I reckoned there was no point in going on. I had nothing to gain and a lot to lose,"* he explained. *"Of course I would have preferred it to end differently, but things did not go as I planned. Formula 1 is in the past for me now and I did the right thing by retiring."* His boss, Eddie Jordan, did not appreciate his driver's attitude and did not even say goodbye after the race, furious at this pointless retirement. It was a long time since the two men had got on, as Hill had lost all motivation a long time ago.

An hour after the end of the race, Damon Hill returned to the pit wall with his wife to wave at a hundred or so fans opposite the Jordan garage. *"We'll never forget you Damon,"* read a giant banner. It was a nice way to pay homage to a great driver.

In Japan, passion for Formula 1 is unequaled. And starts at two years ...

results

PRACTICE TIMES

No	Driver	Car/Engine/Chassis	Practice Friday	Pos.	Practice Saturday	Pos.	Qualifying	Pos.	Warm-up	Pos.
1.	Mika Häkkinen	McLaren/Mercedes/MP4 -14/4	1'41"746	1°	1'39"579	2°	1'37"820	2°	1'40"630	1°
2.	David Coulthard	McLaren/Mercedes/MP4 -14/6	1'41"894	2°	1'40"377	7°	1'38"239	3°	1'41"714	5°
3.	Michael Schumacher	Ferrari/Ferrari/F399/195	1'42"215	3°	1'39"085	1°	1'37"470	1°	1'40"761	2°
4.	Eddie Irvine	Ferrari/Ferrari/F399/194	1'43"375	10°	1'40"667	12°	1'38"975	5°	1'42"060	6°
5.	Alessandro Zanardi	Williams/Supertec/FW21/05	1'42"718	5°	1'41"363	14°	1'40"403	16°	1'43"757	17°
6.	Ralf Schumacher	Williams/Supertec/FW21/06	1'43"399	11°	1'40"570	9°	1'39"717	9°	1'41"680	4°
7.	Damon Hill	Jordan/Mugen-Honda/199/4	1'43"720	16°	1'40"175	5°	1'40"140	12°	1'43"023	11°
8.	Heinz-Harald Frentzen	Jordan/Mugen-Honda/199/5	1'43"235	9°	1'40"139	4°	1'38"696	4°	1'41"372	3°
9.	Giancarlo Fisichella	Benetton/Playlife/B199/07	1'42"953	7°	1'41"001	13°	1'40"261	14°	1'43"551	15°
10.	Alexander Wurz	Benetton/Playlife/B199/04	1'43"430	12°	1'41"562	15°	1'40"303	15°	1'43"333	13°
11.	Jean Alesi	Sauber/Petronas/C18/04	1'43"485	13°	1'40"632	10°	1'39"721	10°	1'43"896	18°
12.	Pedro Diniz	Sauber/Petronas/C18/05	1'44"423	21°	1'41"584	16°	1'40"740	17°	1'43"339	14°
14.	Pedro de la Rosa	Arrows/Arrows/A20/05	1'43"599	14°	1'42"156	19°	1'41"708	21°	1'44"411	19°
15.	Toranosuke Takagi	Arrows/Arrows/A20/02	1'43"804	18°	1'42"222	20°	1'41"067	19°	1'45"508	21°
16.	Rubens Barrichello	Stewart/Ford/SF3/04	1'42"529	4°	1'40"334	6°	1'40"140	13°	1'42"522	7°
17.	Johnny Herbert	Stewart/Ford/SF3/06	1'44"179	20°	1'40"134	3°	1'39"706	8°	1'43"051	12°
18.	Olivier Panis	Prost/Peugeot/AP02/5	1'42"925	6°	1'40"656	11°	1'39"623	6°	1'42"919	10°
19.	Jarno Trulli	Prost/Peugeot/AP02/7	1'43"916	19°	1'40"535	8°	1'39"644	7°	1'42"629	8°
20.	Luca Badoer	Minardi/Ford/M01/01	1'45"543	22°	1'43"077	22°	1'42"515	22°	1'45"596	22°
21.	Marc Gené	Minardi/Ford/M01/04	1'43"652	15°	1'42"895	21°	1'41"529	20°	1'43"708	16°
22.	Jacques Villeneuve	BAR/Supertec/BAR01/07	1'43"047	8°	1'41"938	18°	1'39"732	11°	1'42"844	9°
23.	Ricardo Zonta	BAR/Supertec/BAR01/05	1'43"776	17°	1'41"596	17°	1'40"861	18°	1'44"816	20°

MAXIMUM SPEEDS

No	Driver	P1 Qualifs	Pos	P1 Race	Pos	P2 Qualifs	Pos	P2 Race	Pos	Finish Qualifs	Pos	Finish Race	Pos	Trap Qualifs	Pos	Trap Race	Pos
1.	M. Häkkinen	212,8	1°	207,6	2°	308,3	3°	305,2	4°	281,6	3°	278,0	1°	311,9	5°	309,4	4°
2.	D. Coulthard	210,6	7°	207,0	3°	309,6	1°	306,2	3°	282,3	2°	277,7	2°	315,5	1°	312,9	1°
3.	M. Schum.	210,7	6°	205,5	6°	308,2	4°	307,2	1°	279,1	6°	277,7	3°	312,8	3°	310,7	2°
4.	E. Irvine	211,7	4°	206,0	5°	305,0	7°	303,8	9°	278,9	8°	275,2	6°	308,7	8°	308,0	7°
5.	A. Zanardi	203,8	21°	191,9	22°	303,9	8°			276,7	12°			310,4	6°	250,6	22°
6.	R. Schum.	207,2	14°	201,9	16°	303,6	11°	302,9	10°	277,9	10°	273,9	11°	308,5	9°	309,4	3°
7.	D. Hill	211,4	5°	205,2	7°	303,6	10°	304,3	6°	279,0	7°	275,0	7°	307,3	13°	306,8	9°
8.	H.-H. Frentzen	212,3	2°	204,2	9°	308,0	5°	304,7	5°	283,5	1°	276,2	4°	309,2	7°	308,8	5°
9.	G. Fisichella	205,1	17°	201,3	17°	299,0	18°	301,0	13°	273,6	19°	274,0	9°	304,7	17°	305,4	11°
10.	A. Wurz	206,5	15°	202,7	14°	297,1	21°	301,8	12°	273,5	21°	272,1	13°	302,0	21°	304,1	13°
11.	J. Alesi	208,6	11°	204,7	8°	303,2	12°	302,2	11°	276,2	14°	273,8	12°	307,8	10°	306,9	8°
12.	P. Diniz	207,8	13°	203,4	13°	300,6	16°	304,1	7°	275,4	15°	274,4	8°	305,9	16°	306,7	10°
14.	P. de la Rosa	204,5	20°	200,3	18°	301,2	14°	297,6	16°	275,0	17°	271,5	15°	304,3	19°	301,0	17°
15.	T. Takagi	204,7	19°	200,2	19°	299,5	17°	295,7	19°	275,2	16°	269,3	19°	307,7	11°	303,1	15°
16.	R. Barrichello	209,8	8°	206,1	4°	303,8	9°	306,4	2°	278,3	9°	275,6	5°	306,9	14°	308,1	6°
17.	J. Herbert	212,1	3°	207,6	1°	301,0	15°	303,9	8°	277,1	11°	273,9	10°	307,4	12°	304,9	12°
18.	O. Panis	209,5	9°	203,8	11°	307,7	6°	297,0	18°	281,0	5°	271,1	17°	312,6	4°	300,8	18°
19.	J. Trulli	209,0	10°	199,7	20°	309,1	2°	299,5	15°	281,3	4°	271,4	16°	313,6	2°	303,6	14°
20.	L. Badoer	201,0	22°	199,5	21°	296,2	22°	293,3	20°	271,7	22°	266,6	21°	300,0	22°	297,4	20°
21.	M. Gené	204,7	18°	201,9	15°	297,7	20°	292,1	21°	273,6	20°	266,8	20°	303,2	20°	297,3	21°
22.	J. Villeneuve	208,5	12°	204,0	10°	301,4	13°	299,6	14°	276,4	13°	272,1	14°	306,3	15°	302,7	16°
23.	R. Zonta	206,3	16°	203,8	12°	299,0	19°	297,5	17°	274,1	18°	269,5	18°	304,5	18°	300,0	19°

CLASSIFICATION & RETIREMENTS

Pos	Drivers	Team	Time
1.	Häkkinen	McLaren Mercedes	in 1h31"785
2.	M. Schum.	Ferrari	at 5"015
3.	Irvine	Ferrari	at 95"683
4.	Frentzen	Jordan Mugen Honda	at 98"635
5.	R. Schum.	Williams Supertec	at 99"494
6.	Alesi	Sauber Petronas	at 1 lap
7.	Herbert	Stewart Ford	at 1 lap
8.	Barrichello	Stewart Ford	at 1 lap
9.	Villeneuve	BAR Supertec	at 1 lap
10.	Wurz	Benetton Playlife	at 1 lap
11.	Diniz	Sauber Petronas	at 1 lap
12.	Zonta	BAR Supertec	at 1 lap
13.	de la Rosa	Arrows	at 2 laps

Lap	Drivers	Team	Reason
1	Zanardi	Williams Supertec	electrics problem
4	Trulli	Prost Peugeot	clutch
20	Panis	Prost Peugeot	gearbox
22	Hill	Jordan M. Honda	discouraged
32	Gené	Minardi Ford	gearbox
40	Coulthard	McLaren Mercedes	off
44	Badoer	Minardi Ford	engine
44	Takagi	Arrows	gearbox
48	Fisichella	Benetton Playlife	engine

FASTEST LAPS

	Drivers	Time	Lap
1.	M. Schum.	1'41"319	31
2.	Häkkinen	1'41"577	31
3.	Coulthard	1'42"106	33
4.	R.Schum.	1'42"567	22
5.	Frentzen	1'42"972	22
6.	Panis	1'43"188	4
7.	Irvine	1'43"297	26
8.	Barrichello	1'43"496	22
9.	Alesi	1'43"669	3
10.	Herbert	1'43"706	5
11.	Villeneuve	1'43"898	6
12.	Hill	1'43"939	14
13.	Wurz	1'43"963	11
14.	Diniz	1'44"112	22
15.	Trulli	1'44"304	3
16.	Fisichella	1'44"379	12
17.	Zonta	1'44"869	30
18.	Gené	1'45"359	29
19.	Badoer	1'45"377	30
20.	de la Rosa	1'45"556	25
21.	Takagi	1'46"150	27

All results :
© 1999 Fédération Internationale de l'Automobile, 2, Ch. Blandonnet, 1215 Genève 15, Suisse

LAP CHART

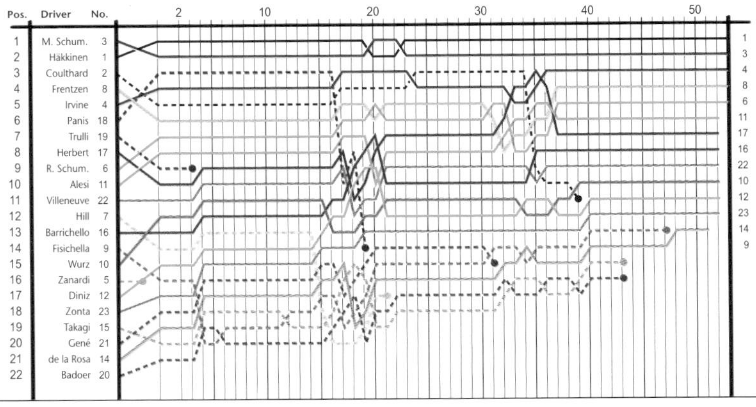

PIT STOPS

	Driver	Time	Lap	Stop n°
1.	Wurz	33"147	15	1
2.	Hill	39"703	15	1
3.	Panis	31"053	16	1
4.	Gené	31"469	16	1
5.	Fisichella	31"821	16	1
6.	Herbert	33"574	17	1
7.	Villeneuve	32"563	17	1
8.	de la Rosa	39"950	17	1
9.	Badoer	32"320	18	1
10.	Häkkinen	32"520	19	1
11.	Frentzen	30"741	19	1
12.	Alesi	33"320	19	1
13.	Zonta	32"729	19	1
14.	Takagi	35"944	19	1
15.	R.Schum.	31"046	20	1
16.	Barrichello	31"230	20	1
17.	Diniz	32"294	20	1
18.	M.Schum.	29"771	22	1
19.	Coulthard	31"042	22	1
20.	Irvine	30"742	23	1
21.	Frentzen	30"362	31	2
22.	Gené	39"882	31	2
23.	Irvine	29"796	32	2
24.	R.Schum.	32"150	32	2
25.	Badoer	37"510	32	2
26.	Barrichello	32"731	33	2
27.	Wurz	33"148	33	2
28.	Zonta	32"300	33	2
29.	Fisichella	32"136	33	2
30.	Coulthard	42"726	34	2
31.	Villeneuve	32"514	34	2
32.	de la Rosa	35"848	34	2
33.	Takagi	34"668	35	2
34.	Herbert	36"468	36	2
35.	Alesi	32"166	36	2
36.	M.Schum.	30"717	37	2
37.	Häkkinen	30"966	38	2
38.	Diniz	31"293	37	2
39.	Badoer	38"561	41	3

THE CIRCUIT

SIXTEENTH ROUND

FUJI TELEVISION JAPANESE GRAND PRIX, SUZUKA

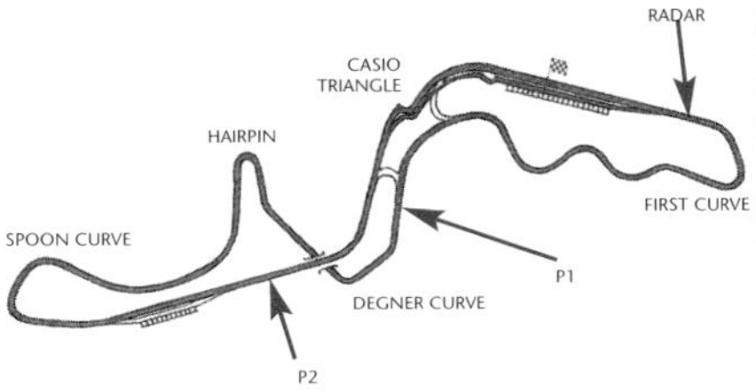

Date : October 31, 1999
Length : 5860 meters
Distance : 53 laps, 310.596 km
Weather : overcast, 18°

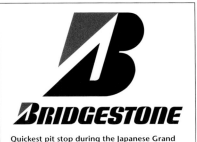

BRIDGESTONE

Quickest pit stop during the Japanese Grand Prix, taking on fuel and four new Bridgestone tyres:
Michael Schumacher, Ferrari, 29"771

CHAMPIONSHIP

(after sixteen rounds)

Drivers :

1. M. Häkkinen 76
2. E. Irvine 74
3. H.-H. Frentzen 54
4. D. Coulthard 48
5. M. Schumacher 44
6. R. Schumacher 35
7. R. Barrichello 21
8. J. Herbert 15
9. G. Fisichella 13
10. M. Salo 10
11. J. Trulli 7
    D. Hill 7
13. A. Wurz 3
    P. Diniz 3
15. O. Panis....................2
    J. Alesi....................2
17. P. de la Rosa....................1
    M. Gené....................1

Constructors :

1. Ferrari....................128
2. McLaren/Mercedes....................124
3. Jordan/Mugen Honda....................61
4. Stewart/Ford 36
5. Williams/Supertec....................35
6. Benetton/Playlife 16
7. Prost/Peugeot....................9
8. Sauber/Petronas 5
9. Arrows 1
   Minardi/Ford 1

RACE SUMMARY

- Michael Schumacher got too much wheelspin at the start, while Hakkinen made an impeccable getaway to take command of the race. The German is second ahead of a fast starting Olivier Panis, Eddie Irvine and David Coulthard.
- Hakkinen and Schumacher pull away from the field. After 14 laps, Schumacher is 6.8s down on Hakkinen, while Panis is 25s down on the Finn and Irvine is 28s behind his championship rival and is coming under attack from David Coulthard.
- The pit stops do not change the order at the front, but they do see Coulthard pass Irvine. The Scotsman would not go far as he crashed off the track, broke his front wing and had to retire soon after.
- Mika Hakkinen fights of Michael Schumacher to the end, to take the race win and the world championship.

WEEKEND GOSSIP

- **Jean Todt is nervous**

For the third time in three years, Scuderia Ferrari was preparing to fight for the world title in the final round of the season. In 1997, it was at Jerez in Spain. Michael Schumacher was up against Jacques Villeneuve. In 1998 at Suzuka again, Michael was fighting against Mika Hakkinen. Both attempts ended in failure. For Jean Todt, Ferrari's Sporting Director, the tension mounted every year. *"We have to stay totally focussed,"* he affirmed on the Thursday before the race. *"We have already missed out on the title in 1997 and 1998. Winning is therefore very important to us. Yes, I am nervous, but after all, I am a human being and I feel the same emotions as anyone else. After so many years of effort, it would be impossible not to be nervous."* Jean Todt's detractors, of which there are many in Italy, had to admit that the Scuderia's boss knew how to confess to his own weaknesses.

- **Arrows consolidates**

In Suzuka, the Arrows team announced that it had employed Dr. John Davis to work in its research department. Davis had just spent three years with Jordan, in charge of R & D. Before that he had worked for Lotus and Ligier. "We were looking for someone to reinforce the team set up over the summer by Mike Coughlan," explained Tom Walkinshaw. This addition was a sign that Arrows was doing all it could for 2000, having given up on developing the 1999 car a long way back in the season. The team had not done any testing since July.

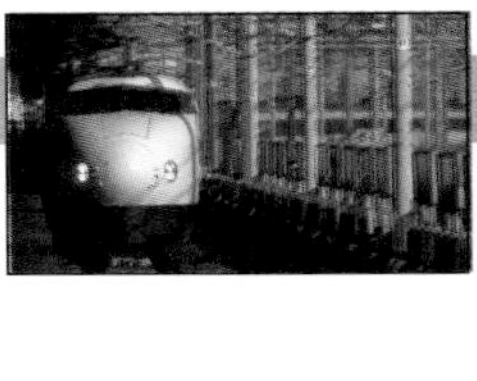

by Pascal Dro

BMW-Williams: a secret force

In carefully avoiding the grand prix circuits or those used in private testing by other F1 teams, since last March the Williams FW20-BMW, or rather the BMW with the Williams FW20 chassis has literally been creeping around the most secret test tracks of Europe. Why? Why avoid comparisons with this year's cars? Because BMW is taking its time and does not want the opposition to learn anything about its activities; neither anything bad if it is quick, nor anything good if it is slow.

So, test driver Jorg Muller, the development

Eddie Irvine and Rubens Barrichello swop seats next year. It was the big transfer of the year.

team set up by Williams and motor sport director Gerhard Berger are not saying anything as they get on with their work. It is an arduous task, colossal even. Trying to beat McLaren or get to their level is harder than climbing Everest. McLaren-Mercedes fumbled around for three years before winning a race. The engine from the three pointed

A Williams fitted with a BMW engine has been running for several months in the South of France, at the private Miramas test track.

star first ran as an Ilmor in a March chassis with the Leyton House team and then in 1990, it appeared in the back of a Sauber and petrol poured out of its injectors. David Coulthard produced its first win in 1997 in Melbourne. That makes a total of six seasons before it won anything. Naturally, Ilmor without the support of DaimlerChrysler progressed more slowly than BMW is likely to do under its own banner. But nevertheless, BMW must try to do in a couple of years what its German rival took much longer to achieve. That's a lot of mountains of experience to climb. In short, just like with BAR and all the other new boys, it will take a huge investment and a lot of time to get on the pace in the ultra-competitive world of F1.

The first opportunity to make a reasonable comparison came in October at the A1-Ring in Austria. It was fifteen degrees cooler than when the grand prix was held there and therefore no conclusions could be drawn. But BMW does scare the opposition. It was they who beat Renault, the inventor of the F1 turbocharged engine after just two years of trying. That was back in 1983, when there was a lot of talk of Brabham running illegal fuel. If that proves anything it's that BMW will stop

at nothing to succeed. They have the time, the budget and in Williams they have a chassis builder as capable as Brabham was back then. In Ralf Schumacher they also have a driver with as much latent talent as a young Nelson Piquet. All the ingredients seem to be in place. In two years time it will be 2001 and the odyssey continues.

Jaguar year zero

Jac Nasser is Ford's workaholic boss. Apparently he gets by on three hours sleep a night! Seeing the huge crowds that fill the grandstands at the grands prix he declared, in a wistful voice: "It makes me green with envy." The colour green might have been a clue and although there was no announcement at that point, the rumour gathered momentum. Thanks to its owners at Ford, Jaguar, seven times a Le Mans winner would be in Formula 1 in the year 2000. The final step in this plan was Ford's acquisition of the Stewart Grand Prix team, announced at the Canadian Grand Prix. It was big news. Since the team had come into existence, Ford had underwritten the Stewart project and now it had decided to take it over completely. It seemed that like all big companies, Ford preferred to have total control. Ford still holds the record as the most successful engine manufacturer in Formula 1. With 175 wins to its name, compared with less than 125 for Ferrari, the blue oval has a big lead, but no one seems aware of the fact. Just as few

of us remember that when Benetton won the world championship it was a Ford V10 engine that powered Michael Schumacher to the title. Along with this record for technical superiority, Ford holds another record: that of the worst marketing and publicity in the history of F1. For a major American company, this is totally unacceptable. So now everything will change. From next year, Stewart Ford becomes Jaguar Racing. If it succeeds on the track and as a marketing exercise, who knows where it could all end. The Jaguars could become Mazdas or Mustangs or Aston Martins. There is even the possibility of seeing a Ford engine in another car with a Volvo badge on it. Ford is not investing for the simple pleasure of winning, because if nobody knows about it, it serves no useful purpose. Jac Nasser and Jackie Stewart both understand that fact. In a way, Stewart's win in the European Grand Prix and the way it snatched fourth place in the Constructors' championship from the prestigious Williams team constitutes a piece of bad news for its

new owner. Getting Stewart off the middle of the grid and into the top end would have been a worthy first achievement for Jaguar. Never mind and all the more credit to Jackie and his son Paul. The father has just given his son a motor racing curriculum vitae. It was the best moment of Jackie's career and that's quite something!

△
Alain Prost with Eddie Jordan. The Irishman has taken Jarno Trulli off the Frenchman's hands.

Honda, while waiting for Toyota

The story ran all year. Last winter, the late Harvey Postlethwaite and his 70 faithful workers in the Honda Research and Development F1 project was hard at work. The former Tyrrell men were working on a chassis built by Dallara fitted with a Honda V10 engine and driven by Jos Verstappen. At that time, it was fully expected that Honda would come back to the sport as a complete team, building both chassis and engine. The constructors' association had even earmarked a a slot for a twelfth team especially to welcome Honda. That was just a few months ago, but since then, a lot of water has flowed under the bridge. When the final budget presentation was made to the Honda board, the Japanese appeared to take fright. The budget was reckoned to be of the order of 135 million dollars over five years. Then, Harvey Postlethwaite died of a heart attack. The Honda R and D project was canned and a few weeks later, BAR announced it would be the official Honda-supplied team from 2000.

So what of the twelfth team? That place now seems to be ready and waiting for Nissan's great rival, Toyota. The European team based in Germany has already started recruiting from scratch. At the end of the year, it announced it would be stopping its rally programme and it seemed that Toyota was even prepared to give up on its Le Mans campaign without ever winning the classic endurance race. We shall see. It still has eighteen months to design and develop a chassis. What is certain is that it cannot afford to do less well than Honda, which owes a great part of its current image to its previous Formula 1 participation. Toyota has been getting ready at its Cologne base since 1998. Because Toyota is also becoming a European constructor with a manufacturing facility in France, this all seems to be falling into place nicely. The only question which remains unanswered is which, if any, European organisation it will team up with. Nothing would be more dangerous for an inexperienced

team than to try and go it alone. There is talk of Arrows or Benetton. But if that was the case, then the twelfth place would remain vacant. That is just one of the mysteries that adds to the charm of Formula 1. That empty seat might have to be filled by an American organisation, but for the moment, Bernie Ecclestone claims he has had no offers from that side of the pond.

△
In 2000, Jean Alesi should fire up the Prost-Peugeot. Fireworks in prospect.

Craig Pollock smiles. 2000 cannot possibly be worse than 1999.
▽

△ *The Schumacher brothers take a close look at a McLaren in parc ferme.*

Recap of the 1999 season

Pos.	Driver	Make	AUS	BRA	SM	MON	ESP	CAN	FRA	GB	AUT	GER	HUN	BEL	ITA	EUR	MAL	JAP	Poles	Wins	Fast. laps	Laps led	Km led	Final
1	Mika HAKKINEN	McLaren Mercedes	A	1	A	3	1	1	2	A	3	A	1	2	A	5	1	1	11	5	6	383	1'881	76
2	Eddie IRVINE	Ferrari	1	5	A	2	4	3	6	2	1	1	3	4	6	7	1	3	1	4	1	132	709	74
3	Heinz-Harald FRENTZEN	Jordan Mugen Honda	2	3	A	4	A	11	1	4	4	3	4	3	1	A	6	4	-	2	-	64	319	54
4	David COULTHARD	McLaren Mercedes	A	A	2	A	2	7	A	1	2	5	2	1	5	A	2	A	2	2	2	145	782	48
5	Michael SCHUMACHER	Ferrari	8	2	1	1	3	A	5	DNS							2	2	3	2	6	176	730	44
6	Ralf SCHUMACHER	Williams Supertec	3	4	A	5	4	4	3	4	A	9	5	2	4	A	5		-	-	1	8	36	35
7	Rubens BARRICHELLO	Stewart Ford	5	A	3	9	8	A	3	8	A	A	5	10	4	3	5	8	1	-	-	67	286	21
8	Johnny HERBERT	Stewart Ford	DNS	A	10	A	A	5	A	12	14	11	11	A	14	1	4	7	-	1	-	17	77	15
9	Giancarlo FISICHELLA	Benetton Playlife	4	A	5	5	9	2	A	7	12	A	A	11	A	A	11	14	-	-	-	4	18	13
10	Mika SALO	BAR Supertec / Ferrari	A	A	-	7	A	-	-	-	-	2	12	7	3	A	9	A	-	-	-	2	13	10
11	Jarno TRULLI	Prost Peugeot	A	A	4	7	6	A	7	9	7	8	12	8	12	2	A	A						7
12	Damon HILL	Jordan Mugen Honda	A	A	4	6	A	7	A	5	8	A	6	6	10	A	8	10						7
13	Alexander WURZ	Benetton Playlife	A	7	A	6	10	A	10	10	5	7	7	14	A	A	8	10						3
14	Pedro DINIZ	Sauber Petronas	A	A	A	A	A	6	A	6	6	A	6	A	A	7	6	A						3
15	Jean ALESI	Sauber Petronas	A	6	A	A	9	A	14	A	8	A	9	9	A	A	6	A						2
16	Olivier PANIS	Prost Peugeot	A	6	A	A	9	8	13	10	6	10	13	11	11	A	A	A						2
17	Marc GENÉ	Minardi Ford	A	9	9	A	8	A	15	11	9	17	16	A	6	9	A	A						1
18	Pedro de la ROSA	Arrows	6	A	A	A	11	A	12	A	A	A	A	15	A	A	13							1

Then, by alphabetical order :

Driver	Make	AUS	BRA	SM	MON	ESP	CAN	FRA	GB	AUT	GER	HUN	BEL	ITA	EUR	MAL	JAP
Luca BADOER	Minardi Ford	A	-	8	A	A	10	10	A	13	10	14	A	A	A	A	A
Stéphane SARRAZIN	Minardi Ford	-	A														
Toranosuke TAKAGI	Arrows	7	8	A	A	12	A	11	16	A	A	A	A	15	8	10	A
Jacques VILLENEUVE	BAR Supertec	A	A	A	A	A	A	A	11	A	A	8	7	A	10	A	12
Alessandro ZANARDI	Williams Supertec	A	A	11	8	A	A	A	11	A	A	8	7	A	10	A	12
Ricardo ZONTA	BAR Supertec	A	F	-	-	A	9	A	15	A	13	A	8	A	12		

Nber of GP contested

Patrese	256
Berger	210
DeCesaris	208
Piquet	204
Prost	199
Alboreto	194
Mansell	187
G. Hill	176
Laffite	176
Lauda	171
Alesi	167
Boutsen	163
Senna	161
Brundle	158
Watson	152
Arnoux	149
Warwick	147
Reutemann	146
E. Fittipaldi	144
Herbert	144
Jarier	135
Cheever	132
Regazzoni	132
Ma. Andretti	128
M. Schumacher	128
Häkkinen	128
Brabham	126
Peterson	123
Ickx	116
Jones	116
Rosberg	114
Tambay	114
Hulme	112
Scheckter	112
Surtees	111
Martini	119
D. Hill	115
Barrichello	113
De Angelis	108
Alliot	107
Mass	105
Bonnier	102
McLaren	101
Stewart	99
Siffert	97
Irvine	97
Frentzen	97
Amon	96
Depailler	95
Katayama	95
Capelli	94
Hunt	92
Panis	91
Coulthard	90
Beltoise	86
Gurney	86
Palmer	84
Surer	82
Trintignant	82
Diniz	82
Johansson	79
Salo	78
Nannini	77
Ghinzani	76
Nakajima	74
Brambilla	74
Gugelmin	74
Stuck	74
Clark	72
Pace	72
Modena	70
Pironi	70
Then :	
J. Villeneuve	64
Fisichella	57
Badoer	50
R. Schumacher	49
Trulli	45
Zanardi	41
Wurz	35
Takagi	31
Gené	16

Nber of poles

Senna	65
Prost	33
Clark	33
Mansell	32
Fangio	28
Lauda	24
Piquet	24
M. Schumacher	23
Häkkinen	21
D. Hill	20
Andretti	18
Arnoux	18
Stewart	17
Moss	16
Ascari	14
Hunt	14
Peterson	14
Brabham	13
G. Hill	13
Ickx	13
J. Villeneuve	13
Berger	12
Rindt	10
Surtees	8
Patrese	8
Coulthard	8
Laffite	7
Fittipaldi	6
P. Hill	6
Jabouille	6
Jones	6
Reutemann	6
Amon	5
Farina	5
Regazzoni	5
Rosberg	5
Tambay	5
Hawthorn	4
Pironi	4
De Angelis	3
Brooks	3
T. Fabi	3
Gonzales	3
Gurney	3
Jarier	3
Scheckter	3
Then :	
Alesi	2
Frentzen	2
Barrichello	2
Fisichella	1

Nber of victories

Prost	51
Senna	41
M. Schumacher	35
Mansell	31
Stewart	27
Clark	25
Lauda	25
Fangio	24
Piquet	23
D. Hill	22
Moss	16
Häkkinen	15
Brabham	14
Fittipaldi	14
G. Hill	14
Ascari	13
Andretti	12
Jones	12
Reutemann	12
J. Villeneuve	11
Hunt	10
Peterson	10
Scheckter	10
Berger	10
Hulme	8
Ickx	8
Arnoux	7
Brooks	6
Laffite	6
Rindt	6
Surtees	6
G. Villeneuve	6
Patrese	6
Coulthard	6
Alboreto	5
Farina	5
Regazzoni	5
Rosberg	5
Watson	5
Gurney	4
McLaren	4
Boutsen	3
P. Hill	3
Hawthorn	3
Pironi	3
Irvine	3
Frentzen	3
Herbert	3
Then :	
Panis	1
Alesi	1

Number of fastest laps

Prost	41
M. Schumacher	38
Mansell	30
Clark	28
Lauda	25
Fangio	23
Piquet	23
Berger	21
Moss	20
D. Hill	19
Senna	19
Regazzoni	15
Stewart	15
Ickx	14
Jones	13
Patrese	13
Arnoux	12
Häkkinen	12
Ascari	11
Surtees	11
Coulthard	11
Andretti	10
Brabham	10
G. Hill	10
Hulme	9
Peterson	9
J. Villeneuve	9
Hunt	8
Laffite	7
G. Villeneuve	7
Farina	6
Fittipaldi	6
Gonzalez	6
Gurney	6
Hawthorn	6
P. Hill	6
Pironi	6
Scheckter	6
Frentzen	6
Pace	5
Watson	5
Alesi	4
Alboreto	4
Beltoise	4
Depailler	4
Reutemann	4
Siffert	4
Then :	
Fisichella	1
Wurz	1
Irvine	1
R.Schumacher	1

Total number of points scored

Prost	798.5
Senna	614
M. Schumacher	570
Piquet	485.5
Mansell	482
Lauda	420.5
Berger	385
Stewart	360
D. Hill	360
Reutemann	310
Häkkinen	294
G. Hill	289
E. Fittipaldi	281
Patrese	281
Fangio	277.5
Clark	274
Brabham	261
Scheckter	255
Alesi	236
Laffite	228
Coulthard	221
Regazzoni	212
Jones	206
Peterson	206
McLaren	196.5
Alboreto	186.5
Moss	186.5
Arnoux	181
Ickx	181
Ma. Andretti	180
Surtees	180
J. Villeneuve	180
Hunt	179
Irvine	173
Watson	169
Frentzen	142
Then :	
Herbert	98
Barrichello	76
R. Schumacher	62
Panis	56
Fisichella	49
Wurz	27
Salo	25
Trulli	11
Diniz	8
Gené	1
de la Rosa	1

Nber of laps in the lead

Senna	2'999
Prost	2'705
Mansell	2'099
Clark	2'039
M. Schumacher	2'012
Stewart	1'893
Lauda	1'620
Piquet	1'572
D. Hill	1'352
G. Hill	1'073
Häkkinen	1'024
Brabham	827
Andretti	799
Peterson	706
Berger	695
Scheckter	671
Reutemann	648
Hunt	634
J. Villeneuve	634
Jones	594
Coulthard	575
Patrese	568
G. Villeneuve	533
Ickx	529
Arnoux	506
Rosberg	506
Fittipaldi	459
Hulme	436
Rindt	387
Regazzoni	361
Surtees	310
Pironi	295
Watson	287
Laffite	279
Alesi	271
Alboreto	218
Tambay	197
Gurney	191
P. Hill	189
Jabouille	184
Amon	183
Brooks	173
Depailler	165
Irvine	156
Frentzen	140
Then :	
Barrichello	71
Herbert	44
Trulli	37
Fisichella	35
Panis	16
R. Schumacher	8
Salo	2

Nber of km in the lead

Senna	13'613
Prost	12'575
Clark	10'189
Mansell	9'642
M. Schumacher	9'193
Stewart	9'077
Piquet	7'465
Lauda	7'188
D. Hill	6'248
Häkkinen	4'903
G. Hill	4'618
Brabham	4'541
Andretti	3'577
Berger	3'456
Reutemann	3'309
Peterson	3'304
Hunt	3'229
Ickx	3'067
J. Villeneuve	2'972
Jones	2'877
Scheckter	2'837
Coulthard	2'834
Patrese	2'571
Arnoux	2'561
G. Villeneuve	2'244
Rosberg	2'137
Surtees	2'131
Fittipaldi	2'122
Rindt	1'905
Hulme	1'900
Regazzoni	1'855
P. Hill	1'715
Brooks	1'525
Gurney	1'518
Laffite	1'476
Alesi	1'297
Watson	1'245
Pironi	1'238
Jabouille	978
Tambay	975
Alboreto	927
Irvine	838
Von Trips	787
Amon	784
Frentzen	698
Then :	
Herbert	226
Fisichella	172
Trulli	160
Barrichello	85
Panis	53
R. Schumacher	36
Salo	13

Abbreviations : A = retired; NQ = not qualified; DNF = not finished; F = forfeit; D = disqualified; NC = finished, but not classified (insufficient distance covered); ARG = Argentina; AUS = Australia; AUT = Autria; BEL = Belgique; BRE = Brésil; CAN = Canada; DAL = Dallas; ESP = Espagne; EUR = Europe; FIN = Finland; FRA = France; GB = England; GER = Germany HOL = The Netherlands; ITA = Italy; JAP = Japon; MEX = Mexico; MON = Monaco; NZ = New-Zealand; PAC = Pacific; POR = Portugal; RSM = San-Marino; SA = South Africa; SUE = Sweden; SUI = Switzerland; USA = Etats-Unis;USAE = East USA ; USAW = West USA; VEG = Las Vegas; NB = Laps in the lead only since 1957.

The 50 World Champions

Year	Driver	Nationality	Make	Nber of races	Nber of poles	Nber of victories	Nber of bestest laps
1950	Giuseppe Farina	ITA	Alfa RomÈo	7	2	3	3
1951	Juan Manuel Fangio	ARG	Alfa RomÈo	8	4	3	5
1952	Alberto Ascari	ITA	Ferrari	8	5	6	5
1953	Alberto Ascari	ITA	Ferrari	9	6	5	4
1954	Juan Manuel Fangio	ARG	Mercedes/Maserati	9	5	6	3
1955	Juan Manuel Fangio	ARG	Mercedes	7	3	4	3
1956	Juan Manuel Fangio	ARG	Lancia/Ferrari	8	5	3	3
1957	Juan Manuel Fangio	ARG	Maserati	8	4	4	2
1958	Mike Hawthorn	GB	Ferrari	11	4	1	5
1959	Jack Brabham	AUS	Cooper Climax	9	1	2	1
1960	Jack Brabham	AUS	Cooper Climax	10	3	5	3
1961	Phil Hill	USA	Ferrari	8	5	2	2
1962	Graham Hill	GB	BRM	9	1	4	3
1963	Jim Clark	GB	Lotus Climax	10	7	7	6
1964	John Surtees	GB	Ferrari	10	2	2	2
1965	Jim Clark	GB	Lotus Climax	10	6	6	6
1966	Jack Brabham	AUS	Brabham Repco	9	3	4	1
1967	Dennis Hulme	NZ	Brabham Repco	11	0	2	2
1968	Graham Hill	GB	Lotus Ford	12	2	3	0
1969	Jackie Stewart	GB	Matra Ford	11	2	6	5
1970	Jochen Rindt	AUT	Lotus Ford	13	3	5	1
1971	Jackie Stewart	GB	Matra Ford	11	6	6	3
1972	Emerson Fittipaldi	BRE	Lotus Ford	12	3	5	0
1973	Jackie Stewart	GB	Tyrrell Ford	15	3	5	1
1974	Emerson Fittipaldi	BRE	McLaren Ford	15	2	3	0
1975	Niki Lauda	AUT	Ferrari	14	9	5	2
1976	James Hunt	GB	McLaren Ford	16	8	6	2
1977	Niki Lauda	AUT	Ferrari	17	2	3	3
1978	Mario Andretti	USA	Lotus Ford	16	8	6	3
1979	Jody Scheckter	SA	Ferrari	15	1	3	1
1980	Alan Jones	AUS	Williams Ford	14	3	5	5
1981	Nelson Piquet	BRE	Brabham Ford	15	4	3	1
1982	Keke Rosberg	FIN	Williams Ford	16	1	1	0
1983	Nelson Piquet	BRE	Brabham BMW Turbo	15	1	3	4
1984	Niki Lauda	AUT	McLaren TAG Porsche Turbo	16	0	5	5
1985	Alain Prost	FRA	McLaren TAG Porsche Turbo	16	2	5	5
1986	Alain Prost	FRA	McLaren TAG Porsche Turbo	16	1	4	2
1987	Nelson Piquet	BRE	Williams Honda Turbo	16	4	3	4
1988	Ayrton Senna	BRE	McLaren Honda Turbo	16	13	8	3
1989	Alain Prost	FRA	McLaren Honda	16	2	4	5
1990	Ayrton Senna	BRE	McLaren Honda	16	10	6	2
1991	Ayrton Senna	BRE	McLaren Honda	16	8	7	2
1992	Nigel Mansell	GB	Williams Renault	16	14	9	8
1993	Alain Prost	FRA	Williams Renault	16	13	7	6
1994	Michael Schumacher	GER	Benetton Ford	14	6	8	9
1995	Michael Schumacher	GER	Benetton Renault	17	4	9	7
1996	Damon Hill	GB	Williams Renault	16	9	8	5
1997	Jacques Villeneuve	CAN	Williams Renault	17	10	7	3
1998	Mika Häkkinen	FIN	McLaren Mercedes	16	9	8	6
1999	Mika Häkkinen	FIN	McLaren Mercedes	16	11	5	6

Constructor's championship des 1999

Position	Team	Nber of points	Nber of poles	Nber of victories	Nber of bestest laps	Nber of laps in the lead	Nber of kil. in the lead
1.	Ferrari	128	3	6	8	310	1'439
2.	McLaren Mercedes	124	11	7	0	528	2'663
3.	Jordan Mugen Honda	61	1	2	0	65	324
4.	Stewart Ford	36	1	1	0	84	363
5.	Williams Supertec	35	0	0	1	8	36
6.	Benetton Playlife	16	0	0	0	4	18
7.	Prost Peugeot	9	0	0	0	0	0
8.	Sauber Petronas	5	0	0	0	0	0
9.	Arrows	1	0	0	0	0	0
10.	Minardi Ford	1	0	0	0	0	0
11.	BAR Supertec	0	0	0	0	0	0

Nb of constructor's championship titles
(exists since 1958)

9 : Williams 1980 - 81 - 86 - 87 -92 93 - 94 - 96 - 97
Ferrari 1961 - 64 - 75 - 76 - 77 - 79 - 82 - 83

8 : McLaren 1974 - 84 - 85 - 88 - 89 - 90 - 91 - 98

7 : Lotus 1963 - 65 - 68 - 70 -72 73 - 78

2 : Cooper 1959 - 60
Brabham 1966 - 67

1 : Vanwall 1958
BRM 1962
Matra 1969
Tyrrell 1971
Benetton 1995

Numberde poles par marque

Ferrari	127
Williams	108
Lotus	107
McLaren	103
Brabham	39
Renault	31
Benetton	16
Tyrrell	14
Alfa RomÈo	12
BRM	11
Cooper	11
Maserati	10
Ligier	9
Mercedes	8
Vanwall	7
March	5
Matra	4
Shadow	3
Lancia	2
Jordan	2
Arrows	1
Honda	1
Lola	1
Porsche	1
Wolf	1
Stewart	1

Number of victories per make

Ferrari	125
McLaren	123
Williams	103
Lotus	79
Brabham	35
Benetton	26
Tyrrell	23
BRM	17
Cooper	16
Renault	1
Alfa RomÈo	10
Maserati	9
Matra	9
Mercedes	9
Vanwall	9
Ligier	9
March	3
Wolf	3
Jordan	3
Honda	2
Hesketh	1
Penske	1
Porsche	1
Shadow	1
Stewart	1

Number of fastest laps per make

Ferrari	139
Williams	110
McLaren	80
Lotus	70
Brabham	41
Benetton	37
Tyrrell	20
Renault	18
BRM	15
Maserati	15
Alfa RomÈo	14
Cooper	13
Matra	12
Ligier	11
Mercedes	9
March	7
Vanwall	6
Surtees	4
Eagle	2
Honda	2
Shadow	2
Wolf	2
Ensign	1
Gordini	1
Hesketh	1
Lancia	1
Parnelli	1
Jordan	1

Family picture of the 1999 championship, a few hours before the finale in Suzuka. Standing, from left to right: Jean Alesi, Pedro Diniz, Jacques Villeneuve, Ricardo Zonta, Rubens Barrichello et Johnny Herbert. Middle, Toranosuke Takagi, Pedro de la Rosa, Alessandro Zanardi, Ralf Schumacher, Heinz-Harald Frentzen, Damon Hill, Luca Badoer, Marc Gené. Sitting: Giancarlo Fisichella, Alexander Wurz, David Coulthard, Mika Häkkinen, Michael Schumacher, Eddie Irvine, Jarno Trulli et Olivier Panis.

Sporting regulations

The FIA will organise the FIA Formula One World Championship (the Championship) which is the property of the FIA and comprises two titles of World Champion, one for drivers and one for constructors. It consists of the Formula One Grand Prix races which are included in the Formula One calendar and in respect of which the ASNs and organisers have signed the organisation agreement provided for in the 1998 Concorde Agreement (...)

LICENCES

10. All drivers, competitors and officials participating in the Championship must hold a FIA Super Licence. Applications for Super Licences must be made to the FIA through the applicant's ASN.

CHAMPIONSHIP EVENTS

11. Events are reserved for Formula One cars as defined in the Technical Regulations.

12. Each Event will have the status of an international restricted competition.

13. The distance of all races, from the start signal referred to in Article 141 to the chequered flag, shall be equal to the least number of complete laps which exceed a distance of 305 km. However, should two hours elapse before the scheduled race distance is completed, the leader will be shown the chequered flag when he crosses the control line (the Line) at the end of the lap during which the two hour period ended. The Line is a single line which crosses both the track and the pit lane.

14. The maximum number of Events in the Championship is 17, the minimum is 8.

16. An Event which is cancelled with less than three months written notice to the FIA will not be considered for inclusion in the following year's Championship unless the FIA judges the cancellation to have been due to force majeure.

17. An Event may be cancelled if fewer than 12 cars are available for it.

WORLD CHAMPIONSHIP

18) The Formula One World Championship driver's title will be awarded to the driver who has scored the highest number of points, taking into consideration all the results obtained during the Events which have actually taken place.

19. Points will not be awarded for the Championship unless the driver has driven the same car throughout the race in the Event in question.

20. The title of Formula One World Champion for Constructors will be awarded to the make which has scored the highest number of points, taking into account all the results obtained by a maximum of 2 cars per make.

21. The constructor of an engine or rolling chassis is the person (including any corporate or unincorporated body) which owns the intellectual property rights to such engine or chassis. The make of an engine or chassis is the name attributed to it by its constructor. If the make of the chassis is not the same as that of the engine, the title will be awarded to the former which shall always precede the latter in the name of the car.

22. Points for both titles will be awarded at each Event according to the following scale :

1st : 10 points; 2nd : 6 points; 3rd : 4 points; 4th : 3 points; 5th : 2 points; 6th : 1 point.

23. If a race is stopped under Articles 155 and 156, and cannot be restarted, no points will be awarded in case A, half points will be awarded in case B and full points will be awarded in case C.

24. Drivers finishing first, second and third in the Championship must be present at the annual FIA Prize Giving ceremony. Any such driver who is absent will be liable to a maximum fine of US $ 50,000.00. All competitors shall use their best endeavours to ensure that their drivers attend as aforesaid.

DEAD HEAT

25. Prizes and points awarded for all the positions of competitors who tie, will be added together and shared equally.

26. If two or more constructors or drivers finish the season with the same number of points, the higher place in the Championship (in either case) shall be awarded to :

a) the holder of the greatest number of first places,

b) if the number of first places is the same, the holder of the greatest number of second places,

c) if the number of second places is the same, the holder of the greatest number of third places and so on until a winner emerges.

d) if this procedure fails to produce a result, the FIA will nominate the winner according to such criteria as it thinks fit.

COMPETITORS APPLICATIONS

42. Applications to compete in the Championship may be submitted to the FIA at any time between 1 November and 15 November each year, on an entry form as set out in Appendix 2 hereto accompanied by the entry fee provided for in the Agreement. Entry forms will be made available by FIA who will notify the applicant of the result of the application no later than 1 December. Successful applicants are automatically entered in all Events of the Championship and will be the only competitors at Events.

44. A competitor may change the make and/or type of engine at any time during the Championship. All points scored with an engine of different make to that which was first entered in the Championship will count (and will be aggregated) for the assessment of Benefits and for determining team positions for pre-qualifying purposes, however such points will not count towards (nor be aggregated for) the FIA Formula One Constructors Championship.

45. With the exception of those whose cars have scored points in the Championship of the previous year, applicants must supply information about the size of their company, their financial position and their ability to meet their prescribed obligations. All applicants who did not take part in the entire Championship for the previous year must also deposit US$500,000.00 with the FIA when submitting their application. This sum will be returned to them forthwith if their application is refused or at the end of their first Championship season provided they have met all the requirements of the Agreement and its schedules.

46. All applications will be studied by the FIA which will publish the list of cars and drivers accepted together with their race numbers on 1 December (or the following Monday if 1 December falls on a week-end), having first notified unsuccessful applicants as set out in article 42.

47. No more than 24 will be accepted from any one competitor.

INCIDENTS

53. Incident means any occurrence or series of occurrences involving one or more drivers, or any action by any driver, which is reported to the stewards by the race director (or noted by the stewards and referred to the race director for investigation) which :

- necessitated the stopping of a race under Article 155;
- constituted a breach of these Sporting Regulations or the Code;
- caused a false start by one or more cars;
- caused an avoidable collision;
- forced a driver off the track;
- illegitimately prevented a legitimate overtaking manoeuvre by a driver;
- illegitimately impeded another driver during overtaking.

54. a) It shall be at the discretion of the stewards to decide, upon a report or a request by the race director, if a driver or drivers involved in an incident shall be penalised.

b) If an incident is under investigation by the stewards, a message informing all Teams of this will be displayed on the timing monitors.

c) If a driver is involved in a collision or Incident (see Article 53), he must not leave the circuit without the consent of the stewards.

55. The stewards may impose a 10 second time penalty on any driver involved in an Incident. However, should such penalty be imposed during the last five laps, or after the end of a race, Artice 56b) below will not apply and 25 seconds will be added to the elapsed race time of the driver concerned.

56. Should the stewards decide to impose a time penalty, the following procedure will be followed :

a) The stewards will give written notification of the time penalty which has been imposed to an official of the team concerned and will ensure that this information is also displayed on the timing monitors.

b) From the time the steward's decision is notified on the timing monitors the relevant driver may cover no more than three complete laps before entering the pits and proceeding to his pit where he shall remain for the period of the time penalty. During the time the car is stationary for the time penalty it may not be worked on. However, if the engine stops, it may be started after the time penalty period has elapsed.

c) When the time penalty period has elapsed the driver may rejoin the race.

d) Any breach or failure to comply with Articles 56 b) or 56 c) may result in the car being excluded.

57. Any determination made or any penalty imposed pursuant to Article 55 shall be without prejudice to the operation of Articles 160 or 161 of the Code.

PROTESTS

58. Protests shall be made in accordance with the Code and accompanied by a fee of 2500.00 Swiss Francs or its equivalent in US Dollars or local currency.

SANCTIONS

59. The stewards may inflict the penalties specifically set out in these Sporting Regulations in addition to or instead of any other penalties available to them under the Code.

CHANGES OF DRIVER

60. During a season, each team will be permitted one driver change for their first car and will be permitted to have three drivers for their second car who may be changed at any time provided that any driver change is made in accordance with the Code and before the start of qualifying practice. After 18.00 on the day of scrutineering, a driver change may only take place with the consent of the stewards. In all other circumstances, competitors will be obliged to use the drivers they nominated at the time of entering the Championship except in cases of force majeure which will be considered separately. Any new driver may score points in the Championship.

PIT LANE

66. a) For the avoidance of doubt and for description purposes, the pit lane shall be divided into two lanes. The lane closest to the pit wall is designated the "fast lane", and the lane closest to the garages is designated the "inner lane", and is the only area where any work can be carried out on a car.

b) Competitors must not paint lines on any part of the pit lane.

c) No equipment may be left in the fast lane. A car may enter or remain in the fast lane only with the driver sitting in the car behind the steering wheel in his normal position, even when the car is being pushed.

d) Team personnel are only allowed in the pit lane immediately before they are required to work on a car and must withdraw as soon as the work is complete.

e) It is the responsibility of the Competitor to release his car after a pit stop only when it is safe to do so.

SPORTING CHECKS

67. Each competitor must have all relevant Super Licences available for inspection at any time during the Event.

SCRUTINEERING

70. Initial scrutineering of the car will take place three days (Monaco : four days) before the race between 10.00 and 16.00 in the garage assigned to each team.

71. Unless a waiver is granted by the stewards, competitors who do not keep to these time limits will not be allowed to take part in the Event.

72. No car may take part in the Event until it has been passed by the scrutineers.

73. The scrutineers may :

a) check the eligibility of a car or of a competitor at any time during an Event,

b) require a car to be dismantled by the competitor to make sure that the conditions of eligibility or conformity are fully satisfied,

c) require a competitor to pay the reasonable expenses which exercise of the powers mentioned in this Article may entail,

d) require a competitor to supply them with such parts or samples as they may deem necessary.

74. Any car which, after being passed by the scrutineers, is dismantled or modified in a way which might affect its safety or call into question its eligibility, or which is involved in an accident with similar consequences, must be re-presented for scrutineering approval.

75. The race director or the clerk of the course may require that any car involved in an accident be stopped and checked.

77. The stewards will publish the findings of the scrutineers each time cars are checked during the Event. These results will not include any specific figure except when a car is found to be in breach of the Technical Regulations.

SUPPLY OF TYRES IN THE CHAMPIONSHIP AND TYRE LIMITATION DURING THE EVENT

78. Supply of tyres : No tyre may be used in the Championship unless the company supplying such tyre accepts and adheres to the following conditions :

- one tyre supplier present in the Championship: this company must equip 100% of the entered teams on ordinary commercial terms.

- two tyre suppliers present : each of them must, if called upon to do so, be prepared to equip up to 60% of the entered teams on ordinary commercial terms.

- three or more tyre suppliers present : each of them must, if called upon to do so, be prepared to equip up to 40% of the entered teams on ordinary commercial terms.

- each tyre supplier must undertake to provide only two specifications of dry-weather tyre and three specifications of wet-weather tyre at each Event, each of which must be of one homogenous compound only;(...)

79. Quantity and type of tyres :

a) The same driver may not use more than a total of thirty two dry-weather tyres and twenty eight wet-weather tyres throughout the entire duration of the Event. Prior to the qualifying practice each driver may use two specifications of dry-weather tyres but must, before qualifying practice begins, nominate which specification of tyre he will use for the remainder of the Event. For qualifying practice, warm up and the race each driver may use no more than twenty eight tyres (fourteen front and fourteen rear).

b) All dry-weather tyres must incorporate circumferential grooves square to the wheel axis and around the entire circumference of the contact surface of each tyre

c) Each front dry-weather tyre, when new, must incorporate 4 grooves which are :

- arranged symmetrically about the centre of the tyre tread ;

- at least 14 mm wide at the contact surface and which taper uniformly to a minimum of 10 mm at the lower surface ;

- at least 2.5 mm deep across the whole lower surface ;

- 50 mm (+/- 1.0 mm) between centres.

Furthermore, the tread width of the front tyres must not exceed 270 mm.

d) Each rear dry-weather tyre, when new, must incorporate 4 grooves which are:

- arranged symmetrically about the centre of the tyre tread ;

- at least 14 mm wide at the contact surface and which taper uniformly to a minimum of 10 mm at the lower surface ;

- at least 2.5 mm deep across the whole lower surface ; - 50 mm (+/- 1.0 mm) between centres.

The measurements referred to in c) and d) above will be taken when the tyre is fitted to a wheel and inflated to 20 psi.

e) A wet-weather tyre is one which has been designed for use on a wet or damp track.

All wet-weather tyres must, when new, have a contact area which does not exceed 300 cm? when fitted to the front of the car and 475 cm? when fitted to the rear. Contact areas will be measured over any square section of the tyre which is normal to and symmetrical about the tyre centre line and which measures 200 mm x 200 mm when fitted to the front of the car and 250 mm x 250 mm when fitted to the rear. For the purposes of establishing conformity, only void areas which are greater than 2.5 mm in depth will be considered.

Prior to use at an Event, each tyre manufacturer must provide the technical delegate with a full scale drawing of each type of wet-weather tyre intended for use. With the exception of race day, wet-weather tyres may only be used after the track has been declared wet by the race director and, during the remainder of the relevant session, the choice of tyres is free.

80. Control of tyres :

a) All tyres which are to be used at an Event will be marked with a unique identification.

b) At any time during an Event, and at his absolute discretion, the FIA technical delegate may select the dry-weather tyres to be used by any Team from among the total stock of tyres which such Team's designated supplier has present at the Event.

c) During initial scrutineering, each competitor may have up to forty four dry-weather tyres and thirty six wet-weather tyres for each of his drivers ready for marking in his garage. Tyres not marked during initial scrutineering can be marked at other times by arrangement with the FIA technical delegate.

d) From among the twenty-eight dry-weather tyres chosen for each car for qualifying practice, warm up and the race, the FIA technical delegate will choose at random sixteen tyres (eight front and eight rear) which are the only dry-weather tyres which such car may use in qualifying practice.

e) A competitor wishing to replace an already marked unused tyre by another unused one must present both tyres to the FIA technical delegate.

f) The use of tyres without appropriate identification is strictly forbidden.

81. Wear of tyres :

The Championship will be contested on grooved tyres. The FIA reserve the right to introduce at any time a method of measuring remaining groove depth if performance appears to be enhanced by high wear or by the use of tyres which are worn so that the grooves are no longer visible.

WEIGHING

82. The weight of any car may be checked during the Event as follows :

a) all drivers entered in the Championship will be weighed, wearing their complete racing apparel, at the first Event of the season. If a driver is entered later in the season he will be weighed at his first Event.

b) During qualifying practice :

1) the FIA will install weighing equipment in an area as close to the first pit as possible, this area will be used for the weighing procedure ;

2) cars will be selected at random to undergo the weighing procedure. The FIA technical delegate will inform the driver by means of a red light at the pit entrance that his car has been selected for weighing

3) having been signalled (by means of a red light), that his car has been selected for weighing, the driver will proceed directly to the weighing area and stop his engine ;

4) the car will then be weighed and the result given to the driver in writing ;

5) if the car is unable to reach the weighing area under its own power it will be placed under the exclusive control of the marshals who will take the car to be weighed ;

6) a car or driver may not leave the weighing area without the consent of the FIA technical delegate.

c) After the race :

Each car crossing the Line will be weighed. If a car is weighed without the driver, the weight determined under a) above will be added to give the total weight required under Article 4.1 of the Technical Regulations.

d) Should the weight of the car be less than that specified in Article 4.1 of the Technical Regulations when weighed under b) or c) above, the car and the driver will be excluded from the Event save where the deficiency in weight results from the accidental loss of a component of the car due to force majeure.

e) No solid, liquid, gas or other substance or matter of whatsoever nature may be added to, placed on, or removed from a car after it has been selected for weighing or has finished the race or during the weighing procedure. (...)

f) Only scrutineers and officials may enter the weighing area. No intervention of any kind is allowed there unless authorised by such officials.

83. Any breach of these provisions for the weighing of cars may result in the exclusion of the relevant car.

SPARE CAR

86. A competitor may use several cars for practice and the race provided that :

a) he uses no more than two cars (one car for a one car Team) for free practice sessions on each of the two practice days held under Article 115 a) and b) ;

b) he uses no more than three cars (two cars for a one car Team) during qualifying practice;

c) they are all of the same make and were entered in the Championship by the same competitor,

d) they have been scrutineered in accordance with these Sporting Regulations,

e) each car carries its driver's race number.

87. Changes of car may only take place in the pits under supervision of the marshals.

88. No change of car will be allowed after the green light (see Article 139) provided always that if a race has to be restarted under Article 157 Case A, the moment after which no car change will be allowed shall be when the green light for the subsequent start is shown.

GENERAL SAFETY

90. Drivers are strictly forbidden to drive their car in the opposite direction to the race unless this is absolutely necessary in order to move the car from a dangerous position. A car may only be pushed to remove it from a dangerous position as directed by the marshals.

91. Any driver intending to leave the track or to go to his pit or the paddock area must signal his intention to do so in good time making sure that he can do this without danger.

93. A driver who abandons a car must leave it in neutral or with the clutch disengaged and with the steering wheel in place.

94. Repairs to a car may be carried out only in the paddock, pits and on the grid.

96. Save as provided in Article 138, refuelling is allowed only in the pits.

99. Save as specifically authorised by the Code or these Sporting Regulations, no one except the driver may touch a stopped car unless it is in the pits or on the starting grid.

101. During the periods commencing 15 minutes prior to and ending 5 minutes after every practice session and the period between the green lights being illuminated (Article 139) and the time when the last car enters the parc fermé, no one is allowed on the track with the exception of :

a) marshals or other authorised personnel in the execution of their duty ;

b) drivers when driving or under the direction of the marshals ;

c) mechanics under Article 140 only.

102. During a race, the engine may only be started with the starter except in the pit lane where the use of an external starting device is allowed (...)

104. A speed limit of 80 km/h in practice and 120 km/h during the warm up and the race, or such other speed limits as the Permanent Bureau of the Formula One Commission may decide, will be enforced in the pit lane. Except in the race, any driver who exceeds the limit will be fined US$250 for each km/h above the limit (this may be increased in the case of a second offence in the same Championship season). During the race, the stewards may impose a time penalty on any driver who exceeds the limit.

105. If a driver has serious mechanical difficulties during practice or the race he must leave the track as soon as it is safe to do so.

106. The car's rear light must be illuminated at all times when it is running on wet-weather tyres.

107. Only six team members per participating car (all of whom shall have been issued with and wearing special identification) are allowed in the signalling area during practice and the race.

109. The race director, the clerk of the course or the FIA medical delegate can require a driver to have a medical examination at any time during an Event.

110. Failure to comply with the general safety requirements of the Code or these Sporting Regulations may result in the exclusion of the car and driver concerned from the Event.

FREE PRACTICE, QUALIFYING PRACTICE AND WARM UP

112. No driver may start in the race without taking part in qualifying practice.

113. During all practices there will be a green and a red light at the pit exit. Cars may only leave the pit lane when the green light is on (...)

115. Free practice sessions will take place :

a) Two days (Monaco : three days) before the race from 11.00 to 12.00 and from 13.00 to 14.00.

b) The day before the race from 09.00 to 09.45 and from 10.15 to 11.00.

116. Qualifying practice will take place :

a) The day before the race from 13.00 to 14.00.

b) Each driver is allowed a maximum of 12 laps qualifying practice. Should a driver complete more than 12 laps all times recorded by the driver will be cancelled.

117. Warm up : a free practice session will take

place on race day; it will last 30 minutes and start 4 hours and 30 minutes before the starting time of the race.

118. The interval between the free and qualifying practice session may never be less than 1 hour and 30 minutes. Only in the most exceptional circumstances can a delay in free practice or other difficulty on race morning result in a change to the starting time of the race.

119. If a car stops during practice it must be removed from the track as quickly as possible so that its presence does not constitute a danger or hinder other competitors. If the driver is unable to drive the car from a dangerous position, it shall be the duty of the marshals to assist him. If any such assistance results in the car being driven or pushed back to the pits, the car may not be used again in that session. Additionally, if the assistance is given during a pre-qualifying or qualifying practice session, the driver's fastest lap time from the relevant session will be deleted. In the event of a driving infringement during practice, the stewards may delete any number of qualifying times from the driver concerned. In this case, a Team will not be able to appeal against the steward's decision.

120. The clerk of the course may interrupt practice as often and for as long as he thinks necessary to clear the track or to allow the recovery of a car. In the case of free practice only, the clerk of the course with the agreement of the stewards may decline to prolong the practice period after an interruption of thiskind.Furthermore, if in the opinion of the stewards, a stoppage is caused deliberately, the driver concerned may have his times from that session cancelled and may not be permitted to take part in any other practice session that day.

122. Should one or more sessions be thus interrupted, no protest can be accepted as to the possible effects of the interruption on the qualification of drivers admitted to start.

123. All laps covered during qualifying practice will be timed to determine the driver's position at the start in accordance with the prescriptions of Article 129. With the exception of a lap on which a red flag is shown (see Article 155), each time a car crosses the Line it will be deemed to have completed one lap.

STOPPING THE PRACTICE

124. Should it become necessary to stop the practice because the circuit is blocked by an accident or because weather or other conditions make it dangerous to continue, the clerk of the course shall order a red flag and the abort lights to be shown at the Line. Simultaneously, red flags will be shown at all marshal posts. When the signal is given to stop, all cars shall immediately reduce speed and proceed slowly back to their respective pits, and all cars abandoned on the track will be removed to a safe place. Any lap during which the red flag is shown will not be counted towards a car's total lap allocation for that session. At the end of each practice session all drivers may cross the Line only once.

PRESS CONFERENCES AND DRIVERS PARADE

125. The FIA press delegate will choose a maximum of five drivers who must attend a press conference in the media centre for a period of one hour at 15.00 on the day before first practice. These driver's Teams will be notified no less than 48 hours before the conference. In addition, a maximum of two team personalities may be chosen by the FIA press delegate to attend this press conference. On the first day of practice, a minimum of three and a maximum of six drivers and/or team personalities, (other than those who attended the press conference on the previous day and subject to the consent of the team principal) will be chosen by ballot or rota by the FIA press delegate during the Event and must make themselves available to the media for a press conference in the media centre for a period of one hour at 15.30.

126. Immediately after qualifying practice the first three drivers in qualifying will be required to make themselves available for television interviews in the unilateral room and then attend a press conference in the media centre for a maximum period of 30 minutes.

THE GRID

128. At the end of qualifying practice, the fastest time achieved by each driver will be officially published (see Article 51).

129. The grid will be drawn up in the order of the fastest time achieved by each driver. Should two or more drivers have set identical times, priority will be given to the one who set it first.

130. The fastest driver will start the race from the position on the grid which was the pole position in the previous year or, on a new circuit, has been designated as such by the FIA safety delegate.

131. Any driver whose best qualifying lap exceeds 107% of the pole position time will not be allowed to take part in the warm up or race. Under exceptional circumstances however, which may include setting a suitable lap time in a previous free practice session, the stewards may permit the car to start the race. Should there be more than one driver accepted in this manner, their order will be determined by the stewards. In either case, a Team will not be able to appeal against the stewards' decision.

132. The starting grid will be published after the warm up on race day. Any competitor whose car(s) is (are) unable to start for any reason whatsoever (or who has good reason to believe that their car(s) will not be ready to start) must inform the clerk of the course accordingly at the earliest opportunity and, in any event, no later than 45 minutes before the start of the race. If one or more cars are withdrawn, the grid will be closed up accordingly. The final starting grid will be published 45 minutes before the start of the race.

134. Any car which has not taken up its position on the grid by the time the ten minute signal is shown, will not be permitted to do so and must start from

the pits in accordance with Article 137.

BRIEFING

135. A briefing by the race director will take place at 10.00 on the first day of practice. All drivers entered for the Event and their Team Managers must be present . Should the race director consider another briefing is necessary, it will take place one hour after the end of warm up. Competitors will be informed no later than three hours after the end of qualifying practice if this is deemed necessary.

STARTING PROCEDURE

136. 30 minutes before the time for the start of the race, the cars will leave the pits to cover a reconnaissance lap. At the end of this lap they will stop on the grid in starting order with their engines stopped. Should they wish to cover more than one reconnaissance lap, this must be done by driving down the pit lane at greatly reduced speed between each of the laps.

137. 17 minutes before the starting time, a warning signal announcing the closing of the pit exit in 2 minutes will be given. 15 minutes before the starting time, the pit exit will be closed and a second warning signal will be given. Any car which is still in the pits can start from the pits, but only under the direction of the marshals. It may be moved to the pit exit only with the driver in position. Where the pit exit is immediately after the Line, cars will join the race when the whole field has passed the pit exit on its first racing lap. Where the pit exit is immediately before the Line, cars will join the race as soon as the whole field has crossed the Line after the start.

138. Refuelling on the starting grid may only be carried out prior to the 5 minute signal and by using one unpressurised container with a maximum capacity of 12 litres. Any such container may not be refilled during the starting procedure and must be fitted with one or more dry break couplings connecting it to the car.

139. The approach of the start will be announced by signals shown ten minutes, five minutes, three minutes, one minute and thirty seconds before the start of the formation lap, each of which will be accompanied by an audible warning.

When the ten minute signal is shown, everybody except drivers, officials and team technical staff must leave the grid. When the five minute signal is shown all cars must have their wheels fitted. After this signal wheels may only be removed in the pits. Any car which does not have all its wheels fitted at the five minute signal must start the race from the

back of the grid or the pit lane. When the one minute signal is shown, engines will be started and all team technical staff must leave the grid.

When the green lights are illuminated, the cars will begin the formation lap with the pole position driver leading. When leaving the grid, all drivers must proceed at a greatly reduced speed until clear of any Team personnel standing beside the track. During the formation lap practice starts are forbidden and the formation must be kept as tight as possible.

Overtaking during the formation lap is only permitted if a car is delayed when leaving its grid position and cars behind cannot avoid passing it without unduly delaying the remainder of the field. In this case, drivers may only overtake to re-establish the original starting order.

Any driver who is delayed leaving the grid may not overtake another moving car if he was stationary after the remainder of the cars had crossed the Line, and must start the race from the back of the grid. If more than one driver is affected, they must form up at the back of the grid in the order they left to complete the formation lap. If the Line is not situated in front of pole position, for the purposes of this Article only, it will be deemed to be a white line one metre in front of pole position.

A time penalty will be imposed on any driver who, in the opinion of the Stewards, unnecessarily overtook another car during the formation lap.

140. Any driver who is unable to start the formation lap must raise his arm and, after the remainder of the cars have crossed the Line, his mechanics may attempt to rectify the problem under the supervision of the marshals. If the car is still unable to start the formation lap it will be pushed into the pit lane by the shortest route and the mechanics may work on the car again.

141. When the cars come back to the grid at the end of the formation lap, they will stop on their respective grid positions, keeping their engines running. Once all the cars have come to a halt the five second signal will appear followed by the four, three, two and one second signals. At any time after the one second signal appears, the race will be started by extinguishing all red lights.

143. Any car which is unable to maintain starting order during the entire formation lap or is moving when the one second light comes on must enter the pit lane and start from the pits as specified in Article 137.

144. If, after returning to the starting grid at the end of the formation lap, a driver's engine stops and he is unable to restart the car, he must immediately raise his hands above his head and the marshal responsible for that row must immediately wave a yellow flag. If the start is delayed, (see Article 145) a marshal with a yellow flag will stand in front of the car concerned to prevent it from moving until the whole field has left the grid. The driver may then follow the procedure set out in Articles 140 and 143. As in Article 141, other cars will maintain their grid positions and the vacant position(s) will not be filled.

Should there be more than one driver in this situation, their new positions at the back of the grid will be determined in accordance with their relative positions on the grid at the start of the formation lap.

145. If a problem arises when the cars reach the starting grid at the end of the formation lap the following procedure shall apply :

a) If the race has not been started, the abort lights will be switched on, all engines will be stopped and the new formation lap will start 5 minutes later with the race distance reduced by one lap. The next signal will be the three minute signal.

b) If the race has been started the marshals alongside the grid will wave their yellow flags to inform the drivers that a car is stationary on the grid.

c) If, after the start, a car is immobilised on the starting grid, it shall be the duty of the marshals to push it into the pit lane by the fastest route. If the driver is able to re-start the car whilst it is being pushed he may rejoin the race.

d) If the driver is unable to start the car whilst it is being pushed his mechanics may attempt to start it in the pit lane. If the car then starts it may rejoin the race. The driver and mechanics must follow the instructions of the track marshals at all times during such a procedure.

147. No refuelling will be allowed on the grid if more than one start procedure proves necessary under Article 145.

148. A time penalty will be imposed for a false start judged using a FIA supplied transponder which must be fitted to the car as specified.

149. Only in the following cases will any variation in the start procedure be allowed :

a) If the track is dry throughout all practice sessions but becomes wet (or vice-versa) after the end of the warm up and at least 60 minutes before the starting time, a 15 minute free practice may be allowed.

b) If it starts to rain after the five minute signal but before the race is started and, in the opinion of the race director Teams should be given the opportunity to change tyres, the abort lights will be shown on the Line and the starting procedure will begin again at the 15 minute point. If necessary the procedure set out in Article 145 will be followed.

c) If the start of the race is imminent and, in the opinion of the race director, the volume of water on the track is such that it cannot be negotiated safely even on wet-weather tyres, the abort lights will be shown on the Line simultaneously with a "10" board with a red background. This "10" board with a red background will mean that there is to be a delay of ten minutes before the starting procedure can be resumed. If weather conditions have improved at the end of that ten minute period, a "10" board with a green background will be shown. The "10" board with a green background will mean that the green light will be shown in ten minutes. Five minutes after the "10" board with the green background is shown, the starting procedure will begin and the normal starting procedure signals (i.e. 5, 3, 1 min., 30 second) will be shown. If however, the weather conditions have not improved within ten minutes after the "10" board with the red background was shown, the abort lights will be shown on the Line and the "10" board with the red background will be shown again which will mean a further delay of ten minutes before the starting procedure can be resumed. This procedure may be repeated several times. At any time when a "10" board (with either a red or green background) is shown, it will be accompanied by an audible warning.

d) If the race is started behind the safety car, Article 154n) will apply.

THE RACE

151. A race will not be stopped in the event of rain unless the circuit is blocked or it is dangerous to continue (see Article 155).

152. If a car stops during the race (except under Article 145c and d), it must be removed from the track as quickly as possible so that its presence does not constitute a danger or hinder other competitors. If the driver is unable to drive the car from a dangerous position, it shall be the duty of the marshals to assist him. If any such assistance results in the engine starting and the driver rejoining the race, the car will be excluded from the results of the race.

153. During the race, drivers leaving the pit lane may only do so when the pit exit light is green and on their own responsibility. A marshal with a blue flag, or a flashing blue light, will also warn the driver if cars are approaching on the track.

SAFETY CAR

154 (...)b) 30 minutes before the race start time the safety car will take up position at the front of the grid and remain there until the five minute signal is given. At this point (except under n) below) it will cover a whole lap of the circuit and enter the pit lane. If Article 149a) applies, the safety car will take up its position at the front of the grid as soon as the 15 minute practice session has finished.

c) The safety car may be brought into operation to neutralise a race upon the decision of the clerk of the course. It will be used only if competitors or officials are in immediate physical danger but the circumstances are not such as to necessitate stopping the race.

d) When the order is given to deploy the safety car, all observer's posts will display immobile yellow flags and a board "SC" which shall be maintained until the intervention is over.

e) During the race, the safety car with its revolving lights on, will start from the pit lane and will join the track regardless of where the race leader is.

f) All the competing cars will form up in line behind the safety car no more than 5 car lengths apart. All overtaking is forbidden (except under n) below), unless a car is signalled to do so from the safety car.

g) When ordered to do so by the clerk of the course the observer in the car will use a green light to signal to any cars between it and the race leader that they should pass. These cars will continue at reduced speed and without overtaking until they reach the line of cars behind the safety car.

h) The safety car shall be used at least until the leader is behind it and all remaining cars are lined up behind him.(...)

i) While the safety car is in operation, competing cars may stop at their pit, but may only rejoin the track when the green light at the pit exit is on. It will be on at all times except when the safety car and the line of cars following it are about to pass or are passing the pit exit. A car rejoining the track must proceed at reduced speed until it reaches the end of the line of cars behind the safety car.

j) When the clerk of the course calls in the safety car, it must extinguish all the revolving lights, this will be the signal to the drivers that it will be entering the pit lane at the end of that lap. At this point the first car in line behind the safety car may dictate the pace and, if necessary, fall more than five car lengths behind it. As the safety car is approaching the pit entrance the yellow flags and SC boards at the observer's posts will be withdrawn and green flags will be displayed for one lap.

k) When the safety car has pulled off the circuit and the cars are approaching the Line, green lights will be shown. Overtaking remains strictly forbidden until the cars pass the green light at the Line.

l) Each lap completed while the safety car is deployed will be counted as a race lap.

m) If the race is stopped under Article 156 Case C, the safety car will take the chequered flag and all cars able to do so must follow it into the pit lane and into the parc fermé.

n) In exceptional circumstances the race may be started behind the safety car. In this case, at any time before the one minute signal, its revolving yellow lights will be turned on. This is the signal to the drivers that the race will be started behind the safety car. When the green lights are illuminated the safety car will leave the grid with all cars following in grid order no more than 5 car lengths apart. There will be no formation lap and race will start when the leading car crosses the line for the first time. Overtaking, during the first lap only, is permitted if a car is delayed when leaving its grid position and cars behind cannot avoid passing it without unduly delaying the remainder of the field. In this case, drivers may only overtake to re-establish the original starting order. Any driver who is delayed leaving the grid may not overtake another moving car if he was stationary after the remainder of the cars had crossed the Line, and must form up at the back of the line of cars behind the safety car. If more than one driver is affected, they must form up at the back of the field in the order they left the grid. A time penalty will be imposed on any driver who, in the opinion of the Stewards, unnecessarily overtook another car during the first lap.

STOPPING A RACE

155. Should it become necessary to stop the race because the circuit is blocked by an accident or because weather or other conditions make it dangerous to continue, the clerk of the course shall order a red flag and the abort lights to be shown at the Line. Simultaneously, red flags will be shown at all marshal posts. When the signal is given to stop all cars shall immediately reduce speed in the knowledge that :

- the race classification will be that at the end of the penultimate lap before the lap in which the signal to stop the race was given,

- race and service vehicles may be on the track,

- the circuit may be totally blocked because of an accident,

- weather conditions may have made the circuit undriveable at racing speed,

- the pit lane will be open.

156. The procedure to be followed varies according to the number of laps completed by the race leader before the signal to stop the race was given :

Case A : Less than two full laps. If the race can be restarted, Article 157 will apply.

Case B : Two or more full laps but less than 75% of the race distance (rounded up to the nearest whole number of laps). If the race can be restarted, Article 158 will apply.

Case C : 75% or more of the race distance (rounded up to the nearest whole number of laps). The cars will be sent directly to the parc fermé and the race will be deemed to have finished when the leading car crossed the Line for the penultimate time before the race was stopped.

RESTARTING A RACE

157. Case A.

a) The original start shall be deemed null and void.

b) The length of the restarted race will be the full original race distance.

c) The drivers who are eligible to take part in the race shall be eligible for the restart either in their original car or in a spare car.

d) After the signal to stop the race has been given, all cars able to do so will proceed directly but slowly to either :

- the pit lane or ;

- if the grid is clear, to their original grid position or ;

- if the grid is not clear, to a position behind the last grid position as directed by the marshals.

e) All cars may be worked on.

f) Refuelling will be allowed until the five minute signal is shown.

158. Case B.

a) The race shall be deemed to be in two parts, the first of which finished when the leading car crossed the Line for the penultimate time before the race was stopped.

b) The length of the second part will be three laps less than the length of the original race less the first part.

c) The grid for the second part will be a standard grid with the cars arranged in the order in which they finished the first part.

d) Only cars which took part in the original start will be eligible and then only if they returned under their own power by an authorised route to either :

- he pit lane or ;

- to a position behind the last grid position as directed by the marshals.

e) No spare car will be eligible.

f) Cars may be worked on in the pits or on the grid. If work is carried out on the grid, this must be done in the car's correct grid position and must in no way impede the re-start.

g) If a car returns to the pits it may be refuelled. If a car is refuelled it must take the re-start from the back of the grid and, if more than one car is involved, their positions will be determined by their order on the penultimate lap before the race was stopped. In this case their original grid positions will be left vacant.

159. In both Case A and Case B :

a) 10 minutes after the stop signal, the pit exit will close.

b) 15 minutes after the stop signal, the five minute signal will be shown, the grid will close and the normal start procedure will recommence.

c) Any car which is unable to take up its position on the grid before the five minute signal will be directed to the pits. It may then start from the pits as specified in Article 137. The organiser must have sufficient personnel and equipment available to enable the foregoing timetable to be adhered to even in the most difficult circumstances.

FINISH

160. The end-of-race signal will be given at the Line as soon as the leading car has covered the full race distance in accordance with Article 13. Should two hours elapse before the full distance has been covered, the end-of-race signal will be given to the leading car the first time it crosses the Line after such time has elapsed.

161. Should for any reason (other than under Article 155) the end-of-race signal be given before the leading car completes the scheduled number of laps, or the prescribed time has been completed, the race will be deemed to have finished when the leading car last crossed the Line before the signal was given. Should the end-of-race signal be delayed for any reason, the race will be deemed to have finished when it should have finished.

162. After receiving the end-of-race signal all cars must proceed on the circuit directly to the parc fermé without stopping, without receiving any object whatsoever and without any assistance (except that of the marshals if necessary). Any classified car which cannot reach the parc fermé under its own power will be placed under the exclusive control of the marshals who will take the car to the parc fermé.

PARC FERME

163. Only those officials charged with supervision may enter the parc fermé. No intervention of any kind is allowed there unless authorised by such officials.

164. When the parc fermé is in use, parc fermé regulations will apply in the area between the Line and the parc fermé entrance.

165. The parc fermé shall be sufficiently large and secure that no unauthorised persons can gain access to it.

CLASSIFICATION

166. The car placed first will be the one having covered the scheduled distance in the shortest time, or, where appropriate, passed the Line in the lead at the end of two hours. All cars will be classified taking into account the number of complete laps they have covered, and for those which have completed the same number of laps, the order in which they crossed the Line.

167. If a car takes more than twice the time of the winner's fastest lap to cover its last lap this last lap will not be taken into account when calculating the total distance covered by such car.

168. Cars having covered less than 90% of the number of laps covered by the winner (rounded down to the nearest whole number of laps), will not be classified.

169. The official classification will be published after the race. It will be the only valid result subject to any amendments which may be made under the Code and these Sporting Regulations.

PODIUM CEREMONY

170. The drivers finishing the race in 1st, 2nd and 3rd positions and a representative of the winning constructor must attend the prize-giving ceremony on the podium and abide by the podium procedure set out in Appendix 3 (except Monaco); and immediately thereafter make themselves available for a period of 90 minutes for the purpose of television unilateral interviews and the press conference in the media centre.

Meaning of the flags

White flag :	service vehicle on track
Blue flag :	(immobile) : a car is close behind you (waving) : a car is about to overtake you
Yellow flag :	(immobile) : overtaking is prohibited, danger (waving) immediate danger, slow down
Red flag :	(by marshals and the Clerk of the race) : stopping of the race on the Line
Green flag :	end of danger, free track
Yellow with red stripes flag :	danger, slippery surface
Black flag :	(with car number) : stop on the next lap
Black with yellow circle flag :	your car is in danger
Black and white flag :	non-sporting behaviour, warning
Chequered flag :	end of the race or of the practice

One man **One car**

Pictures from 1999 season

One tyre

Formula One tyres by Bridgestone

BRIDGESTONE

ULTIMATE PERFORMANCE